Learning Scala Programming

Object-oriented programming meets functional reactive to create Scalable and Concurrent programs

Vikash Sharma

BIRMINGHAM - MUMBAI

Learning Scala Programming

Commissioning Editor: Merint Matthew
Acquisition Editor: Sandeep Mishra
Content Development Editor: Rohit Kumar Singh
Technical Editor: Pavan Ramchandani
Copy Editor: Safis Editing
Project Coordinator: Vaidehi Sawant
Proofreader: Safis Editing
Indexers: Aishwarya Gangawane
Graphics: Tom Scaria
Production Coordinator: Melwyn Dsa

First published: January 2018

Production reference: 1250118

Published by Packt Publishing Ltd.
Livery Place
35 Livery Street
Birmingham
B3 2PB, UK.

ISBN 978-1-78839-282-2

www.packtpub.com

`mapt.io`

Mapt is an online digital library that gives you full access to over 5,000 books and videos, as well as industry leading tools to help you plan your personal development and advance your career. For more information, please visit our website.

Why subscribe?

- Spend less time learning and more time coding with practical eBooks and Videos from over 4,000 industry professionals

- Improve your learning with Skill Plans built especially for you

- Get a free eBook or video every month

- Mapt is fully searchable

- Copy and paste, print, and bookmark content

PacktPub.com

Did you know that Packt offers eBook versions of every book published, with PDF and ePub files available? You can upgrade to the eBook version at `www.PacktPub.com` and as a print book customer, you are entitled to a discount on the eBook copy. Get in touch with us at `service@packtpub.com` for more details.

At `www.PacktPub.com`, you can also read a collection of free technical articles, sign up for a range of free newsletters, and receive exclusive discounts and offers on Packt books and eBooks.

Contributors

About the author

Vikash Sharma is a software developer and open source technology evangelist. He tries to keep things simple, which helps him write clean and manageable code. He has invested a large amount of time learning and implementing Scala code, and he has authored video courses for Scala. He works as a developer at SAP Labs.

First and foremost, I would like to thank the amazing and continuously growing Scala community, the source of continuous enthusiasm. It's a fun and proud feeling to contribute to such a community. Then, to the team, Sandeep Mishra, Rohit Kumar Singh, Vaidehi Sawant, and Pavan Ramchandani—you guys get all the credit for the work done. Special thanks to our reviewer, Vasilis Nicolaou. His comments were helpful. I hope our book will be fun and informative to read.

About the reviewer

Vasilis Nicolaou is a software engineer, and a Linux and FOSS hobbyist and enthusiast. He began his career at CERN as a Linux developer and now works for Rentalcars.com as a senior software engineer developing microservices and distributed system solutions with Scala and Akka.

Packt is searching for authors like you

If you're interested in becoming an author for Packt, please visit `authors.packtpub.com` and apply today. We have worked with thousands of developers and tech professionals, just like you, to help them share their insight with the global tech community. You can make a general application, apply for a specific hot topic that we are recruiting an author for, or submit your own idea.

Table of Contents

Preface

Scala, despite being a general purpose JVM-based language like Java, provides an edge with functional programming primitives. Scala has a rich type system, which makes it more expressive. Using type systems, developers can write applications that are less error prone at runtime. Once you have spent enough time learning and practicing concepts, working with Scala is fun. Rich constructs and abstractions have made it powerful, and even framework and library developers enjoy working with Scala.

Keeping these points in mind, this book provides you with all the essentials you need to write programs using Scala. It has all the basic building blocks someone new to Scala might want to know about it, along with the reasons for using it. One of the major goals of this book is to enable you to choose a particular construct above another.

This book will be a companion on your journey towards learning and writing good software using Scala. We believe it'll be a fun journey for you all.

Who this book is for

This book is for programmers who want to get to grips with Scala to write concurrent, scalable, and reactive programs. No prior experience with any programming language is required to learn the concepts explained in this book. However, knowledge of any programming language will help the reader to understand concepts more quickly.

What this book covers

Chapter 1, *Getting Started with Scala Programming*, introduces you to programming paradigms and explains why choosing Scala gives you an edge over other languages. This chapter ends with demonstrating our first Scala program.

Chapter 2, *Building Blocks of Scala*, explains the basic constructs required to write a simple program. We'll discuss data types, variables, and literals, with a little bit on type inference.

Chapter 3, *Shaping our Scala Program*, takes you through looping constructs, control structures, and, most importantly, pattern matching.

Chapter 4, *Give Meaning to Programs with Functions*, discusses the important functions, function literals, and function call mechanisms. We'll end the chapter with a discussion on partial functions.

Chapter 5, *Getting Familiar with Scala Collections*, introduces you to Scala's rich collections. We'll discuss mutable and immutable collections, and talk about choosing the most suitable collection.

Chapter 6, *Object-Oriented Scala Basics*, introduces you to object-oriented Scala. We'll talk about objects, classes, and case classes.

Chapter 7, *Next Steps in Object-Oriented Scala*, talks about default and parameterized constructors. We will also be introduced to class fields, inheritance, and traits.

Chapter 8, *More on Functions*, differentiates between functions and methods. We'll talk about partially applied functions, closures, and higher-order functions.

Chapter 9, *Using Powerful Functional Constructs*, covers some of the important topics in Scala, such as tail-call optimization and currying. Then, we'll discuss combinators and end the chapter with an introduction to parameterized types.

Chapter 10, *Advanced Functional Programming*, takes you into depth of variance and types. We'll also discuss abstract versus parameterized types.

Chapter 11, *Working with Implicits and Exceptions*, discusses these two important topics, though they are not related, but are essential to the language. An introduction to implicits and understanding how they work will be the key points of this chapter. We'll also discuss the way we handle exceptions in Scala.

Chapter 12, *Introduction to Akka*, discusses one of the most talked about toolkits the Scala ecosystem provides. Akka is based on the Actor Model, and that's the main attraction of this chapter.

Chapter 13, *Concurrent programming in Scala*, takes you deeper into concurrent programming. We'll also cover asynchronous programming using Futures and Promises.

Chapter 14, *Programming with Reactive Extensions*, talks about reactive programming and the API available in Scala for reactive programming. We'll discuss RxScala, a reactive extension, with a few examples.

Chapter 15, *Testing in Scala*, covers testing. Our approach will be test-driven. We'll use ScalaTest and try out the library to write test cases for our Scala programs.

To get the most out of this book

This book is an introduction to the Scala language, where you start from learning the basic building blocks of the language and end up learning about frameworks written in Scala. Regardless of whether Scala is your first or second programming language, you're going to enjoy the book. No prior programming knowledge is required. This book has been written with the intention that its chapters are read sequentially, but if you're aware of some of the concepts and want to go skip a particular topic, feel free to do so.

Download the example code files

You can download the example code files for this book from your account at www.packtpub.com. If you purchased this book elsewhere, you can visit www.packtpub.com/support and register to have the files emailed directly to you.

You can download the code files by following these steps:

1. Log in or register at www.packtpub.com.
2. Select the **SUPPORT** tab.
3. Click on **Code Downloads & Errata**.
4. Enter the name of the book in the **Search** box and follow the onscreen instructions.

Once the file is downloaded, please make sure that you unzip or extract the folder using the latest version of:

- WinRAR/7-Zip for Windows
- Zipeg/iZip/UnRarX for Mac
- 7-Zip/PeaZip for Linux

The code bundle for the book is also hosted on GitHub at https://github.com/ PacktPublishing/Learning-Scala-Programming. We also have other code bundles from our rich catalog of books and videos available at https://github.com/PacktPublishing/. Check them out!

Conventions used

There are a number of text conventions used throughout this book.

`CodeInText`: Indicates code words in text, database table names, folder names, filenames, file extensions, pathnames, dummy URLs, user input, and Twitter handles. Here is an example: "In Scala, `Unit` is the same as the `void`, it does not represent any type."

A block of code is set as follows:

```
object First {
  def main(args: Array[String]): Unit = {
  val double: (Int => Int) = _ * 2
    (1 to 10) foreach double .andThen(println)
  }
}
```

When we wish to draw your attention to a particular part of a code block, the relevant lines or items are set in bold:

```
package lsp

object FirstApp extends App {
  val double: (Int => Int) = _ * 2
  (1 to 10) foreach double .andThen(print)
}
```

Any command-line input or output is written as follows:

```
sbt console
```

Bold: Indicates a new term, an important word, or words that you see onscreen. For example, words in menus or dialog boxes appear in the text like this. Here is an example: "Click on the **Create New Project** function."

Warnings or important notes appear like this.

Tips and tricks appear like this.

Get in touch

Feedback from our readers is always welcome.

General feedback: Email feedback@packtpub.com and mention the book title in the subject of your message. If you have questions about any aspect of this book, please email us at questions@packtpub.com.

Errata: Although we have taken every care to ensure the accuracy of our content, mistakes do happen. If you have found a mistake in this book, we would be grateful if you would report this to us. Please visit www.packtpub.com/submit-errata, selecting your book, clicking on the Errata Submission Form link, and entering the details.

Piracy: If you come across any illegal copies of our works in any form on the Internet, we would be grateful if you would provide us with the location address or website name. Please contact us at copyright@packtpub.com with a link to the material.

If you are interested in becoming an author: If there is a topic that you have expertise in and you are interested in either writing or contributing to a book, please visit authors.packtpub.com.

Reviews

Please leave a review. Once you have read and used this book, why not leave a review on the site that you purchased it from? Potential readers can then see and use your unbiased opinion to make purchase decisions, we at Packt can understand what you think about our products, and our authors can see your feedback on their book. Thank you!

For more information about Packt, please visit packtpub.com.

1
Getting Started with Scala Programming

"When you don't create things, you become defined by your own tastes rather than ability, your tastes only narrow and exclude people. So create."

- Why the Lucky Stiff

Scala is easy to get into but too deep to get a grip on. As the name suggests, Scala means *A Scalable Language*, a programming language that grows with your programming abilities. This chapter introduces you to this very popular language.

In this chapter, we will cover the following topics:

- Introduction to Scala
- Scala advantages
- Working with Scala
- Running our first program

Introduction to Scala

Consider a scenario where you get a paragraph and a word and you are asked to get the number of occurrences for that word. You're lucky enough to know a language such as Java. Your solution might look like this:

```
String str = "Scala is a multi-paradigm language. Scala is scalable too."
int count = 0;
for (stringy: str.split (" ")) {
    if (word.equals (stringy))
        count++;
}
System.out.println ("Word" + word + " occurred " + count + " times.")
```

That was easy, wasn't it? Now our Scalable language has a simple way of accomplishing this. Let's take a look at that:

```
val str = "Scala is a multi-paradigm language. Scala is scalable too."
println ("Word" + word + " occurred " + str.split(" ").filter(_ ==
word).size + " times.")
```

That's it, a one-liner solution for the same problem. The code may not look familiar right now, but gradually you'll have command over it. By the end of this chapter, we'll understand everything that's needed to run a Scala program, not just a `Hello World` program, but one that does something.

Scala's no different. It runs on **Java Virtual Machine** (**JVM**), so Java folks must have an idea about it. If not, JVM is defined as an abstract computing machine that operates on a set of instructions (Java Bytecode). It enables a machine to run a Java program. So here's the conclusion: when we write Scala programs and compile them, they are converted into Java Bytecode and then run on JVM. Scala interoperates with all Java libraries. It's easier and, of course, possible to write our own Scala code and also incorporate library functions written in Java.

Scala is a multi-paradigm language; it's a mixture of object-oriented and functional programming. But what good is it to us?

A programming paradigm

A paradigm is simply a way of doing something. So a programming paradigm means a way of programming or a certain pattern of writing programs. There are a number of programming paradigms in existence, but four of them have gained popularity:

- **Imperative Paradigm**: First do this and then do that
- **Functional Paradigm**: Evaluate and use
- **Logical Paradigm**: Answer through solution
- **Object-Oriented Paradigm**: Send messages between objects to simulate temporal evolution of a set of real-world phenomena

Object-oriented versus functional paradigms

With its roots in the mathematics discipline, the functional programming paradigm is simple. It works on the theory of functions which produce values that are immutable. Immutable values mean they can't be modified later on directly. In the functional paradigm, all computations are performed by calling self/other functions. Functions are first-class citizens in the functional world. This opens up a new world of possibilities where all computations are driven by a certain need.

The object-oriented planet revolves around encapsulation and abstractions. The logical grouping of components makes maintenance of larger and complex programs easier. Data and models are encapsulated in objects. Information hiding is effective for containing an object's properties. Inheritance hierarchies, the concept of classes, and messaging between objects makes the whole model/pattern of object-oriented programming a partial success.

Scala is multi-paradigm

Scala, being a multi-paradigm language, supports both paradigms. As we're learning Scala, we have the power of both of these paradigms. We can create functions as we need them, and also have objects talking to other objects. We can have class hierarchies and abstractions. With this, dominance over a particular paradigm will not affect another.

Today the need for concurrency, immutability, heterogeneity, reactiveness, and fault tolerant architectures with ever-shrinking development life cycles has drastically increased. In this era, languages such as Scala do more than they need to with their support for functional as well as object-oriented programming.

For a programmer like us, a language is a tool to create something meaningful. We tend to reuse and manipulate other tools as well, in our case let's say other libraries. Now, we would like to work with a language which provides us extensibility and flexibility in terms of its use. Scala does this. This powerful language lets you mix in newly created traits (you may not have heard about this, but you can compare it to Java's interfaces). There are a number of ways we can make our code more meaningful and of course concise. If used smartly, you can create your own custom constructs with native language features. So this language is as exciting as you are!

This is one of the reasons to learn it. There are other reasons behind why we would choose Scala over any other languages, and there's quite a few. Let's take them one by one. But first let's get confused:

> *"Scala is a functional language, supports multiple paradigms, and every function in Scala is an object."*

Great! Now you know three main characteristics of this language. But it's hard to swallow. It's a functional language, and every function is an object. Really?

The following is an example of a `trait` defined in Scala, called `Function1`:

```
package scala
trait Function1[A, B] {
        def apply(x: A) : B
}
```

There are more of these, from `Function0` to `Function22`. There's a certain way of using these. We'll be using them many times in this book. We also refer to these as *A => B* (we call it, A to B). It means this function takes a parameter of type `A`, does some operation as defined, and returns a value of type `B`:

```
val answer = new Functional[Int, Int] {
        def apply(x: Int): Int = x * 2
}
```

This feels a bit too much to start with but getting familiar with these constructs is a good idea. `val` is a keyword used to declare a value type. It means, once declared and instantiated, you can't change it further. This `answer = (x: Int) => x * 2` becomes a function literal that can be passed to another function. We get to this point because we were able to instantiate an object of our `Function1` trait (we'll see how this works in Chapter 7, *Next Steps in Object-Oriented Scala*).

Think of any two lucky numbers, now represent how you can add them. Suppose your numbers were 42 + 61. Here, your numbers 42 and 61 are objects of type `Int` and + is a method on type `Int`. This is the way you and Scala are going to treat entities. We'll treat entities as objects and operations performed on them as methods. And this is what makes this language scalable.

We can perform functional operations where inputs are transformed to outputs rather than changing data/state of them. With this in mind, most of our operations (almost all) will not depend on state change; means functions are not going to have side effects. One example could be a function which takes your date of birth and returns your age in terms of the number of years and months:

```
class YearsAndMonths(years: Int, months: Int)
def age(birthdate: Date): YearsAndMonths = //Some Logic
```

This is a pure function because it does not manipulate the input. It takes input, transforms, and gives output. Case class is just to help us here define the age in a certain manner. With this, we can introduce more terminology called **referentially transparent methods**. Our `age` method can be called *referentially transparent*. These method calls can be replaced by the result without changing any meaning/semantics of your program.

Pure functions, the concept of immutability, and referential transparency are here only to make this language more powerful. There are more reasons to choose this language as a tool for your next application.

Scala advantages

We're smart programmers. We've already set expectations on the choice of our language. Our language should be extensive and flexible enough. It should be friendly, support libraries written in languages such as Java, be easy to work with, have good online support, and a whole lot more. And guess what! Scala gives you the complete package.

Runs on JVM

Consider efficiency and optimization as factors for a language to be well performant. Scala utilizes JVM for this. JVM uses **Just in Time (JIT)** compilation, adaptive optimization techniques for improved performance. Running on JVM makes Scala interoperable with Java. You've multitudinous libraries available as tools for reuse.

If anywhere in your mind you're comparing Java and Scala's performance, let's get it clear. Both Java and Scala programs are compiled into bytecode. JVM understands bytecode and runs it for you. So it mostly depends on the way you write a program. Scala blends in some syntax sugar, compiler logic that can cause your program to be more/less performant than Java. Mix-ins using traits can be an asset to your program architecture but may affect your program's performance. But alternatives in Java may cost the same or more. So it is more about your core understanding of constructs and how your code is going to compile and perform. It takes some time and effort to understand so the choice is yours; as a smart programmer, you may go for a syntactically powerful language.

Super smart syntax

You are going to write succinct code with Scala. There are a lot of examples we can look at to see Scala's syntax conciseness. Let's take an example from Scala's rich collections and create a `Map`:

```
val words = Map ("Wisdom" -> "state of being wise")
println(words("Wisdom"))

> state of being wise
```

The preceding code is creating a map of words and their meaning. Only `Map ("Wisdom" -> "state of being wise")` is the amount of code we have to write to make it possible. No need to add semicolons. We did not even mention the type of our value and the Scala compiler was able to infer it. **Type inference** is a characteristic of this language. Because of Type inference, a lot of times we omit type declaration and use a value directly. This way, using only a minimal set of words/tokens you can express the logic to implement them. Constructs like case classes and pattern matching take away the extra effort one might have to make and makes writing code joyful. It also helps you reduce written code by a good margin.

Best of both worlds

Scala is a mixture of functional and object-oriented worlds. It gives two benefits. First, you can leverage the power of functional constructs: higher-order functions, nested functions, pure functions, and closures. You get to work with more available (and recommended) immutable data structures. Working with immutable code helps in eliminating code that can introduce side effects or state change. This also makes this language suitable for concurrent programming. This is just another advantage Scala provides. Second, you've all the object-oriented goodies available.

You can define traits, mix them in with classes or objects, and achieve inheritance. The creation of objects, defining abstracts, and sub-classing is also possible in Scala.

Type is the core

In the early days (great, if even in the present) you may have come across this:

```
f : R -> N
```

This is the mathematical representation of a function. This is how we denote any function *f's* domain and co-domains. In this case a function, f maps values from a set of *real numbers* to a set of *natural numbers*. With this deep abstraction level, you can think of Scala's rich type system. Some of the numerous types available are parameterized, structural, compound, existential, path-dependent, higher-kinded, and yes, we are discussing abstract types. An explanation of all these is beyond the scope of this book. But if you're curious, you may refer to Scala documentation at https://www.scala-lang.org/documentation/. Knowledge of these helps a lot when designing frameworks or libraries.

Concurrency made easy

Scala recommends the use of immutable data structures, immutable collections, use of value types, functional compositions, and transformations. Along with these, the use of actors and other concurrent constructs have made it so easy to write concurrent programs. Mostly, programmers do not have to deal with the complication of thread life cycle management, because of modern constructs such as actors and reactors available in the form of native support and through libraries. Akka is one of these toolkits available, written in Scala. Also, the use of futures and promises enables writing asynchronous code.

Asynchronous code

Simply defined, asynchronous code is where your program control returns immediately after calling a block of instruction (that is a function), having started some parallel/ background effort to complete your request. This means your program flow will not stop because of a certain function taking time to complete.

Asynchronous versus parallel versus concurrent programming

Asynchronous programming involves some calculations time-intensive tasks, which on the one hand are engaging a thread in the background but do not affect the normal flow of the program.

Parallel programming incorporates several threads to perform a task faster and so does concurrent programming. But there's a subtle difference between these two. The program flow in parallel programming is deterministic whereas in concurrent programming it's not. For example, a scenario where you send multiple requests to perform and return responses regardless of response order is said to be concurrent programming. But where you break down your task into multiple sub-tasks to achieve parallelism can be defined as the core idea of parallel programming.

Now available for the frontend

Scala.js is specifically designed for the frontend and helps you avoid type-based mistakes as Scala.js is able to infer to types. You can leverage performance optimization and interoperability with some already available JavaScript frameworks such as Angular and React. Then added to that, you have macros available that help you extend the language.

Smart IDEs

There are many options available to make your programming journey easier. Scala IDE provides numerous editing and debugging options for development of Scala-based applications. The Scala IDE is built on top of a known Eclipse IDE. There are also plugins available to write Scala applications. We'll take a look at how to install and use IDE for Scala development in the coming sections.

Extensive language

Scala is very deep. Rich type abstractions, reflection, and macros all help you build some really powerful libraries and frameworks. Scala documentation explains everything to you: from parameterized types to reflection components. Understanding compile-time reflection (macros) and runtime reflection are essential for writing frameworks using Scala. And it's fun.

Online support

One of the biggest reasons for the growth of Scala as a programming language and its success is the vast online support available. The Scala team has put in a good amount of work and have come up with rich documentation. You can find documentation at `http://docs.scala-lang.org`

Learning Scala is challenging but fun. It brings out the best in you as a programmer. Isn't it fun to think and write shorter and smarter syntax with almost the same performance capabilities?

Working with Scala

In this book, we're using Scala version 2.12.2. Scala 2.12 requires your system to have Java version 8 installed. Older Scala versions support Java version 6 and above. Support for Java version 9 is still a topic of discussion for the Scala 2.13 roadmap.

Scala 2.12 was a step up from previous versions, mainly for support of Java and Scala lambda interoperability. Traits and functions are compiled directly to their Java 8 equivalents.

Java installation

Do the needful. If Java is not already installed on your machine, you may refer to Oracle's website at `https://docs.oracle.com/javase/8/docs/technotes/guides/install/install_overview.html` for instructions on how to install Java for your operating system.

SBT installation

SBT, as the name suggests, is a **Simple Build Tool**. From managing all source files to their compiled target versions to downloading all dependencies, SBT helps you create a Scala application with ease. You can configure how your test cases run. SBT comes with various commands for such tasks.

To install SBT on your machine, perform the following:

1. Go to `http://www.scala-sbt.org/download.html`.
2. You may choose from the available options suitable for your operating system.

After installation, you may check the version, so open a command prompt/terminal and type this:

```
sbt sbt-version
[info] 0.13.11
```

You should get the corresponding version number.

Scala REPL

There is more than one way of interacting with Scala. One of them is using Scala Interpreter (REPL). To run Scala REPL using SBT, just give the following command in the command prompt/terminal:

```
sbt console
```

This command will run Scala REPL.

To run Scala REPL using Scala binary, perform the following:

1. Go to `https://www.scala-lang.org/download/`.
2. Download the latest Scala archive.
3. Extract the archive to any directory.
4. Set the directory path as environment variables as shown in `https://www.scala-lang.org/download/install.html`.
5. Try running the `scala` command, it should look something like this:

```
● ● ●                    🏠 vika — java · scala — 80×24
Vikashs-MacBook-Air:~ vika$ scala
Welcome to Scala 2.12.2 (Java HotSpot(TM) 64-Bit Server VM, Java 1.8.0_60).
Type in expressions for evaluation. Or try :help.

scala>
```

If so, congrats. You've done it. Now it's asking you to type any expression. You may try typing any expression. Try anything, like 1 + 2 or 1 + "2". REPL is your playground to learn Scala.

Scala IDEs

After getting familiar with Scala REPL, now is the time to install IDE (Integrated Development Environment). There are options available to work with Scala in IDE. Choose what fits the best for you. Eclipse lovers can go for Scala IDE. To download:

1. Go to `http://scala-ide.org/download/sdk.html`.
2. You may choose from the available options suitable for your operating system.

If you're accustomed to IntelliJ IDE, you may go for the plugin download for SBT. This will enable you to create Scala applications. To get started with Scala development on IntelliJ IDE:

1. Go to `https://www.jetbrains.com/idea/download/`.
2. You may choose from the available options suitable for your operating system.
3. After installation, go to **File | IntelliJ IDEA | Preferences | Plugins** and search for `Scala`.
4. Click on **Install | Apply**.

With this, you're ready to work with Scala on IntelliJ IDE. If you're IDE neutral, you may choose whichever suits the best. We'll use IntelliJ IDE (Community Edition) version 2017.1 with SBT version 0.13.15 and Scala 2.12.2 version.

Running our first program

Time to do some real work. The recommended way of getting started with a Scala project is to use an `activator/gitor8` seed template. For `gitor8`, you require SBT version 0.13.13 and above. Using SBT, give the command `sbt new` providing the name of the template. A list of templates can be found at `https://github.com/foundweekends/giter8/wiki/giter8-templates/30ac1007438f6f7727ea98c19db1f82ea8f00ac8`.

For learning purposes, you may directly create a project in IntelliJ. For that, you may first start the IDE and start with a new project:

1. Click on the **Create New Project** function:

2. Select the **Scala | IDEA** option and click **Next**:

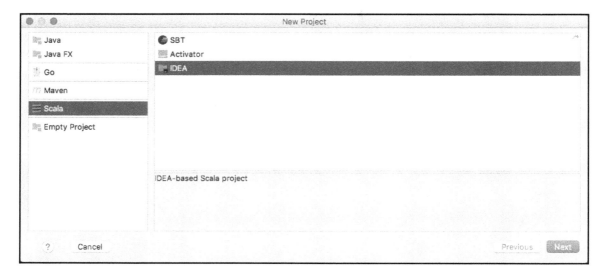

3. Give **Project name**, **Project location**, select/locate **Scala SDK**, and **Finish**:

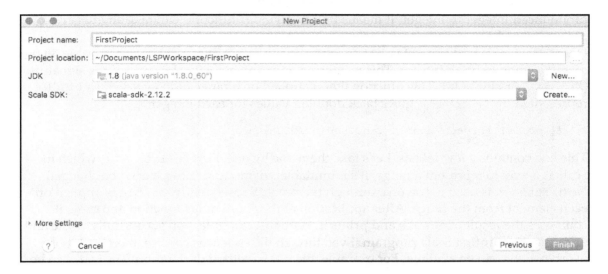

You're ready to write your first program.

Let's write some code:

```
package lsp

object First {
  def main(args: Array[String]): Unit = {
  val double: (Int => Int) = _ * 2
    (1 to 10) foreach double .andThen(println)
  }
}
```

The preceding program does nothing but print doubles of numbers ranging from 1 to 10. Let's go through the code. First, we gave the package declaration with a name `lsp`. In the next line, we created an `object` named `First`. An object in Scala is a singleton container of code which cannot take any parameters. You are not allowed to create instances of an `object`. Next, we used the `def` keyword to define the `main` method that works as an entry point to our application. The `main` method takes an array of String as parameters and returns `Unit`. In Scala terminology, `Unit` is the same as the `void`, it does not represent any type.

In the definition of this method, we defined a function literal and used it. A value named `double` is a function literal (also called **anonymous function**) of type `Int => Int` pronounced Integer to Integer. It means this anonymous function will take an integer parameter and return an integer response. An anonymous function is defined as `_ * 2`. Here `_` (that is an underscore) is sort of syntactic sugar that infers any expected value, in our case, it's going to be an integer. This is inferred as an integer value because of the signature (`Int => Int`) Int to Int. This function literal applied on a range of integer values 1 to 10, represented by (`1 to 10`), gives back doubled values for each integer:

```
(1 to 10) foreach double .andThen(println)
```

This line contains a few tokens. Let's take them one by one. First is (`1 to 10`), which in Scala is a way to represent a range. It's immutable, so once produced it can't be changed. Next, `foreach` is used to traverse through the range. Subsequently, `double` is applied on each element from the range. After application of the anonymous function `andThen`, it composes the result of `double` and prints it. With this example, you successfully wrote and understood your first Scala program. Even though the code was concise, there's a bit of overhead that can be avoided. For example, the `main` method declaration. The code can be written as follows:

```scala
package lsp

object FirstApp extends App {
  val double: (Int => Int) = _ * 2
  (1 to 10) foreach double .andThen(print)
}
```

Here, the same code is written in an object that extends the `App` trait. By extending the `App` trait available, you don't have to explicitly write the `main` method.

Summary

This chapter was an introduction to Scala for us. We started learning about programming paradigms. After that, we discussed Scala's advantages over other available languages. Then we got our development environment ready. Finally, we wrote our first Scala program.

In the next chapter, we'll take our Scala journey ahead and learn about literals, data types, and the basic building blocks of Scala.

2
Building Blocks of Scala

"You can't build a great building on a weak foundation. You must have a solid foundation if you're going to have a strong superstructure."

- Gordon B. Hinckley

Our aim as programmers is to provide a solution to a problem through some logical implementation. Programming languages work as a tool for just that. When we implement a solution to a problem, we must be able to describe the problem (specification) so that a programming language can verify (verification) whether the solution indeed solves the problem.

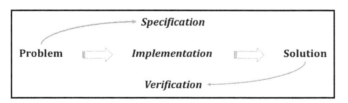

Problem Solution

For implementation, we use various programming constructs, which are basic entities with some syntactic rules. These entities work as building blocks for any programming language. In Scala, we have similar syntax to almost any other programming language. We use `keyword/name/classifier/bound-entity`. In this chapter, our aim is to get familiar with some of the building blocks. We'll go through:

- The `val` and `var` keywords
- Literals
- Data types

- Type Inference
- Operators
- Wrapper classes
- String interpolation

What is underneath a Scala program?

A Scala program is a tree of nested definitions. A definition may start with a keyword, definition's name, a classifier, and if it's a concrete definition, then also an entity to which that definition is bound. So the syntax is regular, just like any other programming language has `keyword/name/classifier/bound-entity`. Let's take an example. We'll use Scala REPL to see how a simple Scala program is built. For that, let's import a Scala package named `universe`:

```scala
scala> import scala.reflect.runtime.universe._
import scala.reflect.runtime.universe._
```

This `import` clause brings all the definitions within the `universe` package in scope. It means that the required functions we are going to use are in scope, and available for us to use. Then we'll use a `reify` method, which returns an `Expr` to construct `tree` out of our simple Scala program expression. We passed a Scala class to our `reify` method. Let's pretend that a Scala class encapsulates some members like a value with the name `segment` and a `name` definitions. We'll talk about all these members as we go along in subsequent sections. For now, let's execute this line and see what we get in response:

```scala
scala> val expr = reify {class Car {val segment="SUV"; def name="Q7"}}
expr: reflect.runtime.universe.Expr[Unit] =
Expr[Unit]({
  class Car extends AnyRef {
    def <init>() = {
      super.<init>();
      ()
    };
    val segment = "SUV";
    def name = "Q7"
  };
  ()
})
```

The preceding code shows Scala's `reify` method's response. It looks like alien code (only for now) that we have no idea about, so let's find out what's meaningful to us. We know which is somewhat using the class `Car` that we passed to generate some code. We recognize this `Car` class and that it's extending some construct named `AnyRef`. Every class we define in Scala is a subclass of `AnyRef`, hence we can see the interpreter has shown the explicit view of our class definition with modifiers, constructors, and members that we defined. We'll use the `showRaw(expr.tree)` method to print tree:

```
scala> showRaw(expr.tree)
res0: String = Block(List(ClassDef(Modifiers(), TypeName("Car"), List(),
Template(List(Ident(TypeName("AnyRef"))), noSelfType,
List(DefDef(Modifiers(), termNames.CONSTRUCTOR, List(), List(List()),
TypeTree(), Block(List(Apply(Select(Super(This(typeNames.EMPTY),
typeNames.EMPTY), termNames.CONSTRUCTOR), List())),
Literal(Constant(())))), ValDef(Modifiers(), TermName("segment"),
TypeTree(), Literal(Constant("SUV"))), DefDef(Modifiers(),
TermName("name"), List(), List(), TypeTree(), Literal(Constant("Q7"))))))),
Literal(Constant(())))
```

Now, we'll take a closer look at the response `res0`. The expression started with `Block`, that's a tree representing the class we defined. Our class `Car` contained a value declaration named `segment`, and a method named `name`. The representation of our class as a tree contains all the entities that we defined. And these together construct our program. A tree that we got using the method `showRaw(tree)` give us the skeleton of the program we wrote. The tree has String literals like `SUV` and `Q7`, value definitions like `segment`, and other meaningful constructs. We'll learn the basics of these literals and types of data in Scala in this chapter.

Vals and vars

While writing our Scala programs, we can define our member fields using either `val` or `var` keywords. When we use a `val` keyword to assign a value to any attribute, it becomes a value. We're not allowed to change that value in the course of our program. So a `val` declaration is used to allow only immutable data binding to an attribute. Let's take an example:

```
scala> val a = 10
a: Int = 10
```

Here, we have used a `val` keyword with an attribute named a, and assigned it a value 10. Furthermore, if we try to change that value, the Scala compiler will give an error saying: `reassignment to val`:

```
scala> a = 12
<console>:12: error: reassignment to val
    a = 12
```

Scala recommends use of `val` as much as possible to support immutability. But if an attribute's value is going to change in the course of our program, we can use the `var` declaration:

```
scala> var b = 10
b: Int = 10
```

When we define an attribute using a `var` keyword, we're allowed to change its value. The `var` keyword here stands for variable, which may vary over time:

```
scala> b = 12
b: Int = 12
```

If you take a closer look at our declaration of value a, you will find that we're not providing the *type* information anywhere, but still the Scala interpreter is able to infer the type of defined value, which in our case is an integer. That happens because of the Scala compiler's type inference characteristic. We'll learn about Scala's type inference later on in this chapter. Scala's compiler is able to infer the type of declared value. So it's up to the programmer if he/she wants to explicitly give type information for good readability of the code, or let Scala do this job for him/her. In Scala, we can explicitly give types after the attribute's name:

```
scala> val a: String = "I can be inferred."
a: String = I can be inferred.
```

This is a bit different to how we declare fields in Java. First, we use a `val` or `var` keyword , then we give its type, and then give a literal value. Here, it's a `String` literal. When we explicitly define type information for an attribute, then the value we give to it should justify to the type specified:

```
scala> val a: Int = "12"
<console>:11: error: type mismatch;
found : String("12")
required: Int
    val a: Int = "12"
```

The preceding code is not going to work for us, because the type specified is `Int`, and the literal bound to our attribute is a `String`, and as expected, Scala gifted an error saying type mismatch. Now that we know that the bound value to our attribute is a literal, I think we're ready to discuss literals in Scala.

Literals

In the previous discussion, we've seen a String literal and an Integer too. Here, we'll discuss all available literals, and how to define them in Scala. If you're coming from a Java background, then quite a few will be the same for you: Integer, Floating point, Boolean, Character, and String are similar. Along with those, the Tuple and Function literals can be treated as something new to learn. All the literals are listed as follows:

- Integer literals
- Floating point literals
- Boolean literals
- Character literals
- String literals
- Symbol literals
- Tuple literals
- Function literals

We'll discuss them one by one. Let's start with Integer literals.

Integer literals

Numeric literals can be expressed in the form of decimal, octal, or hexadecimal forms. These are basic integer values that can be signed or unsigned. Octal values are deprecated since version 2.10, so if you try out a numeric with a leading 0, it'll give you a compile time error:

```
scala> val num = 002
<console>:1: error: Decimal integer literals may not have a leading zero.
(Octal syntax is obsolete.)
val num = 002
    ^
```

If you define a literal with prefix `0x` or `0X`, it's going to be a hexadecimal literal. Also, the Scala interpreter prints these values as a decimal value. For example:

```
scala> 0xFF
res0: Int = 255
```

The value to be printed is converted to its decimal equivalent, and then printed. Hexadecimal literals can contain digits (0 to 9) and letters (A to F) in upper/lower case. Integer literals are further classified into different types such as `Int`, `Long`, `Byte`, and `Short` literals. These literals are divided based on the range of values. The following table shows the minimum and maximum values for specified types:

Type	Minimum value	Maximum value
`Int`	-2^{31}	$2^{31} - 1$
`Long`	-2^{63}	$2^{63} - 1$
`Short`	-2^{15}	$2^{15} - 1$
`Byte`	-2^7	$2^7 - 1$

If we try to define any literal outside of these ranges for specified types, the compiler is going to give some error stating type mismatch:

```
scala> val aByte: Byte = 12
aByte: Byte = 12
```

Here, we defined a normal `Byte` value with type information given explicitly. If we try to give a value that is out of the range for a `Byte`, the compiler will try to convert that value to an integer, and then try to assign it to the attribute, but will fail to do so:

```
scala> val aByte: Byte = 123456
<console>:20: error: type mismatch;
found  : Int(123456)
required: Byte
    val aByte: Byte = 123456
```

This happened because the compiler tries to assign the converted value of Int (123456) to aByte, which is of Byte type. Hence, the types do not match. If we do not use type explicitly, then Scala itself is capable of inferring the type due to type inference. What if we try to assign an attribute, an integer value that does not come under any of the mentioned ranges? Let's try:

```
scala> val outOfRange = 123456789101112131415
<console>:1: error: integer number too large
val outOfRange = 123456789101112131415
```

In these cases, the Scala compiler is smart enough to sense that things are out of control, and gives this error message stating integer number too large.

To define long literals, we put the character L or l at the end of our literal. Otherwise, we can also give type information for our attribute:

```
scala> val aLong = 909L
aLong: Long = 909

scala> val aLong = 909l
aLong: Long = 909

scala> val anotherLong: Long = 1
anotherLong: Long = 1
```

The Byte and Short values can be defined by explicitly telling the interpreter about the type:

```
scala> val aByte : Byte = 1
aByte: Byte = 1

scala> val aShort : Short = 1
aShort: Short = 1
```

Floating point literals

Floating point literals include a decimal point that can be at the beginning or in between decimal digits, but not at the end. What we mean by this is that if you write the following statement, it won't work:

```
scala> val a = 1. //Not possible!
```

It won't work if you try this in Scala REPL, the expression will be continued in the next line. A quick trick: if you give two more returns in REPL, it'll start a new command. But this is how we cannot create a floating point in Scala, so now let's see how we can define a `Double` or a `Float` value. By default, Scala treats decimal point values as `Double`, if we don't specify it to be a `Float`:

```
scala> val aDoubleByDefault = 1.0
aDoubleByDefault: Double = 1.0
```

We can specify our values to be of `Float` type the same way we did for `Long` literals but with an invisible asterisk. Let's check that condition:

```
scala> val aFloat: Float = 1.0 //Compile Error!
scala> val aFloat: Float = 1.0F //Works
scala> val aFloat: Float = 1.0f //Works
```

All three were supposed to work and give us `Float` values but unfortunately only the latter two give back a `Float` value. The first one is going to give a type mismatch error stating what you specified is a `Float`, and what you bound is of `Double` type. So in Scala, to specify a literal to be of `Float` value, we'll have to give suffix `f` or `F`:

```
scala> val aFloat: Float = 1.0
<console>:11: error: type mismatch;
found  : Double(1.0)
required: Float
    val aFloat: Float = 1.0
        ^
```

Then we can optionally append `D` or `d` for a `Double` value, but we hardly do so. Floating point literals can also have an exponential part in it. That is going to be an `e` or `E` followed by an optional + or −, then few digits. `E` or `e` indicates the power of 10. So a value 3.567e2 means 3.567 multiplied by 10^2, which is 356.7, that is, 3.567 times 100.

Boolean literals

These are simple, they indicate 0 or 1, which mean true or false. The basic use of Boolean literals is for operating on comparisons, or conditions. These two are called Boolean literal, which can't be replaced by 0 or 1:

```
scala> val aBool: Boolean = 1
<console>:11: error: type mismatch;
found  : Int(1)
```

```
required: Boolean
    val aBool: Boolean = 1
        ^
```

To define a Boolean value, we simply give `true` or `false`:

```
scala> val aBool = true
aBool: Boolean = true
scala> val aBool = false
aBool: Boolean = false
```

That's all for Boolean literals.

Character literals

What if you want to break down some words and spaces into separate characters? If you do so, you're creating Character literals. We represent Character literals in single quotes. Any Unicode character or escape sequence can be represented as a Character literal. What's an escape sequence, by the way? Let's take this `backslash` for example. If we try this:

```
scala> val aChar = '\'
<console>:1: error: unclosed character literal
val aChar = '\'
```

This will not work at all, because this `'\'` is an escape character. By definition, an escape sequence or character is something that does not represent itself in String or Character literal. To define these characters, we use this sequence:

```
scala> val doublequotes = "\""
doublequotes: String = "
scala> val aString = doublequotes + "treatme a string" + doublequotes
aString: String = "treatme a string"
```

In the preceding code, we used our `doublequotes` as prefix and suffix to our string `treatme a string`, and get a response.

We've a list of escape sequence characters shown in the following table:

Sequence	Value	Unicode
\b	Backspace	\u0008
\t	Horizontal Tab	\u0009
\r	Carriage Return	\u000D

\n	Line Feed	\u000A
\f	Form Feed	\u000C
\"	Double Quote	\u0022
\\	Backslash	\u005C
\'	Single Quote	\u0027

You can also use the hex code to represent a Character literal, but we need to put a \u preceding it:

```
scala> val c = '\u0101'
c: Char = ā
```

String literals

We've already used String literals in several places at this point. So here, apart from a formal introduction to what a String literal is, we'll take a look at how String literals in Scala are different, since there's more than one way to write String literals. Up till now we've declared String literals within double quotes:

```
scala> val boringString = "I am a String Literal."
boringString: String = I am a String Literal.
```

So let's start with a String literal declaration within triple quotes. Sounds interesting! Isn't it? Take a look at this:

```
scala> val interestingString = """I am an Interesting String
     | Also span in multiple Lines!
     | Ok, That's it about me"""
interestingString: String =
"I am an Interesting String

Also span in multiple Lines!
Ok, That's it about me"
```

Got an idea about it after seeing it? A string quoted in triple quotes can be spanned over multiple lines, thus they are called multi-line string literals. These are also called raw strings, because if you try to give any escape character inside triple quotes, these multi-line string literals treat them as normal characters:

```scala
scala> val aString = """ / " ' """
aString: String = " / " ' "
scala> println(aString)

 / " '
```

So these escape characters are treated as defined if inside multi-line strings. This can contain any character, even spaces. There's more to strings, such as string interpolation, where we can dynamically assign values to a string from the current scope. For that, we use interpolators. We'll study these further a little later on in this chapter.

Symbol literals

A symbol has a name, and it can be defined as a single quote (') followed by alphanumeric identifier:

```scala
scala> val aSymbol = 'givenName
aSymbol: Symbol = 'givenName

scala> aSymbol.name
res10: String = givenName
```

We don't use symbols a lot in normal Scala programs. If we try to dig down deeper into symbols in Scala, we get to know that everything that we define in Scala and give a name to is a symbol. We can check the absolute type for a symbol:

```scala
scala> import scala.reflect.runtime.universe._
import scala.reflect.runtime.universe._

scala> typeOf[Symbol]
res12:reflect.runtime.universe.Type= scala.reflect.runtime.universe.Symbol
```

So this `Symbol` is from Scala's reflection package. We're not going to dig any deeper. If you're curious though, I would recommend going through the Scala documentation at http://docs.scala-lang.org/overviews/reflection/symbols-trees-types.html.

So that's all about Symbol literals.

Tuple literals

Tuple is a data type in Scala. We'll discuss the type in this chapter later on. First, let's take a look at how we can define a literal of the same type:

```scala
scala> val aTuple = ("Val1", "Val2", "Val3")
aTuple: (String, String, String) = (Val1,Val2,Val3)
scala> println("Value1 is: " + aTuple._1)
Value1 is: Val1
```

Here, we defined a `Tuple3`, which took three parameters that are in parentheses and comma separated. Its type is going to be `Tuple3`, the same way we can define `TupleN` with `N` being 1 to 22. Take a closer look at the REPL response for the first declaration:

```scala
aTuple: (String, String, String) = (Val1,Val2,Val3)
```

Here `aTuple` has a `Type` (`String, String, String`), so as we assigned values to our identifier, `aTuple` Scala was able to construct type based on values we gave. Tuple values can be accessed using a special underscore syntax. Here, we use the tuple attribute name, along with an underscore (_), followed by the index of value. In our example, we're using `val1`, so we gave `aTuple._1 value`.

A tuple with two elements is also called a **Pair**, it can be defined using the *arrow assoc (->)* operator:

```scala
scala> val smartPair = 1 -> "One"
smartPair: (Int, String) = (1,One)
```

Function literals

Function literals are a syntactical way of representing a function. The basic structure of a function is something that can take some parameters and return a response. If we've to represent a function that takes an `Int` value and respond in `String`, it will be like this:

```scala
Int => String
```

The left-hand side represents the input parameters, and the right-hand side gives parameters that are response type. The type of preceding function literal is `Function1[Int, String]`, and parameters `Int` and `String` are representing input and output parameters respectively. We'll discuss these more when we talk about functions in subsequent chapters.

We have discussed how literals are represented in Scala, and now that we know this, we've got a heads up to go ahead with data types.

Data types

We have just covered literals in Scala, and with that, we've almost covered the introduction to all the data types existing as well. We discussed how to define Int, Long, Short, and Byte data types. Along with these, we also covered Float and Double type. Together, all these are called numeric data types. The Byte, Short, and Char are called **sub-range types**. We also talked about Boolean, character, and strings:

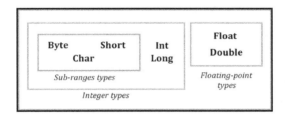

Numeric value types

In Java, these numeric types are called **Primitive Types**, and then there are user-defined types as well. But in Scala, these somewhat similar types to primitives, are called **value types**. Objects of these value types are not represented by an object in the underlying runtime system. Thus, arithmetic operations performed are in the form of methods defined for Int, and other numeric value types. Think about it, it means that we can perform method operations on these. So let's take an example:

```
scala> val x = 10 //x is an object of Type Int
x: Int = 10   //x is assigned value 10

scala> val y = 16 //y is an object of Type Int
y: Int = 16 //y is assigned value 16

scala> val z = x + y //z is addition of x and y's value
z: Int = 26
```

As you can see, x and y are two Integer objects created, and there's another named z. The result is *z*, addition of x and y. The sign + here is a method on the `Int` object, which means more than just an operator, it's a method that is defined for `Int` types and expects a parameter of `Int` type. This is going to have a definition similar :

```
scala> def +(x: Int): Int = ??? //Some definition
$plus: (x: Int)Int
```

What do we get from this? It means that the construct is more powerful because the methods look more natural and can also be written for other types. And that's how it's written for `Int`. Let's try this:

```
scala> val aCharAndAnInt = 12 + 'a'
aCharAndAnInt: Int = 109
```

This happened because there's a method + overloaded for the type character. Something like this:

```
scala> def +(x: Char): Int = ???
$plus: (x: Char)Int
```

You may refer to the class `Int.scala` at `http://www.scala-lang.org/api/2.12.0/scala/Int.html`, and go through how these methods are structured. I would recommend taking a closer look at the source of this class, and see if there's anything particular.

Scala's class hierarchy

Let's discuss Scala's class hierarchy, and also a few extra types that exist, such as bottom types in Scala. Scala has a unified type hierarchy, which means there's only one top-level class that's `Any`, and all other types extend directly or indirectly from this top-level type. It also means that any class that we define or a class pre-existing in Scala, has access to universal methods defined in the top-level class `Any`. Two variants of a relationship shown in the following figure are **subtypes** and **view**. The first one, *subtypes* depicts a relationship between two types, whereas the latter one shows that one type can be typecasted to another one. View relations are shown for value types, where a `Char` can be typecasted into `Int`.

The following figure shows the relationship between classes in Scala:

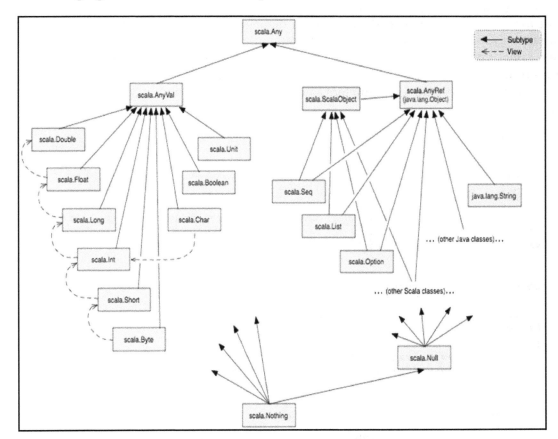

Scala class hierarchy

Any

A little excerpt from Scala's official website about the *root* of all classes:

"Class Any is the root of the Scala class hierarchy. Every class in a Scala execution environment inherits directly or indirectly from this class. Starting with Scala 2.10 it is possible to directly extend Any using universal traits. A universal trait is a trait that extends Any, only has defs as members, and does no initialization."

Yes, `Any` is the super class of all the existing or defined classes in Scala. If you don't know what inheritance or super class is, here's a quick example for you. Let's say we defined a type *Item* for our newly opened store's order management application. Each *Item* has some parameters such as `id`. We further want to categorize our items and come up with several item categories, such as `ElectronicItem` and others. Now, `ElectronicItem` can be a subtype of `Item`, and `Item` will be called a super type of `ElectronicItem`, hence it doesn't have to declare those three parameters again, and can use them directly to assign values. Take a look:

```scala
import java.util.UUID

class Item {
  val id: UUID = UUID.randomUUID()
}

class ElectronicItem(val name: String, val subCategory: String) extends
Item {
val uuid: String = "Elec_" + id
}

object CartApp extends App {

  def showItem(item: ElectronicItem) = println(s"Item id: ${item.id} uuid:
${item.uuid} name: ${item.name}")

  showItem(new ElectronicItem("Xperia", "Mobiles"))
  showItem(new ElectronicItem("IPhone", "Mobiles"))
}
```

The following is the result:

```
Item id: 16227ef3-2569-42b3-8c5e-b850474da9c4 uuid:
Elec_16227ef3-2569-42b3-8c5e-b850474da9c4 name: Xperia

Item id: 1ea8b6af-9cf0-4f38-aefb-cd312619a9d3 uuid:
Elec_1ea8b6af-9cf0-4f38-aefb-cd312619a9d3 name: IPhone
```

This example shows what we intended with inheritance. "The `ElectronicItem` function extends `Item`" that means "every `ElectronicItem` is an item." That's why we're able to refer to ID, UUID, and the name from an `ElectronicItem` instance. We've used the `import` statement to bring UUID type in scope of our compilation unit, so that when we use UUID, it should not give a compile-time error.

Now, as we discussed, every class is a subclass of Any. Hence, we have access to all non-private members of Any. Methods like != , ==, asInstanceOf, equals, isInstanceOf, toString, and hashCode are defined in Any class. These are in the form of:

```
final def  !=  (that: Any): Boolean
final def  ==  (that: Any): Boolean
def isInstanceOf[a]: Boolean
def equals(that: Any): Boolean
def ##: Int
def hashCode: Int
def toString: String
```

And yes! You can override these non-final methods, which means you can have your own definition of these.

AnyVal and AnyRef

Both AnyVal and AnyRef are two subclasses of root class Any. These two represent two families of types in Scala: the first ones are object references, the latter are value classes.

AnyRef

The AnyRef class represents all values that are/can be represented as objects in the underlying runtime system. It includes all user-defined classes that explicitly do not inherit from AnyVal. Some standard reference classes are String, Tuple, Function, and Array. The Scala compiler either provides syntactic sugar for them, or generates special code at the time of compilation for their operations. We've already seen a bit of syntactic sugar such as Tuple2, which can be represented as (A, B) where A and B are type parameters. An applied form of this Tuple2 can be (String and Int). In Scala, we represent this as Tuple2[String, Int].

AnyVal

The latter, AnyVal, represents values not implemented as objects in the underlying runtime system. Scala has some predefined numeric and non-numeric value classes as shown in the class hierarchy.

It's possible to define user-defined value types as well, with some conditions applied. Remember I asked you to take a closer look at the source of the Int.scala file? You may have noticed that there are no val or var declarations in the class Int that extends AnyVal. This is one of the constraints of defining a subtype of AnyVal. One of the reasons you might consider defining an AnyVal type is to avoid object instantiation at runtime. Some of the constraints are:

- It must have a single val parameter that is the underlying representation. It means that if you declare class Num(val underlying: Int) extends AnyVal, then the compile time representation of it will be of type Num, but at runtime it'll be converted to Int, and methods defined within will be used as statics.
- It must define only def, no val, var, nested classes, traits, or objects.
- It can only extend *universal traits, traits* that extend only the super type *Any*.
- It can't be used for pattern-matching, or type tests.

Scala's implementation of AnyVal includes nine implementations. Out of them, Byte, Short, Int, Long, Char, Float, and Double are numeric value types, while Boolean and Unit are non-numeric types.

Unit

Scala's Unit is a subtype of AnyVal, and the implementation contains the equals method, which returns a true value if the passed argument is also a Unit which means a value (), that is, just a pair of parentheses otherwise false. Other methods are hashCode and toString, which return an implementation-specific hash code and () respectively, because Unit has only one value: (), which is equivalent to Java's void type.

Boolean

A Boolean represents two values: true and false. As expected, it implements Boolean arithmetic methods such as *and, or, strict and, strict or, equality, inequality*, and negation in the form of &&, ||, &, |, ==, !=, and unary_! respectively. Boolean also implements equals, hashCode, and toString from the class Any.

The equals method checks for argument evaluation and returns its result, while hashCode returns a fixed implementation-specific hash code based on value true or false.

Null and Nothing

Null and Nothing are called **Bottom types** in Scala. Why do we need these Bottom types? Take a look at the code snippet:

```
def checkIF10AndReturn20(x: Int): Int =  {
  if(x == 10)
    x * 2
  else
    throw new Exception("Sorry, Value wasn't 10")
}
```

The method `checkIf10AndReturn20` expects a returned value of `Int` type, but what's happening here is different. If the passed argument value is not 10, we are throwing an exception, yet still the compiler is OK with our code. How can this be possible?

This is because of Type Inference. It always looks for common types in both branches of an `if` statement, so if in the other branch, the type extends everything, then the inferred type will automatically be the first one. In Scala, `Nothing` is a subtype of everything, hence the inferred type automatically becomes of type `Int`. Let's visualize this:

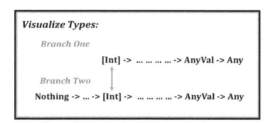

Visualizing Types Inferred

With this, it's important to understand that Type Inference plays an important role in Scala's ecosystem.

Type inference

We can call type inference a built-in Scala feature that permits us to omit type information while writing code. This means we don't have to specify the type while declaring any variables; Scala compiler can do it for us:

```
scala> val treatMeAString = "Invisible"
treatMeAString: String = Invisible
```

We did not specify our `val`, to be of `String` type, but seeing the value of `Invisible`, Scala compiler was able to infer its type. Also with some constraints, we can also omit the method's return types:

```
defcheckMeImaString(x: Boolean) = if(x) "True"else "False"
```

Here we did not give the return type, as Scala compiler was able to infer its type. But for recursive methods, this doesn't work. The famous factorial method expects you to specify the return type if implementation is recursive:

```
def recursiveFactorial(n: Int) = if(n == 0) 1 else recursiveFactorial(n-1)
//Recursive method recursiveFactorial needs result type
```

Scala uses a constraints-driven algorithm to implement type inference. It means that Scala compiler tries to infer constraints, and then attempts to unify the type. We're talking about *constraints*, but what are they? A constraint is a statement about the types of expression. And even if it's not an expression, for example, when we bind a value to a variable, we must deduce their type too. But first think about what we can deduce from the type of an expression:

- If it is related to the type of some identifier
- If it is related to the type of some other expression
- If it is a base type, such as numbers and Booleans
- If it is a constructed type such as a function, whose domain and range types are further constrained

Scala compiler uses this approach to deduce constraints and then apply unification (explanation is beyond the scope of this book) to infer the type. In instances where we can't take out any statements about an expression, inferring type is impossible:

```
scala> val x = x => x
<console>:11: error: missing parameter type
       val x = x => x
```

Because of type inference only, we're able to use *syntactic sugar* for cases where we're not expected to specify types:

```
scala> List(1,4,6,7,9).filter(_+1 > 5)
res0: List[Int] = List(6, 7, 9)
```

Exciting, isn't it? This way, we've performed our logic simply with less information about types. The underscore (_) used is syntactic sugar, and it's possible to use here because of type inference.

We'll continue our good work and learn about implementing this, perform operations using all these types, and strengthen our basics.

Operators in Scala

Based on the way we use them, the Scala operators can be classified into three types:

- Infix operators
- Prefix operators
- Postfix operators

We use operators to perform some operation on operands, which is obvious, and the way we implement makes them infix, prefix, or postfix. A basic example of an infix operator is addition +:

```
scala> val x = 1 + 10
x: Int = 11
```

We have two operands (1 and 10) on which this addition operation is being performed. We've already discussed that *operators are methods*. It means that somehow the operation is being performed as 1.+(10), and 1 + 10 is just syntactic sugar of how we can write this. This is possible because the method + is defined for the given types. Here, in our case, the addition (+) method is defined for Int. Along with this, there are several versions of overloaded methods that support other numeric value types as well. It means that we can pass in any other type and it'll be a normal addition operation performed, given that the overloaded version of that method is present:

```
scala> val y = 1 + 'a'
y: Int = 98
```

Here, the method def+(arg: Char): Int is invoked and has given an Int as a result. Think about it, if these methods are not native Scala operators and are methods, then we can also create methods like these that work as operators. This makes you feel powerful. Let's try this:

```
class Amount(val amt: Double) {

  def taxApplied(tax: Double) = this.amt * tax/100 + this.amt

  }

object Order extends App {
```

```
    val tax = 10
    val firstOrderAmount = 130

    def amountAfterTax(amount: Amount) = amount taxApplied tax

    println(s"Total Amount for order:: ${amountAfterTax(new
Amount(firstOrderAmount))}")
    }
```

The following is the result:

```
    Total Amount for order:: 143.0
```

Great! `taxApplied` is the first operator that we defined, it is defined for the type `Amount`. Our program has a class `Amount` that is just a `Double` value, and defines a method `taxApplied`. This method expects a double value for `tax` to be applied on `this` which is going to be the current value for the amount. Operators are a way we can use methods, which is why we have this operator. We've used it in object, `Order` while defining a function, `amountAfterTax`:

```
    > amount taxApplied tax
```

It can also be written as `amount.taxApplied(tax)`. There are also a few examples in Scala; for example, the `indexOf` operator that works on `String`:

```
scala> val firstString = "I am a String"
firstString: String = I am a String

scala> firstString indexOf 'a'
res1: Int = 2
```

We've talked about *infix* operators, where the operator sits between two operands. Now let's take a look at another way of using operators, that is, *prefix* and *postfix*. The first one, *prefix* operators, sits before an operand. Examples of these are –, !, and so on:

```
scala> def truthTeller(lie: Boolean) = !lie
truthTeller: (lie: Boolean)Boolean

scala> truthTeller(false)
res2: Boolean = true
```

Here, `!lie`, uses the *prefix* operator `!`, and this is the way we put an operand to the right of our operator. But this is getting invoked as a method. What happens in the background is that Scala uses `unary_` to call these operators, and that's obvious because these operators use only one operand. So our implementation looks something like the following:

```scala
scala> def truthTeller(lie: Boolean) = lie.unary_!
truthTeller: (lie: Boolean)Boolean
```

The operator `!` is defined for Boolean types, hence we were allowed to make calls on Boolean. The other way is where the operand sits on the left side, called *postfix* operators. Examples of these operators are convertors such as `toLowerCase`, `toInt`, `toString`, and so on:

```scala
scala> 1.toString
res4: String = 1

scala> "1".toInt
res5: Int = 1

scala> "ABC".toLowerCase
res7: String = abc
```

It means that these operators are defined as methods in the corresponding types. This is one way to classify operators in Scala. Now we'll go and have a quick look at types of operators based on the context they are used in programming languages. These are basically classified as:

- Arithmetic operators
- Relational operators
- Logical operators
- Bitwise operators

Arithmetic operators

We can perform arithmetic operations using the arithmetic operators. Arithmetic operators contain operators for addition (+), subtraction (-), multiplication (*), division (/), and remainder (%). We've already seen many examples for addition, not mentioning that these operators are methods!

Let's take examples of others:

```
scala> val x = 10 - 1
x: Int = 9

scala> val y = 10 * 1
y: Int = 10

scala> val z = 10 / 1
z: Int = 10

scala> val yx = 10 % 9
yx: Int = 1
```

These operators have their overloaded versions also defined, to see that we may try with different types as operands. Let's take an `Int` and `Double`:

```
scala> val yx = 10 % 9.0
yx: Double = 1.0
```

Here, the first operand is an `Int`, and the second one is a `Double`, and since `Int` is view-bounded to `Double`, the result is converted to `Double`.

Relational operators

Relational operators are used to compare two operands. We have quite enough of these, ==, !=, >, <, >= and <=. Let's try them:

```
scala> val equal_op = 10 == 10
equal_op: Boolean = true

scala> val not_eq_op = 10 != 10
not_eq_op: Boolean = false

scala> val gt_than_op = 10 > 10
gt_than_op: Boolean = false

scala> val gt_than_op = 11 > 10
gt_than_op: Boolean = true

scala> val lt_than_op = 11 < 10
lt_than_op: Boolean = false

scala> val gt_eq_op = 11 >= 11
gt_eq_op: Boolean = true
```

```
scala> val lt_eq_op = 11 <= 11
lt_eq_op: Boolean = true
```

With these operators, we compare two operands for their values, and these operations yield a Boolean result.

Logical operators

Logical operators include ! (NOT), && (AND), and || (OR), and obviously we use these to perform logical operations on operands. These methods are written for Boolean, so they expect Boolean operands:

```
scala> val log_not = !true
log_not: Boolean = false

scala> val log_or = true || false
log_or: Boolean = true

scala> val log_and = true && true
log_and: Boolean = true
```

Logical AND and OR are short-circuiting operators. It means that these are only evaluated till the result is undetermined. This is achievable in Scala even though operators are methods, because of a feature of function calls named *by-name parameters*. It allows us to pass parameters by name that get evaluated later on when required at the time of method call.

Bitwise operators

We can perform operations on individual bits of Integer types using Bitwise operators. These includes Bitwise AND (&), OR (|), and XOR (^):

```
scala> 1 & 2
res2: Int = 0

scala> 1 | 2
res3: Int = 3

scala> 1 ^ 2
res5: Int = 3
```

These operators can be performed only on `Int`. If you try this on `Double`, it'll throw an error: *value & is not a member of Double*. These operators perform operations on individual bits; in our case, 1 is converted into bits as 01 and 2 as 10, and then AND, OR, and XOR operations are performed:

- 0001 AND 0010 resulted into 00 means 0
- 0001 OR 0010 resulted into 11 means 3
- 0001 XOR 0010 resulted into 11 means 3

We can perform a logical not-operating using ~ operator:

```
scala> ~2
res8: Int = -3
```

There are also *three shift methods* for `Int` types named *shift right (>>), shift left (<<) and unsigned-shift right (>>>)*. These are binary operators working on two operands. Bits of operand on the left are shifted by value to the right.

Operator precedence

Operations such as *2 + 3 * 4 / 2 - 1* can give different results if there's no rule for evaluation of these. Hence we have some precedence-based rules for these. We're going to talk about it in this part:

```
scala> 2 + 3 * 4 / 2 - 1
res15: Int = 7
```

For reference purposes, we have the preceding expression. The evaluation gives back the result 7. How?

The expression *(2 + ((3 * 4) / 2))) - 1* is evaluated in the following steps:

1. *(2 + (12 / 2)) - 1*
2. *(2 + 6) - 1*
3. *8 - 1*
4. *7*

It's based on operator precedence. That's in the following order:

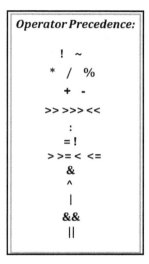

Operator precedence

As shown in the preceding figure, Scala operator expressions are evaluated based on the precedence shown. As per the figure, *, /, and % are of top priority, then comes + and -.

Other operators also follow the same precedence as shown. If operators of the same precedence level appear together, the operands are evaluated from left to right. It means that the expression 1 + 2 + 3 * 3 * 4 - 1 will result in 38:

```
scala> 1 + 2 + 3 * 3 * 4 - 1
res16: Int = 38
```

The expression *(1 + 2) + ((3 * 3) * 4) - 1* will be evaluated in the following steps:

1. *1 + 2 + 9 * 4 - 1*
2. *1 + 2 + 36 - 1*
3. *3 + 36 - 1*
4. *39 - 1*
5. *38*

This gives clarity of evaluation of expressions in Scala.

Wrapper classes

In Scala, we can create our own universe, apart from the native methods provided, we can add our own implementations, which we call *Rich Wrapper* classes. This is possible because of *Implicit Conversions*. First, we'll list out some *Wrappers* available already:

Rich Wrapper Classes:	
Base Type	**Wrapper**
Byte	scala.runtime.RichByte
Short	scala.runtime.RichShort
Char	scala.runtime.RichChar
Int	scala.runtime.RichInt
Boolean	scala.runtime.RichBoolean
Float	scala.runtime.RichFloat
Double	scala.runtime.RichDouble
String	scala.collection.immutable.StringOps

Rich wrappers

To see how it happens, let's see an example:

```
scala> val x = 10
x: Int = 10

scala> x.isValidByte
res1: Boolean = true
```

The preceding expression tries to check if the value of x can be converted into a `Byte`, and suffices range of a `Byte`, and finds it to be `true`:

```
scala> val x = 260
x: Int = 260

scala> x.isValidByte
res2: Boolean = false

scala> val x = 127
x: Int = 127

scala> x.isValidByte
res3: Boolean = true
```

As you know, range for a `Byte` is -128 to 127. If you try to assign it to a value that's out of range of a `Byte` and expect it to behave like a `Byte`, it won't work. Thus, the result for the preceding expression is `false`.

Apart from this `isValidByte`, there are a number of utility methods present in the class `RichByte` wrapper class.

These wrappers methods look like they're natively defined for the types existing. One of the examples is a wrapper around a `String` that is `StringOps`. A String in Scala is nothing more than an instance of `java.lang.String`, so it's clear that all methods implemented for `java.lang.String` are applicable here as well. For example, the `charAt` method does pretty good here:

```
scala> val x = "I am a String"
x: String = I am a String
scala> x.charAt(5)
res13: Char = a
```

Now let's try some methods from `StringOps`:

```
scala> x.capitalize
res14: String = I am a String

scala> x.toUpperCase
res15: String = I AM A STRING

scala> x.toLowerCase
res16: String = i am a string
```

The three methods `capitalize`, `toUpperCase`, and `toLowerCase` are defined in the `StringOps` class and not in `String` classes, but still it works the same way as calling a native method for a `String` type. There are more of these methods that work as a utility method for `Strings`. This is because of the power of *Implicit Conversions*. We'll learn how *Implicits* work in Scala in later chapters.

One of the ways to create a `Range` class out of `Int` types can be achieved using a method *to*. We call these **rich methods**. It's really simple to use them, and based on the purpose they solve, we can also name them:

```
scala> val rangeOfNumbers = 1 to 199
rangeOfNumbers: scala.collection.immutable.Range.Inclusive = Range 1 to 199

scala> val rangeOfNumbersUntil = 1 until 199
rangeOfNumbersUntil: scala.collection.immutable.Range = Range 1 until 199
```

```
scala> rangeOfNumbers contains 1
res17: Boolean = true

scala> rangeOfNumbersUntil contains 1
res18: Boolean = true

scala> rangeOfNumbersUntil contains 199
res19: Boolean = false

scala> rangeOfNumbers contains 199
res20: Boolean = true
```

The preceding are few examples of methods from the `Range` class, which provide rich methods for `Int` to create a `Range` with. The `Range` can contain values inclusive of those. It's built with, and can also exclude, those values. Methods for building these are `to` and `until`. The first includes both values we use to build a `Range`; the latter includes only the beginning value. We've tried all these. As you can see, `rangeOfNumbersUntil` does not contain `199`. We can also create a `Range` with some `step` difference:

```
scala> 1 to 10 by 2 foreach println
```

The following is the result:

```
1
3
5
7
9
```

This is pretty simple; pretty and simple. Especially with the syntax, we are able to write concisely because of *Implicit Conversions* and *Type Inference* happening at the backend. Scala Compiler is taking care of all those parts, leaving us with the simple job of writing code in a beautiful way. Another way of utilizing conciseness while writing a String is by using String Interpolators.

String Interpolators

We've already used String Interpolators, it's hard to avoid using them when they are available to you. Remember when we used them? Yes! When we were learning to create operators on our own:

```
println(s"Total Amount for order:: ${amountAfterTax(new
Amount(firstOrderAmount))}")
```

This little s here is a String interpolator. While using these, we precede our String with a character named s, and inside double quotes of the String, we can use any variable with a $ and it'll be replaced by its value:

```
scala> val myAge = s"I completed my $age."
myAge: String = I completed my 25.
```

This is an example of how we can use interpolators. The s is not the only interpolator existing in Scala. We have a couple more interpolators. We'll go through them one by one.

- The s interpolator
- The f interpolator
- The raw interpolator

The s interpolator

First, we'll look at the s interpolator. We've already seen how we can create a processed String with variables. Now, let's take an example that takes on expressions:

```
scala> val nextYearAge = s"Next Year, I'll complete ${age + 1}."
nextYearAge: String = Next Year, I'll complete 26.
```

Here, we used ${...} where a $ sign is followed by a pair of braces {<expression>}, consisting of the expression to be evaluated. It can be any expression. An arithmetic operation like we just did, or a method call:

```
scala> def incrementBy1(x: Int) = x + 1
incrementBy1: (x: Int)Int

scala> val nextYearAge = s"Next Year, I'll complete ${incrementBy1(age)}."
nextYearAge: String = Next Year, I'll complete 26.
```

Here, we defined a method named incrementBy1 that increments any Int passed by 1 and gives back the result. We've called that method from our interpolator. By the way, it's good to know that our interpolator s is a method just like any other operator in Scala. We're allowed to create our own interpolators in Scala.

f Interpolator

To have something like `printf` styled formatting in Scala, we can use the `f` interpolator. We do this by using a `f` preceding the double quotes of our string, and then within the String we can use one of the format specifiers:

```
scala> val amount = 100
amount: Int = 100
scala> val firstOrderAmount = f"Your total amount is: $amount%.2f"
firstOrderAmount: String = Your total amount is: 100.00
```

From the preceding example, it's clear that we use *f* as a prefix to our string and use $ followed by the expression that includes our format specifier. This works as a formatter for our strings.

A few format specifiers are listed as following:

Format Specifiers	
Specifiers	**Description**
%c	**Characters**
%d	**Decimal Numbers**
%e	**Exponentials**
%f	**Floating Point Numbers**
%i	**Integers**
%f	**Octal Numbers**
%u	**Unsigned decimal number**
%x	**Hexadecimal Number**

Format Specifiers

The raw interpolator

The final one pre-existing interpolator in Scala is the `raw` interpolator. This interpolator does not allow you to use any escape sequence characters in your string, it means that if you try to give an escape sequence character, it'll be treated as a normal literal and nothing more. The way we write `raw` interpolator is almost similar to the other two interpolators. We precede our String with a *raw* keyword and it works for us:

```
scala> val rawString = raw"I have no escape \n character in the String \n "
rawString: String = "I have no escape \n character in the String \n "
```

Here, in the string escape character, \n was treated as a normal literal, and in the resulting string it remained the same. In a normal string, \n would have converted into a *newline* character.

```
scala> val rawString = "I have no escape \n character in the String \n "
rawString: String =
"I have no escape
character in the String
"
```

Using this raw interpolator, we can avoid escape sequences. These constructs give us a way to write code more efficiently and concisely.

Summary

So, let's summarize what we have learned in this chapter. We started with the most basic `val` and `var` variable constructs. Then, we learned how we can write literals, and what data types we have in Scala. We then studied the interesting class hierarchy in Scala, in which we talked about unified class hierarchy and value and reference type classes. Later, we learned one of the most important concepts of Type Inference in Scala. After that, we started with operators, and their precedence. We learned how wrapper classes provide all the richness of functionalities to us as programmers. Finally, we learned a simple, but useful way of processing our String literals using interpolators. Now, it's clear that with some more practice of all these constructs that we've learned we'll be ready to go further and learn about some logical and looping constructs that shape up our programs.

In the next chapter, we'll discuss some looping constructs in Scala, logical constructs, and an introduction to pattern matching and how we can control our program flow using pattern matching and enabling us to strengthen our programs on logical ground.

3
Shaping our Scala Program

"I conclude that there are two ways of constructing a software design: One way is to make it so simple that there are obviously no deficiencies and the other way is to make it so complicated that there are no obvious deficiencies. The first method is far more difficult."

- C. A. R. Hoare

A program is a solution specific to a problem. The solution we write is broken down to different tasks. Tasks can be specific to a step or a part of the solution. While coding for such tasks, we use constructs as tools to make them easier, readable, and performant. These tools make it possible to shape up your program at hand.

To code for a task that is repetitive requires either a construct that can repeat a given logic for you, or write the same snippet of code by hand again and again. I bet the first one is far better and that's why we have a few constructs, we call them looping constructs. Scala supports *for*, `while`, and `do while` loops. We'll see how these loops work in Scala. From there, we'll have a quick look at `for` expressions. We'll also go through the FP (functional programming) way of doing loops through recursion. Then, we'll start taking a look at Scala's conditional statements `if` and `end`, with learning how we can shape up program flow using pattern matching. Here's a quick card for what's in there for us in this chapter:

- Looping
    - `for`, `while`, and `do while` loops
- The `for` expressions: a quick go-through
- Recursion
- Conditional statements
    - `if`, and `if else`
- Pattern matching

Looping

Standing in front of a printer, you give it an instruction to print pages with indexes 2 to 16 from your book. The printer, which is programmed to do so, uses an algorithm to print pages for you; it checks for the document and the number of pages you asked to print. It sets the starting point as 2 and the last point as 16, and it starts printing till the last point is reached. Printing pages we can call repetitive, thus printing each page from your document can be well programmed using a looping construct. As in any other language, Scala supports `for`, `while`, and `do while` loops.

Take a look at the following program:

```scala
object PagePrinter extends App {

  /*
   * Prints pages page 1 to lastIndex for doc
   */
  def printPages(doc: Document, lastIndex: Int) = ??? //Yet to be defined

  /*
   * Prints pages page startIndex to lastIndex for doc
   */
  def printPages(doc: Document, startIndex: Int, lastIndex: Int) = ???

  /*
   * Prints pages with given Indexes for doc
   */
  def printPages(doc: Document, indexes: Int*) = ???

  /*
   * Prints pages
   */
 private def print(index: Int) = println(s"Printing Page $index.")

}

 /*
  * Declares a Document type with two arguments numOfPages, typeOfDoc
  */
case class Document(numOfPages: Int, typeOfDoc: String)
```

We have created an object named `PagePrinter`. We use the syntax `/* ... */` to declare multi-line comments and `//` for single line comments in Scala. We declared three methods, which are supposed to do what the comment says. These methods are yet to be defined and we have communicated that to the Scala compiler, how? Using the syntax "???", that is, three question mark symbols, we tell the Scala compiler we're yet to define the method.

Let's come back to our methods. The first one takes a document, the number of pages to print as arguments, and prints pages up to the passed index. The second one takes the start and end indexes of pages to print and does so. The third method can take random indexes to print and prints pages from those indexes. In the third method, we've used an asterisk `*` to make our Int argument a vararg, that is, a variable argument. Now, the task is to define these methods. We can also see that to define what a document is, we have used a case class—we'll learn about case classes when we go deeper into Scala's object-oriented part in the next few chapters. For now, it'll be helpful to know that a case class let's you create a class with all the boilerplate code already available for you; it means you can access the members, in our case, `numOfPages` and `typeOfDoc`. Well, there's a lot to know about case classes, but we'll go through it later. We'll use our looping constructs to define our `PagePrinter`.

Let's take a look at our looping constructs. We'll first go through the `for` loop.

The for loop

In Scala, a `for` loop, also called `for` comprehension takes a sequence of elements, and performs an operation on each of them. One of the ways we can use them is:

```
scala> val stocks = List("APL", "GOOG", "JLR", "TESLA")
stocks: List[String] = List(APL, GOOG, JLR, TESLA)

scala> stocks.foreach(x => println(x))
APL
GOOG
JLR
TESLA
```

We defined a list named stocks with a few stock names. Then we used a simple `for` loop to print out each stock from that list. Take a look at the syntax: we have `stock <- stocks` that represents a single value from the list at the left-hand side of the generator sign `<-` and the list or sequence at the right-hand side. Then finally, we can provide any operation to be performed, in our case we printed the names. Now that we've seen how to write a simple `for` loop, let's define our set of `printPages` methods:

```scala
object PagePrinter extends App{

    /*
     * Prints pages page 1 to lastIndex for doc
     */
    def printPages(doc: Document, lastIndex: Int) = if(lastIndex <=
doc.numOfPages) for(i <- 1 to lastIndex) print(i)

    /*
     * Prints pages page startIndex to lastIndex for doc
     */
    def printPages(doc: Document, startIndex: Int, lastIndex: Int) =
if(lastIndex <= doc.numOfPages && startIndex > 0 && startIndex < lastIndex)
for(i <- startIndex to lastIndex) print(i)

    /*
     * Prints pages with given Indexes for doc
     */
 def printPages(doc: Document, indexes: Int*) = for(index <- indexes if
index <= doc.numOfPages && index > -1) print(index)

  /*
   *  Prints pages
   */
  private def print(index: Int) = println(s"Printing Page $index.")

  println("---------Method V1-----------")
  printPages(Document(15, "DOCX"), 5)

  println("---------Method V2-----------")
  printPages(Document(15, "DOCX"), 2, 5)

  println("---------Method V3-----------")
  printPages(Document(15, "DOCX"), 2, 5, 7, 15)

 }

/*
  * Declares a Document type with two arguments numOfPages, typeOfDoc
```

```
    */
    case class Document(numOfPages: Int, typeOfDoc: String)
```

The following is the output:

```
---------Method V1-----------
Printing Page 1.
Printing Page 2.
Printing Page 3.
Printing Page 4.
Printing Page 5.
---------Method V2-----------
Printing Page 2.
Printing Page 3.
Printing Page 4.
Printing Page 5.
---------Method V3-----------
Printing Page 2.
Printing Page 5.
Printing Page 7.
Printing Page 15.
```

We have a utility `print` method, which does nothing but print a simple string with index numbers, you're free to imagine a real printer printing the pages though.

Our definition for `printPages` method version 1 merely consists of a condition check that the document consists of the pages to be printed. That's done via an `if` conditional statement. More on `if` statements later in this chapter. After the conditional statement, there's a loop on indexes which ranges from 1 to the `lastIndex` passed. The same way the other method version 2 is also defined that takes `startIndex` and `lastIndex` and prints pages for you. For the last method version 3 of `printPages`, we're looping on the indexes passed and we have a condition guard that starts with an `if` statement. This checks whether the page index is less than the number of pages in the document passed as an argument, and prints it. Finally, we got the result expected from our methods.

The while Loop

Like in most other languages, the `while` loop is another looping construct used. The `while` loop can do any repetitive task until a condition is satisfied. It means that the condition provided has to be true for the code execution to stop. Generic syntax for the `while` loop is:

```
while (condition check (if it's true))
        ... // Block of Code to be executed
```

The condition to be checked is going to be a Boolean expression. It gets terminated when the condition is `false`. One of the ways we can use them is:

```scala
scala> val stocks = List("APL", "GOOG", "JLR", "TESLA")
stocks: List[String] = List(APL, GOOG, JLR, TESLA)

scala> val iteraatorForStocks = stocks.iterator
iteraatorForStocks: Iterator[String] = non-empty iterator

scala> while(iteraatorForStocks.hasNext) println(iteraatorForStocks.next())
APL
GOOG
JLR
TESLA
```

We've used our list of stocks with a few stock names. Then we called the `iterator` method on the list to get an iterator for our sequence. Here `iteraatorForStocks` of Type `Iterator[String]` is a non-empty iterator that we can use to iterate over the list. Iterators have `hasNext` methods to check if there's a component remaining in sequence. Calling `next` on the iterator gives the resulting element. We've printed by iterating over the elements of our stock list. Let's take a look at `do while` loops.

The do while loop

The `do while` loop does not differ a lot from the `while` loop. Generic syntax for `do while` loop is:

```
do
        ... // Block of Code to be executed
        while(condition check (if it's true))
```

The `do while` loop ensures that the code in block gets executed at least once and then checks for the condition defined in a `while` expression:

```scala
scala> do println("I'll stop by myself after 1 time!") while(false)
```

The following is the result:

```
I'll stop by myself after 1 time!
```

It's a simple example where our statement is getting printed just once before the condition passed to the `while` loop is `false`. This is how we can use `do while` loops in Scala.

You may want to try out the `PagePrinter` example using the `while` and `do while` loops.

The for expressions

We've seen the `for` loops, and how simple it is to use them in Scala. There's much more we can do with the `for` syntax. Here's an example:

```
object ForExpressions extends App {

    val person1 = Person("Albert", 21, 'm')
    val person2 = Person("Bob", 25, 'm')
    val person3 = Person("Cyril", 19, 'f')

    val persons = List(person1, person2, person3)

    for {
      person <- persons
      age = person.age
      name = person.name
      if age > 20 && name.startsWith("A")
    } {
      println(s"Hey ${name} You've won a free Gift Hamper.")
    }

  case class Person(name: String, age: Int, gender: Char)
  }
```

The following is the result:

```
Hey Albert You've won a free Gift Hamper.
```

In the preceding example, we used a generator, definitions, and filters in the `for` expression. We used a `for` expression on a list of persons. We proposed a gift hamper for a person whose name starts with A and who is older than 20 years of age.

The first expression in `for` is a generator expression which generates a new person from the persons list and assigns to person. Second is age and name definitions. Then finally we apply filters using the `if` statement to put conditions for our winner:

For Expressions		
Term	**Ex.**	**Description**
Generator	*person <- persons*	**Generates a new element from sequence**
Definition	*age = person.age*	**Defines a value in scope**
Filter	*if age > 20*	**Filters out a value from scope**

The for expressions

What if we want a couple more prizes for our people. In that case we may want to get a sub list of winners. That's possible by introducing `yield`.

The for yield expressions

Here's an example of a `for yield` expression where we're listing the names of winners. The criteria for winning a prize is the age, which should be more than 20:

```
object ForYieldExpressions extends App {

    val person1 = Person("Albert", 21, 'm')
    val person2 = Person("Bob", 25, 'm')
    val person3 = Person("Cyril", 19, 'f')

    val persons = List(person1, person2, person3)

    val winners = for {
      person <- persons
      age = person.age
      name = person.name
      if age > 20
    } yield name

    winners.foreach(println)
    case class Person(name: String, age: Int, gender: Char)
}
```

The following is the result:

```
Albert
Bob
```

Here, `yield` does the trick and results in a list of people with satisfying criteria. That's how `for yield` expressions work in Scala.

But these iterations are not what Scala or any other functional programming language recommends. Let's check out why this is and the alternative to iterative loops.

Recursion

Recursion is a function's call to itself. In simple words, a recursive function is a function which calls itself. Functional programming recommends use of recursion over the use of iterative looping constructs. For the same obvious reasons, Scala also recommends use of **recursion**. Let's first take a look at a recursive function:

```
object RecursionEx extends App {

    /*
     * 2 to the power n
     * only works for positive integers!
     */
    def power2toN(n: Int): Int = if(n == 0) 1 else 2 * power2toN(n - 1)

    println(power2toN(2))
    println(power2toN(4))
    println(power2toN(6))
}
```

The following is the result:

```
4
16
64
```

We've defined a function `power2toN` which expects an integer n, checks for n value and if it's not 0, the function calls itself, decrementing n integer's value till the number n becomes 0. Then comes multiplying the value with 2 with each recursive call to get the desired result.

Consider the following:

```
def power2toN(n: Int) = if(n == 0) 1 else (2 * power2toN(n - 1))
```

The Scala compiler gives an error stating `Recursive method power2N needs result type`. This is a required condition by the Scala compiler. We have to explicitly define the response type of a recursive function—that's the reason we have to give the return type with the method definition.

Why recursion over iteration?

Given the statement *functional programming recommends recursion over iteration*, let's discuss why this is the case. If you take a closer look at our definition:

```
def power2toN(n: Int): Int = if(n == 0) 1 else 2 * power2toN(n - 1)
```

The function definition consists of some conditional statement and finally a call to itself. There's no mutation of states for any variables. Functional programming recommends pure functions, which means functions with no side effects. Side effects can be mutating a state of a variable, performing I/O operations. This is not possible in iteration. Iteration, consists of mutation of its counter/index variable mutating over repetitions. Recursion, on the other hand, can be done without performing any such state changes. This makes it powerful and usable in functional languages. Operations via recursive functions can be performed with all the power of multiple cores executing them without the worry of the same variable state change by different threads. Hence recursion is recommended. But there's a glitch in recursion.

Limitations of recursion

With smaller repetitions or fewer levels of calling functions, recursion is considered to be ok, but with more levels it ends up filling the stack. What's that?

A function call in a program adds a new element to call a stack. A call stack keeps track of information about the function call. For each recursive call, a new call gets added to a stack, hence it works fine for a smaller number of recursive calls. But as the level goes deeper for recursive calls, the call stack reaches its limits and the program gets terminated. That's something unintended and breaks our program. So, shall we avoid *recursion* or use it?

The ideal way to write recursive functions

The complication with *recursion* is filling up the space of the call stack. If we find a way which can free up the current stack for each recursive call and use it for all subsequent recursive calls, we can somewhat optimize the use of a call stack and that can result in better performance of recursive functions. Let's try to understand it this way: we have the definition of our recursive function `power2N`:

```
if(n == 0) 1 else 2 * power2toN(n - 1)
```

As shown in the definition, after a call to itself, `power2toN` needs to keep track of its call stack, because the result of it needs to get multiplied by 2 to finalize the step and get the desired result. To avoid this and make an efficient use of the call stack, we can define a helper function as the very last step to be executed in the recursive function. In other words, if we make our function call a tail call, we will be able to optimize the use of call stack, hence resulting in better recursion. This phenomenon is called tail call optimization:

```scala
package chapter3

import scala.annotation.tailrec

object TailRecursionEx extends App {

  /*
   * 2 to the power n
   * @tailrec optimization
   */
  def power2toNTail(n: Int): Int = {
    @tailrec
    def helper(n: Int, currentVal: Int): Int = {
      if(n == 0) currentVal else helper(n - 1, currentVal * 2)
    }
    helper(n, 1)
  }

  println(power2toNTail(2))
  println(power2toNTail(4))
  println(power2toNTail(6))
}
```

The following is the result:

```
4
16
64
```

Above is the *tail optimized* version of our method `power2toN`. The annotation used here `@tailrec` is to explicitly tell the Scala compiler to recognize a tail recursive function and optimize accordingly. What's different here is the use of a nested, `helper` method, that's recursive and contains a tail call. After a call to `helper(n-1, currentVal * 2)`, there's no further need for that call stack. Hence, the Scala compiler is free to optimize accordingly. More on tail recursion and tail call optimization in `Chapter 9`, *Using Powerful Functional Constructs*.

This is the preferred way of writing recursive functions in Scala. It takes more effort in understanding the requirement and writing one than simply writing an iterative version of your method. But it's worth it in the functional world.

Conditional statements

We've already used conditionals many times. It's hard to have your program make sense without a conditional or logical statement. These statements help keep the flow of the program intact. Moreover, logic implementation is also easier with the use of these. Scala supports `if` and `else` conditional statements.

The if else conditional expression

In Scala, you can use `if else` to control program flow. The generic syntax for an `if else` statement goes as follows:

```
if (condition (is true))
        ... //Block of code to be executed
else
        ... //Block of code to be executed

scala> val age = 17
age: Int = 17

scala> if(age > 18) println("You're now responsible adult.") else
println("You should grow up.")
You should grow up.
```

Above, we defined a variable `age` with value 17. In the next line, we checked a condition `age > 18`. If age is greater than 18 then we printed some string. You're now a responsible adult, or some other string. Instead of just printing out strings, we can perform any operation as part of the control flow. In Scala, we can also declare and assign a value to our variables using `if else` expressions:

```
scala> val marks = 89
marks: Int = 89

scala> val performance = if(marks >= 90) "Excellent" else if(marks > 60 &&
marks < 90) "Average" else "Poor"
performance: String = Average
```

Here we assigned a value to a variable `performance` on the fly using conditional expressions. We checked if marks are greater than 90, or in between 60 to 90, or less than 90 and based on that assigned the value for performance. This happens because in Scala, conditionals are expressions—the result of an `if` statement, is an expression.

There's another way to control the flow of our program in Scala that uses matching of an expression or construct to a value and evaluation of a corresponding block of code on a successful match. We call it pattern matching in Scala.

Pattern matching

Pattern matching is more like Java's `switch` statements with a few differences. With one expression/value to match against several case statements, whenever a match happens, the corresponding block of code is executed. This gives more than one option for our program flow to follow. Java's switch is a fall-through statement, which means it executes all the statements after the very first match until it confronts a `break` statement. In Scala, there's no `break` statement. Also, there's no default case in Scala's pattern matching. Instead, a wildcard "_" is used that matches against any other case that has not been covered in previous `case` statements.

Let's have a look at the syntactical difference between Java's switch and Scala's pattern matching statements:

Java's switch vs Scala's Pattern Matching	
Java's switch statements	**Scala's Pattern Matching**

switch (expression){
  case value1: *//code to be executed:*
    break; *//optional*
 	
  case value2: *//code to be executed:*
    break; *//optional*
 	
  case value3: *//code to be executed:*
    break; *//optional*
 	
  default:
    //code to be executed if all cases
  above are not matched;
}
	value **match** {
	  case value1 => *//Code Block to be*
	  executed
	  case value2 => *//Code Block to be*
	  executed
	  case value3 => *//Code Block to be*
	  executed
	  case _ => *//Code Block to be executed*
	}

The difference is obvious, as we already discussed. In Scala, we have to provide a case matching to our expression, otherwise the compiler will throw an error, `MatchError`:

```scala
object PatternMatching extends App {

  def matchAgainst(i: Int) = i match {
    case 1 => println("One")
    case 2 => println("Two")
    case 3 => println("Three")
    case 4 => println("Four")
  }

  matchAgainst(5)
}
```

The following is the result:

```
Exception in thread "main" scala.MatchError: 5 (of class java.lang.Integer)
        at PatternMatching$.matchAgainst(PatternMatching.scala:6)
        at
PatternMatching$.delayedEndpoint$PatternMatching$1(PatternMatching.scala:13
)
        at
PatternMatching$delayedInit$body.apply(PatternMatching.scala:4)
        at scala.Function0.apply$mcV$sp(Function0.scala:34)
        at scala.Function0.apply$mcV$sp$(Function0.scala:34)
        at
scala.runtime.AbstractFunction0.apply$mcV$sp(AbstractFunction0.scala:12)
```

In the preceding example, we didn't cover all cases possible so the compiler gave this error back. To cover all the cases, we can add the wildcard "_" as the last `case` clause. This will work fine. Let's try that:

```
object PatternMatching extends App {

    def matchAgainst(i: Int) = i match {
      case 1 => println("One")
      case 2 => println("Two")
      case 3 => println("Three")
      case 4 => println("Four")
      case _ => println("Not in Range 1 to 4")
    }

    matchAgainst(1)
    matchAgainst(5)
  }
```

The following is the result:

```
One
Not in Range 1 to 4
```

After covering every `case` clause, pattern matching works a charm. We got a response; for value 1 we got a corresponding `One`, and for 5 we got `Not in Range 1 to 4`. There's more to pattern matching in Scala. We'll go through pattern matching in detail and learn several constructs to match against in `Chapter 9`, *Using Powerful Functional Constructs*.

Summary

We can conclude our chapter; let's go through what we have learned. We started learning about looping constructs in Scala. We discussed native looping constructs such as `for`, `while`, and `do while` loops. After that, we saw `for` expressions, along with `for yield` expressions. Then we understood alternatives to iteration, that is, *recursion*. We wrote a few recursive functions as well. Finally, we looked at `if else` conditional statements and pattern matching. We know there's much more to come, but with these concepts we're on our way to understanding Scala language constructs better. We'll continue doing that in our next chapter. There we'll take a look at the core of functional programming: functions. We will see how functions are defined and used. It'll show the variety of functional constructs we have available in Scala. We'll try to give meaning to our programs using functions.

4
Giving Meaning to Programs with Functions

"Object-oriented programming makes code understandable by encapsulating moving parts; functional programming makes code understandable by minimizing moving parts."

- Michael Feathers

Scala, as a mixed paradigm language, motivates you to reuse the code that you write and, at the same time, expects you to follow the motive behind functional programming. That motive is that your program should be decomposed into smaller abstractions to complete a well-defined task. This can be achieved using functions. A function is nothing but a logical construct that performs a certain task and can be reused as needed.

There are certain ways these functions can be introduced and applied into our programs. There are many reasons why functions can be used in our programs. Functions, well-written with the exact number of needed arguments, with well-defined scope and privacy make your code look good. Moreover, these functions give meaning to your program. There are specific evaluation strategies based on our needs that can be incorporated using some syntactical changes. For example, evaluation of a function if, and only if, it is needed, or lazy evaluation, means expressions are going to be evaluated when they are first accessed. Let's get ready to be introduced to functions in Scala. In this chapter, we'll become familiar with:

- Function syntax
- Calling a function
- Function literals/anonymous functions

- Evaluation strategies
- Partial functions

So let's start our discussion with what it takes to write a function.

Function syntax

Functions in Scala can be written using the `def` keyword, followed by the name of the function, with some arguments supplied as inputs to the function. Let's take a look at the generic syntax for a function:

```
modifiers...
def function_name(arg1: arg1_type, arg2: arg2_type,...): return_type = ???
```

The preceding syntax shows the generic function signature in Scala. First, we give modifiers for the function. Modifiers can be understood as properties defined for the function. Modifiers come in different forms. A few of them are as follows:

- Annotations
- Override modifier
- Access modifiers (`private`, and so on)
- The `final` keyword

It's recommended practice to use the preceding modifiers on an as-needed basis and in the given order. After specifying modifiers, we use the `def` keyword to denote a function followed by the name of the function. After giving the function name, we specify the parameters. The parameters are specified in parenthesis: first, the name of the parameter and then its type. This is a bit different from Java. In Java, this order is the exact opposite. Finally, we specify the return type of our function. We can also omit the return type, as Scala can infer it. Apart from some exceptional cases, it'll work fine. For good readability of our programs, we can make it a practice to have the return type be a part of your function signature. After declaring the function, we can give the definition body. Let's take a look at some concrete examples:

```
def compareIntegers(value1: Int, value2: Int): Int = if (value1 == value2)
0 else if (value1 > value2) 1 else -1
```

The preceding example simply defines a function that expects two integer values, compares them, and returns an integer response. The definition is also simple where we are checking equality for inputs provided. If the values are equal, then 0 is returned; if the first value is greater than the second one we return 1, otherwise we return -1. Here, we've not used any modifiers for our function. By default, Scala treats its functions as `public`, which means you can access them from any other class and override them.

If you take a closer look at the function body, it's inline. We defined the function directly, and there are two reasons for this:

- To make our code simple and readable
- The definition was small enough to define on one line

A recommended practice to define your function definition inline is when your function signature, along with the definition, is 30 characters or so. If it's more but still concise, we can start the definition on the next line, as follows:

```
def compareIntegersV1(value1: Int, value2: Int): Int =
   if (value1 == value2) 0 else if (value1 > value2) 1 else -1
```

So the choice is yours; to make your code more readable, you may choose to define functions inline. If there are multiple lines in a function body, you may choose to encapsulate them within a pair of curly braces:

```
def compareIntegersV2(value1: Int, value2: Int): Int = {
   println(s" Executing V2")
   if (value1 == value2) 0 else if (value1 > value2) 1 else -1
}
```

Here, we have two statements in the function definition. The first is printing and the latter is evaluating the comparison. Hence, we encapsulated them using a pair of curly braces. Let's take a look at the whole program:

```
object FunctionSyntax extends App{
 /*
  * Function compare two Integer numbers
  * @param value1 Int
  * @param value2 Int
  * return Int
  * 1  if value1 > value2
  * 0  if value1 = value2
  * -1 if value1 < value2
  */
   def compareIntegers(value1: Int, value2: Int): Int = if (value1 ==
value2) 0 else if (value1 > value2) 1 else -1
```

```
def compareIntegersV1(value1: Int, value2: Int): Int = {
  if (value1 == value2) 0 else if (value1 > value2) 1 else -1
}

def compareIntegersV2(value1: Int, value2: Int): Int =
  if (value1 == value2) 0 else if (value1 > value2) 1 else -1

println(compareIntegers(1, 2))
println(compareIntegersV1(2, 1))
println(compareIntegersV2(2, 2))

}
```

The following is the result:

```
-1
1
0
```

When we define a function's body, the very last expression works as the return type for the function. In our case, the evaluation of `if else` expression, that is, an integer, will be the return type for the `compareIntegers` function.

Nesting of functions

Wherever we have the possibility of wrapping our logic, we transform the snippet into a function. If we do so a number of times, we may pollute our code. Also, when we decompose our functions into smaller helper units, we tend to give almost similar names. Let's take an example:

```
object FunctionSyntaxOne extends App {

  def compareIntegersV4(value1: Int, value2: Int): String = {
 println("Executing V4")
    val result = if (value1 == value2) 0 else if (value1 > value2) 1 else
-1
    giveAMeaningFullResult(result, value1, value2)
  }

  private def giveAMeaningFullResult(result: Int, value1: Int, value2: Int)
= result match {
    case 0 => "Values are equal"
    case -1 => s"$value1 is smaller than $value2"
    case 1 => s"$value1 is greater than $value2"
    case _ => "Could not perform the operation"
```

```
    }

    println(compareIntegersV4(2,1))
}
```

The following is the result:

```
Executing V4
2 is greater than 1
```

In the preceding program, we defined the `compareIntegersV4` function, in which, after the evaluation of a comparison between two integers, we called a helper function named `giveAMeaningFullResult`, passing a result and two values. This function responds back with a meaningful string based on the result. The code works fine, but if you take a closer look and think about it, you may find that this private method is only meaningful to `compareIntegersV4`, hence it's better if the definition of `giveAMeaningFullResult` can be defined inside the function itself. Let's refactor our code to define the helper function in a nested manner inside `compareIntegersV5`:

```
object FunctionSyntaxTwo extends App {

    def compareIntegersV5(value1: Int, value2: Int): String = {
    println("Executing V5")

        def giveAMeaningFullResult(result: Int) = result match {
            case 0 => "Values are equal"
            case -1 => s"$value1 is smaller than $value2"
            case 1 => s"$value1 is greater than $value2"
            case _ => "Could not perform the operation"
        }

        val result = if (value1 == value2) 0 else if (value1 > value2) 1 else
-1
        giveAMeaningFullResult(result)
    }

    println(compareIntegersV5(2,1))
}
```

The following is the result:

```
Executing V5
2 is greater than 1
```

As you can see in the preceding code, we defined the nested function as `giveAMeaningFullResult`, which has also been changed a bit. Now it's expecting only one parameter of integer type that responds back with a meaningful string. We're allowed to access all the variables of the enclosing function; that's why we omitted passing `value1` and `value2` to our nested helper function. This has made our code look cleaner. We were able to make a call to our function directly passing arguments, in our case 2 and 1. There are a variety of ways we can make a function call; why don't we go ahead and take a look at them?

Calling a function

We can call a function to perform the task we defined for it. While calling, we pass the arguments that the function takes as input parameters. This can be achieved in a variety of ways: we can specify a variable number of arguments, we can specify the name of the argument, or we can specify a default value to consider in case the argument is not passed while calling the function. Let's take a scenario where we are not sure about the number of arguments to be passed to a function for evaluation but we are sure about the type of it.

Passing a variable number of arguments

If you remember, we've already seen an example for functions that take a variable number of arguments and perform operations on them in the previous chapter:

```
/*
 * Prints pages with given Indexes for doc
 */
def printPages(doc: Document, indexes: Int*) = for(index <- indexes if
index <= doc.numOfPages) print(index)
```

Our method takes index numbers and prints those pages from the document passed as the first parameter. Here, the parameter `indexes` is called a **vararg**. This indicates that we can pass any number of arguments of the type specified; in this case, we specified `Int`. While calling this function, we can pass any number of arguments of type `Int`. We've already tried that. Now, let's think of a mathematical function that expects a number of integers and responds back with the average of all the numbers. How should it look?

It may be a signature with the `def` keyword, with a name and parameters, or just one *vararg*:

```
def average(numbers: Int*): Double = ???
```

The preceding code is the signature for our `average` function. The body for the function is yet to be defined:

```
object FunctionCalls extends App {

    def average(numbers: Int*) : Double = numbers.foldLeft(0)((a, c) => a +
c) / numbers.length


    def averageV1(numbers: Int*) : Double = numbers.sum / numbers.length

    println(average(2,2))
    println(average(1,2,3))
    println(averageV1(1,2,3))

}
```

The following is the result:

```
2.0
2.0
2.0
```

Let's look at the first `average` function; it expects a variable argument of type `Int`. It has been called with arguments 2 and 2. Here the number of arguments was 2. We're allowed to provide any number of arguments to perform the operation. The definition of our function uses the `fold` operation to perform summing of all the numbers passed. We'll see the details of how `fold` works in the next chapter, when we discuss the functions for our collections. For now, just understand that it traverses through each element of a collection and performs operations with a supplied argument, that is, 0 in our case. We called the function with a different number of arguments. In the same way, we can define our function to support a variable number of arguments of any type. We can call the function accordingly. The only requirement is that the *vararg* parameter should come last in the function signature's parameters list:

```
def averageV1(numbers: Int*, wrongArgument: Int): Double = numbers.sum /
numbers.length
```

This means that `numbers`, that is, a variable parameter, should be declared last and declaring `wrongArgument` after that will give a *compile time error*.

Calling a function with a default parameter value

We're allowed to give default parameter values at the time of declaring a function. If we do so, we can avoid passing an argument for that parameter while calling the function. Let's see how this works with an example. We've already seen this example, where we're going to compare two integers. Let's give the second parameter a default value of 10:

```scala
def compareIntegersV6(value1: Int, value2: Int = 10): String = {
  println("Executing V6")

  def giveAMeaningFullResult(result: Int) = result match {
    case 0 => "Values are equal"
    case -1 => s"$value1 is smaller than $value2"
    case 1 => s"$value1 is greater than $value2"
    case _ => "Could not perform the operation"
  }

  val result = if (value1 == value2) 0 else if (value1 > value2) 1 else -1
  giveAMeaningFullResult(result)
}

println(compareIntegersV6(12))
```

The following is the result:

```
Executing V6
12 is greater than 10
```

Here, while declaring the `compareIntegersV6` function, we gave a default value of 10 to parameter `value2`. At the end while calling the function, we passed only one argument:

```scala
compareIntegersV6(12)
```

While calling the function, we passed only one argument, 12, which is the value for `value1`. In these situations the Scala compiler looks for a value bound to the other argument. In our case, the compiler was able to infer that for the other parameter there's already a value of 10 by default, so the function application will evaluate based on these two values. Giving default values and using them works only if the Scala compiler can infer the values. In cases of ambiguity, it does not allow you to call a function. Let's take an example:

```scala
def compareIntegersV6(value1: Int = 10, value2: Int) = ???
```

For this function, let's try to call using the following function call:

```scala
println(compareIntegersV6(12)) // Compiler won't allow
```

The Scala compiler will throw an error if we try to call a function in this way, because the compiler was not able to bind the value 12 to value2, because of the ordering of the argument. If somehow we can tell the compiler that the argument that we passed is bound to the parameter named value2, our function will work. To achieve this, we call the function passing the argument by name.

Calling a function while passing named arguments

Yes, while calling a function, we can directly name the arguments. This ensures freedom from the correct ordering of arguments passed. Let's call our function:

```
def compareIntegersV6(value1: Int = 10, value2: Int): String = {
 println("Executing V6")

  def giveAMeaningFullResult(result: Int) = result match {
    case 0 => "Values are equal"
    case -1 => s"$value1 is smaller than $value2"
    case 1 => s"$value1 is greater than $value2"
    case _ => "Could not perform the operation"
  }

  val result = if (value1 == value2) 0 else if (value1 > value2) 1 else -1
  giveAMeaningFullResult(result)
}

println(compareIntegersV6(value2 = 12))
```

The following is the result:

```
Executing V6
10 is smaller than 12
```

The reason behind this is simple: the only thing to ensure is that the Scala compiler is able to infer. This can also allow you to pass arguments regardless of the order in which they appear in the function signature. So it's possible to call our function like this:

```
println(compareIntegersV6(value2 = 12, value1 = 10))
```

The following is the result:

```
Executing V6
10 is smaller than 12
```

This gives us more than one way to define and call our functions. The good news is that you can also pass functions into a function in the form of literals; we call them function literals. Let's go through what function literals look like.

Function literals

We can pass a function in the form of a literal to another function, to work for us. Let's take the same `compareIntegers` function example:

```
def compareIntegersV6(value1: Int = 10, value2: Int): Int = ???
```

We know what our function is supposed to do: take two integer numbers as input and return an integer response telling us the result of our comparison. If we take a look at the abstract form of our function, it will look like this:

```
(value1: Int, value2: Int) => Int
```

This means that the function is expecting two integers, and returning an integer response; our need is the same. It's an abstract form that indicates that elements on the left are inputs and elements on the right are the response type for our function. We can say that this is in its literal form, also called **function literals**. Hence, it's also possible to assign this literal to any variable:

```
val compareFuncLiteral = (value1: Int, value2: Int) => if (value1 ==
value2) 0 else if (value1 > value2) 1 else -1
```

Remember in `PagePrinter` from the last chapter, we had a `print` function that took an index and printed that page:

```
private def print(index: Int) = println(s"Printing Page $index.")
```

If we look at the form our function takes, it takes an integer and prints pages. So the form will look as follows:

```
(index: Int) => Unit
```

The `Unit` keyword here represents that our literal does not respond back with any value. Now let's take a scenario where the requirement is to tell the printer to print a page in color or simple. We'll refactor our code to support using function literals:

```
object ColorPrinter extends App {

  def printPages(doc: Document, lastIndex: Int, print: (Int) => Unit) =
if(lastIndex <= doc.numOfPages) for(i <- 1 to lastIndex) print(i)
```

```
    val colorPrint = (index: Int) => println(s"Printing Color Page $index.")
    val simplePrint = (index: Int) => println(s"Printing Simple Page
$index.")

    println("---------Method V1-----------")
    printPages(Document(15, "DOCX"), 5, colorPrint)

    println("---------Method V2-----------")
    printPages(Document(15, "DOCX"), 2, simplePrint)
}

case class Document(numOfPages: Int, typeOfDoc: String)
```

The following is the result:

```
---------Method V1-----------
Printing Color Page 1.
Printing Color Page 2.
Printing Color Page 3.
Printing Color Page 4.
Printing Color Page 5.
---------Method V2-----------
Printing Simple Page 1.
Printing Simple Page 2.
```

We refactored our `printPages` method and now it takes a *function literal*. The function literal represents our `print` function's form. We represented two forms of our `print` function, the first one prints *colored* pages and the latter prints *simple* pages. This made it simple to call the same function of `printPages` and pass a *function literal* as needed. All we had to do was tell the function this form of function can be passed and, while calling the function, we can pass a *function literal* of the same form.

Scala also uses *function literals* in default constructs. One example is the `filter` function for collections. The `filter` function expects a predicate that checks for a condition and responds with a Boolean response, based on which we filter out elements in a list or collection:

```
scala> val names = List("Alice","Allen","Bob","Catherine","Alex")
names: List[String] = List(Alice, Allen, Bob, Catherine, Alex)

scala> val nameStartsWithA = names.filter((name) => name.startsWith("A"))
nameStartsWithA: List[String] = List(Alice, Allen, Alex)
```

The part where we checked if the name starts with A is an example of a *function literal:*

```
(name) => name.startsWith("A")
```

The Scala compiler only requires extra information where it is needed to infer type information; with this, it allows us to omit the parts that are just extra syntax, hence it's possible to write the proceeding syntax as:

```
scala> val nameStartsWithA = names.filter(_.startsWith("A"))
nameStartsWithA: List[String] = List(Alice, Allen, Alex)
```

In the proceeding snippet, we omitted the name of the parameter and used a `placeholder` syntax instead. What if we pass a function literal as an argument and want it to be evaluated only when it's needed, for example, a predicate that gets evaluated only if a certain functionality is active? In that case, we can pass the parameter as a named parameter. Scala does provide this functionality in the form of *call by name* parameters. These parameters get evaluated lazily whenever needed or first called. Let's take a look at some evaluation strategies provided by Scala.

Evaluation strategies

When functions have some parameters defined in them, those function calls expect us to pass arguments while calling. And as we know, we can pass a *function literal* that gets evaluated at the time of the call or at the time when it is used. Scala supports *call by value* and *call by name* for functions. Let's discuss them in detail.

Call by name

Call by name is an evaluation strategy where we substitute the literal at the place from where we call our function. The literal gets evaluated when it first appears and gets called. We can understand this with a simple example. First, let's take our `ColorPrinter` application and pass a Boolean function literal that checks if the printer is switched on. For that we can refactor our function:

```
def printPages(doc: Document, lastIndex: Int, print: (Int) => Unit,
isPrinterOn: () => Boolean) = {

  if(lastIndex <= doc.numOfPages && isPrinterOn()) for(i <- 1 to lastIndex)
print(i)

}
```

To call this function, we can use:

```
printPages(Document(15, "DOCX"), 16, colorPrint, () => !printerSwitch)
```

There are two problems with this kind of approach. First, it looks odd; using a `()  =>` `expression` here, when we already know that it's going to be a Boolean function literal. Second, we may not want our expression to get evaluated until it's used. For that, we'll make a small change in our `printPages` function signature:

```
object ColorPrinter extends App {

  val printerSwitch = false

  def printPages(doc: Document, lastIndex: Int, print: (Int) => Unit,
isPrinterOn: => Boolean) = {

    if(lastIndex <= doc.numOfPages && isPrinterOn) for(i <- 1 to lastIndex)
print(i)

  }

  val colorPrint = (index: Int) => {
    println(s"Printing Color Page $index.")
  }

  println("---------Method V1-----------")
  printPages(Document(15, "DOCX"), 2, colorPrint, !printerSwitch)

}

case class Document(numOfPages: Int, typeOfDoc: String)
```

The following is the result:

```
---------Method V1-----------
Printing Color Page 1.
Printing Color Page 2.
```

Take a closer look and you'll be able to see that we removed the `()` parenthesis and added `=>` in our function signature. This makes our code understand that this is a *by name* parameter, and to evaluate it only when it's called. This is the reason we are allowed to make this call:

```
printPages(Document(15, "DOCX"), 2, colorPrint, !printerSwitch)
```

This call consists of a Boolean expression as a last argument. And because our function expects it to be of *by name* type, it's going to be evaluated later when the call is actually made.

Call by value

Call by value is a simple and common evaluation strategy, where an expression is evaluated and the result is bound to the parameter. At the place where the parameter is used, the bound value is simply substituted with that. We've already seen many examples for this strategy:

```
def compareIntegers(value1: Int, value2: Int): Int =
      if (value1 == value2) 0 else if (value1 > value2) 1 else -1

compareIntegers(10, 8)
```

Calls made to this function are examples of the *call by value* strategy. We simply give values as arguments that get substituted in the function by parameter values.

These strategies give us a variety of ways we can call a function. Also, evaluating an expression only when it's needed is characteristic of functional languages; it's called *lazy evaluation*. We'll learn about *lazy evaluation* in more detail in `Chapter 9`, *Using Powerful Functional Constructs*, when we'll discuss *powerful functional constructs*.

Functional programming supports this analogy of writing functions that are valid and work for input values rather than failing them with an error. And to support this, Scala has a feature to define partial functions.

Partial functions

Partial functions do not suffice for every input given, which means these are defined to serve a purpose for a specific set of input parameters. To understand more, let's first define a partial function:

```
scala> val oneToFirst: PartialFunction[Int, String] = {
     | case 1 => "First"
     | }
oneToFirst: PartialFunction[Int, String] = <function1>

scala> println(oneToFirst(1))
First
```

In the preceding code, we defined a partial function named `oneToFirst`. We also specified type parameters for our partial function; in our case we passed `Int`, `String`. The `PartialFunction` function is a trait in Scala, defined as:

```
trait PartialFunction[-A, +B] extends (A) => B
```

The trait as shown expects two parameters A and B, that become the input and output types of our partial function. Our `oneToFirst` partial function simply expects 1 and returns a string representation for 1 as first. That's why when we try to call the function by passing 1, it works fine; but if we try to pass any other argument, let's say 2, it'll throw a `MatchError`:

```
scala> println(oneToFirst(2))
scala.MatchError: 2 (of class java.lang.Integer)
  at scala.PartialFunction$$anon$1.apply(PartialFunction.scala:254)
  at scala.PartialFunction$$anon$1.apply(PartialFunction.scala:252)
  at $anonfun$1.applyOrElse(<console>:12)
  at $anonfun$1.applyOrElse(<console>:11)
  at
scala.runtime.AbstractPartialFunction.apply(AbstractPartialFunction.scala:3
4)
```

This is because our partial function is only applicable for a single value, that is, 1; and for others it's not. To ensure that our function does not throw an error, we can check whether the partial function is applicable for a value or not using the `isDefinedAt` method:

```
scala> oneToFirst.isDefinedAt(1)
res3: Boolean = true

scala> oneToFirst.isDefinedAt(2)
res4: Boolean = false
```

For values that our partial function supports, `isDefinedAt` gives `true`; for other values, it returns `false`. These partial functions can also be composed. For that, the trait `PartialFunction` defines two methods: `orElse` and `andThen`:

```
object PartialFunctions extends App {

  val isPrimeEligible: PartialFunction[Item, Boolean] = {
    case item => item.isPrimeEligible
  }

  val amountMoreThan500: PartialFunction[Item, Boolean] = {
    case item => item.price > 500.0
  }

  val freeDeliverable = isPrimeEligible orElse amountMoreThan500

  def deliveryCharge(item: Item): Double = if(freeDeliverable(item)) 0 else
50

  println(deliveryCharge(Item("1", "ABC Keyboard", 490.0, false)))
```

```
}

case class Item(id: String, name: String, price: Double, isPrimeEligible:
Boolean)
```

The following is the result:

```
50.0
```

In the preceding program, we defined the partial functions named `isPrimeEligible` and `amountMoreThan500`, and then composed another partial function using the `orElse` method , which checks if the item is deliverable for free or not. Thus, partial functions provide us with ways to compose and define functions to serve specific purposes for a set of values. Moreover, partial functions give us a way to define separate logic from a given set of input values based on some distinction. It's important to keep in mind that our partial function works on only one operand. Hence, this is a form of unary function and it's the programmer's responsibility to check whether for a specific value, the function is defined or not.

Summary

It's time to conclude our chapter. In this chapter, we had a brief introduction to the important concept of *functions* in Scala. We started with the syntax for defining a function. It is important to know that we're allowed to nest functions and make our code look cleaner. We learned about how we can make function calls in a variety of ways, for example with a variable number of arguments, with a default parameter value, and with a named argument. Then we learned how to write function literals in Scala. Afterwards, we discussed a couple of evaluation strategies for functions in Scala, where we talked about *call by name* and *call by value*. Finally, we discussed another important concept of defining a *partial function* in Scala.

With this chapter, we have completed the first part of our journey. Learning all these concepts has certainly increased our ability to write and understand a mature piece of Scala code. In later parts, we will continue to do so. The second part is about Scala's rich collections hierarchy. In the next chapter, we'll learn about the number of collections Scala provides and various methods to use collections in a variety of ways.

5

Getting Familiar with Scala Collections

"The code that you write should absorb more meaning without becoming bloated or losing comprehensibility."

- Anonymous

In any programming language, one of the essential requirements is to have a way of working with a set of data, or, in other words, a collection of data. If you have worked with any programming language, you must already know the importance of its collection framework. Scala has a rich variety of collections; a rich set of helper functions makes it a lot easier to work with any Scala collection. In this chapter, we'll go through all the essentials of Scala collections. We'll be able to distinguish between several collection options, and also make efficient use of all collections. Along the way, we'll learn about:

- Immutable and mutable Scala collections
- Scala's collection hierarchy
- Commonly used collections in Scala
- Rich operations performed on collections
- Parallel collections
- Conversion from a Java to a Scala collection
- Choosing a collection
- Collection performance

Motivation

Before we start learning about immutable and mutable collections in Scala, we'll try to solve a simple problem using powerful methods provided by Scala collections. For that, let's take a look at a scenario:

```
("GET", "/user/:id"),
("GET", "user/:id/profile/:p_id"),
("POST", "/user"),
("POST", "/profile"),
("PUT", "/user/:id")
```

```
"POST" -> List("/user", "/profile")
"GET"  -> List("/user/:id",
"/user/:id/profile/:p_id")
"PUT"  -> List("/user/:id")
```

RESTful APIs

As shown in the preceding image, we have a set of APIs with method types such as GET, POST, and PUT, and their associated URIs. As these are two entities (method and URI), think of all these as a list of tuples. Now we want to segregate them, so we can create a map, as shown in the right column of the preceding image. A map is a collection that stores values in a key-value pair. Hence, on the right side you can see API information as key-value pairs, where key is the method name, and the value is a list of URIs for that particular request type. So, the idea is to convert List[(String, String)] to Map[String, List[String]]. You may want to think about the solution, and come up with your own.

Meanwhile, let's see if Scala helps us in any way with our solution:

```scala
object RESTFulAPIs extends App {
    //List of Method and URI
    val listOfAPIs = List(("GET", "/user/:id"),
                          ("GET", "user/:id/profile/:p_id"),
                          ("POST", "/user"),
                          ("POST", "/profile"),
                          ("PUT", "/user/:id"))

    /*
     * Returns a scala.collection.immutable.Map[String,
List[(String,String)]]
     */
    val groupedListOfAPIs = listOfAPIs.groupBy(_._1)
    println(s"APIs grouped to a Map :: $groupedListOfAPIs")

    /*
     * Returns a scala.collection.immutable.Map[String, List[String]]
```

```
      */
      val apisByMethod = groupedListOfAPIs.mapValues(_.map(_._2))
      println(s"APIs By Method :: $apisByMethod")
  }
```

Here's the result:

```
APIs grouped to a Map :: Map(POST -> List((POST,/user), (POST,/profile)),
GET -> List((GET,/user/:id), (GET,user/:id/profile/:p_id)), PUT ->
List((PUT,/user/:id)))
APIs By Method :: Map(POST -> List(/user, /profile), GET -> List(/user/:id,
user/:id/profile/:p_id), PUT -> List(/user/:id))
```

If you have come up with a set of `for` loops or recursive methods to accomplish what can be done using a single method, you may want to rethink, or take a look at the solution we have here. Here, we used two utility methods that fulfill our purpose. The first one is `groupBy`, defined in the `TraversableLike` trait, which converts our `List[(String, String)]` to a `Map[String, List[String]]` grouped by the first element of the tuple, the method names. This `groupBy` operation gives us this:

```
Map(POST -> List((POST,/user), (POST,/profile)), GET ->
List((GET,/user/:id), (GET,user/:id/profile/:p_id)), PUT ->
List((PUT,/user/:id)))
```

The latter is the `mapValues` method from `MapLike` trait, which is used to wrap the given map with the same key. The value for each key is simply `f(this(key))`:

```
def mapValues[W](f: V => W): Map[K, W]
```

These two methods were enough to provide the solution, and helped us avoid many traversals using loops. This is just one example, and a lot can be done within only few lines of code that would otherwise have taken several lines. This really makes Scala collections powerful. Scala's collection framework is easy to use; most of the helper methods are universal, with a few exceptions. Also, there is no compromise with performance; these are performance-tuned methods. One can rely on these methods to accomplish any logic; it makes your code look nicer. But that's not all, it's just the beginning. Usually, collections are prone to code that is written with the current environment in mind. That usually makes it hard to debug what went wrong, specifically when mutable collections are in place. So, just to remove this complication, Scala has these immutable data collections. Once created, the immutable collections can't be updated. But how do they work, and how are they different from mutable collections? Let's go through and try to understand.

Immutable and mutable collections

A collection is used to contain data that is used by the program later in time. In a multithreaded environment, if multiple threads try to access a collection at the same time, this can give you a hard time debugging what went wrong. That is a problem programmers usually face when working with collections in a multithreaded environment. But there's a universal solution for that, which expects you to use an immutable collection. Immutable means you can't change/mutate it. Scala provides you options to choose from: `root`, `mutable`, and `immutable` collections. These three are variants that exist in three separate packages: `scala.collection`, `scala.collection.mutable`, and `scala.collection.immutable`. If you don't specify the collection and use one, it'll be an immutable one by default. But how do these work, exactly? Let's take a look:

```scala
scala> val studentsPresent = List("Alex", "Bob", "Chris")

studentsPresent: List[String] = List(Alex, Bob, Chris)
```

A collection that does not allow us to update or delete its elements is of not much use. So, why do we say these are rich collections? The reason is that even though these are immutable collections, there are ways to add and remove elements, but these actions return a new collection altogether. We'll see how these are constructed and then how adding an element affects the collection later in this chapter; but for now, it's important to know that immutable collections can be updated, although doing so returns another collection with the same set of elements, along with the updated collection.

On the other hand, we have mutable collections, which work similar to most object-oriented programming languages. You can declare and instantiate a collection with a few elements. Then, based on any requirements afterwards, you can change its elements, or remove them. With these mutable collections, Scala gives you a choice to make when selecting a collection to work with. When you use mutable collections, you get an extra set of methods to mutate the collection. Be sure, though, about the instances where you may mutate collections. That'll make your program world free of mutability complications.

The third variant, root collections, resides in the `scala.collection` package. When you use a root collection, it can be mutable or immutable. What does that mean? It means that a particular collection is a superclass of a collection from the same family residing in both the `scala.collection.mutable` and `scala.collection.immutable` packages. To understand what we just said, take a look at the following method:

```
def afunction(xs: scala.collection.Iterable[String]) = ???
```

The `afunction` function can take both mutable and immutable collections, as long as they are Iterable, which is one of the traits available in Scala's collection hierarchy.

There are few extra methods that let you mutate your collection, and as we may expect, those are defined only for collections in the `scala.collection.mutable` package, not the `scala.collection` or `scala.collection.immutable` packages. In that case, it's clear that while writing your root collection, the Scala compiler is not going to allow you to update your collection. We talked about one of the use cases of root collections where, regardless of the type of your collection, you can define a function—that is, `afunction`, that takes all sorts of collections. There are more ways we can find the use cases, or differentiate root and immutable collections.

Differences between the root and immutable collections

The differences between the `root` and `immutable` collection use cases are easy to understand with the help of a scenario. Think of a scenario where:

- A function declaration expects a collection as a parameter
- The function is not going to mutate the collection as part of the definition
- The function can work well, regardless of the fact that the collection values can be changed by other threads in time

If these three scenarios are fulfilled, you're welcome to use the `root` collection type as the parameter for your function definition. It means that the following declaration will work for you:

```
def afunction(xs: scala.collection.Iterable[String])
```

If the third scenario is not what you wish for, then use `scala.collection.immutable`. The scenario explains where we can use root collections. Just because you don't have access to methods that mutate collections, it doesn't put a constraint on the runtime modification of the collection.

It's also important to know that even in these three packages, collections are present in a hierarchical manner. So, let's take a look at the hierarchy of collections in Scala.

Hierarchy of collections in Scala

The hierarchical structure of Scala collections is easy to understand. When you start working with collections, it becomes easy to use any method that is already defined in a super trait, and for specific implementations you can define your own versions. The structure has been classified in three distinct categories, that is: `root`, `mutable`, and `immutable`. We've discussed the differences between them. To strengthen our discussion, let's take a look at the hierarchy of `root` package collections:

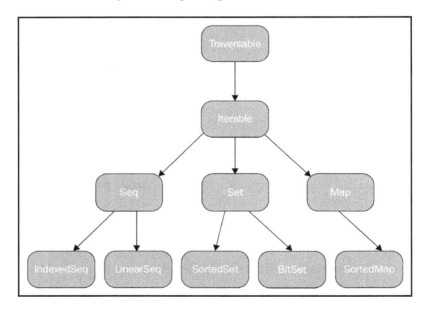

Root collection hierarchy

The preceding hierarchy is for collections in the `root` package. All the collections inherited from the super trait are called **Traversable**. Traversable defines the `foreach` abstract method, along with other helper methods that can relate to any collection in the hierarchy. So, it's clear that every other collection needs to give a definition of the `foreach` method in its implementation. We'll have a look at Traversable *trait* in the next few topics.

After Traversable, there's a *trait* named **Iterable**, which inherits *Traversable*, implements the `foreach` method from Traversable, and has its own *iterator* abstract method. From there, the hierarchy splits into three different categories:

- `Seq`
- `Set`
- `Map`

These three categories are different in implementation, context, and use cases. The first one is a sequence that's used to contain a sequence of elements, such as a sequence of numbers. Sequences are further classified as `LinearSeq` and `IndexedSeq`. The second one is a set, and it is a collection of distinct elements, which means elements can't be repeated. Sets are classified as `SortedSet` and `BitSet`. The last one is a map, which is a key-value-based collection that can have a `SortedMap`. These are all part of the `scala.collection` package.

After the root package, let's take a look at the collections hierarchy in the `scala.collection.mutable` package:

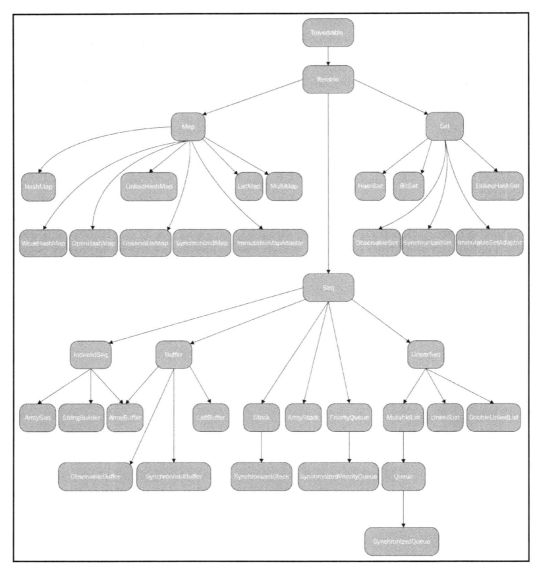

The scala.collection.mutable collections package

It may be frightening when you first see these, but it works as a utility when you use these collections wisely. Collections in the `scala.collection.mutable` package, as expected, contain methods that can be used to add/remove elements in the collection. The hierarchy of this package is similar to `Seq`, `Set`, and `Map` traits. Afterwards, more concrete implementations that are specific to some use cases are part of the package. The figure itself is self-explanatory; more and more implementations of these collection traits are there for us to use. `IndexedSeq` has more implementations now, such as `ArraySeq`, `StringBuilder`, and `ArrayBuffer`. Another trait, named `Buffer`, is introduced. A few implementations, such as `Stack`, `ArrayStack`, and `PriorityQueue` extend directly from `Seq` trait. In the same way, the other two traits, Set and Map, also have a few concrete implementations. HashSet and BitSet are for sets, and HashMap, LinkedHashMap, and ListMap extend Map.

Finally, let's take a look at the hierarchy of the `scala.collection.immutable` package:

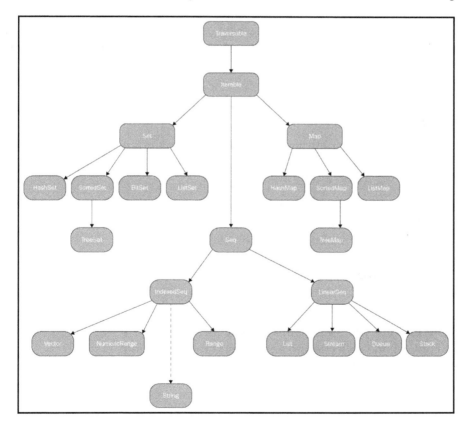

The scala.collection.immutable package

The collections hierarchy is similar to mutable collections apart from the fact that *immutable* collections, don't have the `Buffer` trait; the difference is that these collections do not have methods that let you mutate the same collection. Though it's possible to transform collections, it means that these collections have higher-order methods that can traverse and apply a function to each element, resulting in another collection. This is one of the ways to deal with immutable collections.

This hierarchy also has the *Traversable* and *Iterable* super traits. These traits consist of most helper methods. These are universal methods that can be used with almost any collection in Scala. By default, Scala assumes a collection to be of the `immutable` type. It's good if you use them. It's good to know that you can also create your own custom collections. For this, there's a sub-package named `generic` in the `scala.collection` package that consists of the helpers required to create a collection implementation.

When we implement these collections, we assume there are ways to use and manipulate these collections, and indeed there are many higher-order helper functions that let you do so. Most of the basic and universal helpers are defined in super traits that other collections implement. Let's take a look at these traits.

Traversable

This is a super trait of all other implementations for collections in Scala. Traversable defines a few methods that help to access collection elements, or perform operations on them. These operations can be categorized as follows:

- **Additions**: Methods that append two traversables together. For two traversable collections, such as `xs` and `ys`:
    - For example, `xs ++ ys`

- **Transformations**: Methods such as `map`, `flatMap`, and `collect` come in this category:
    - For example, `xs.map(elem => elem.toString + "default")`
- **Conversions**: Methods with a format such as `toXXX` *or* `mkString`. These are used to convert one collection to another suitable collection:
    - For example, `xs.toArray`, `xs.mkString`, and `xs.toStream`

- **Copying**: Helper methods that copy elements from a collection to another collection, such as an array or buffer:
  - For example, `xs.copyToBuffer(arr)`
- **Information retrievals**: Methods that retrieve information such as size, or whether the collection has elements or not:
  - For example, `xs.isEmpty`, `xs.isNonEmpty`, and `xs.hasDefiniteSize`
- **Element retrievals**: Methods that retrieve an element from a collection:
  - For example, `xs.head` and `xs.find(elem => elem.toCharArray.length == 4)`
- **Sub collections**: Methods that return a sub-collection, based on ordering, or a predicate:
  - For example, `xs.tail`, `xs.init`, `xs.filter(elem => elem.toCharArray.length == 4)`
- **Folding**: Methods that apply a binary operation on each of the successive elements of a collection. Also, there are some special forms of folding operations:
  - For example, `xs.foldLeft(z)(op)`, and `xs.product`

We'll go through implementation details of almost all these methods later in the chapter. For now, it's important to know that the `Traversable` trait mixes in with `TraversableLike` and few other traits. If you don't understand what a mix-in of traits is, we'll discuss that when we talk about object-oriented programming in Scala in subsequent chapters:

```
trait Traversable[+A] extends TraversableLike[A, Traversable[A]] with
GenTraversable[A] with TraversableOnce[A] with
GenericTraversableTemplate[A, Traversable]
```

Traversable has an abstract `foreach` method. Any implementation that mixes in `Traversable` needs to define this abstract `foreach` method:

```
def foreach[U](f: Elem => U)
```

As shown in the `foreach` method signature, it has a type parameter, `U`, which stands for the type of data that we'll impose when we'll use the method. The `foreach` method traverses the collection, applying a function to each of its elements.

Iterable

Iterable is also a trait that other collections mix in with. Iterable mixes in *Traversable,* and also defines the `foreach` abstract method. Iterable also has an abstract method named `iterator`. Implementations that mix in the *Iterable* trait have to define this abstract method:

```
def iterator: Iterator[A]
```

You can see that the `iterator` method returns an `Iterator`, which has the `hasNext` and `next` methods. Using an Iterator, we can fetch all elements one by one, or perform an operation. A closer look will tell you that Traversable can traverse the whole collection in one go, while for an Iterable, the pull approach works well. Each iteration gives an element.

Of course, Iterables support all methods from *Traversable.* Along with that, there are a few more methods:

- **Sub-iterations**: Methods that return another chunked iterator:
  - For example, `xs.grouped(size)`, and `xs.sliding(size)`
- **Sub-collections**: Methods that return parts of collections:
  - For example, `xs.takeRight(n)`, and `xs.dropRight(n)`
- **Zipping**: Methods that return iterable collection elements in pairs:
  - For example, `xs.zip(ys)`, and `xs.zipWithIndex`
- **Comparisons**: Methods that compare two iterable collections according to the order of elements:
  - For example, `xs sameElements ys`

One possible declaration of `Iterable` is as follows:

```
trait Iterable[+A] extends Traversable[A] with GenIterable[A] with
GenericTraversableTemplate[A, Iterable] with IterableLike[A, Iterable[A]]
```

As you can see, the `Iterable` trait mixes in `Traversable`, along with a few others. That's how it exists in the hierarchy. The following Iterables are three traits, named `Seq`, `Set`, and `Map`. Let's go through them.

Seq

The `Seq` represents a sequence of elements. Its signature is as follows:

```
trait Seq[+A] extends PartialFunction[Int, A] with Iterable[A] with
GenSeq[A] with GenericTraversableTemplate[A, Seq] with SeqLike[A, Seq[A]]
```

As shown, Seq extends PartialFunction, but what does that mean? Remember, we discussed partial functions in the previous chapter. These functions are defined for a particular set of values from the domain. In the case of Seq, that domain is the length −1. It is clear from the signature that a Seq can take an Int, and responds with an element of type A. Here, A is the type of the collection element. Let's look at an example:

```
scala> val aSeq = scala.collection.LinearSeq[Int](1,2,3,4)
aSeq: scala.collection.LinearSeq[Int] = List(1, 2, 3, 4)

scala> aSeq(1)
res0: Int = 2
```

In the preceding example, when we define the sequence, it becomes a partial function of type PartialFunction[Int, Int]. It means that passing any value from its length - 1 as a parameter to our sequence will result in a value from the sequence of type A, which in our case, is also an Int. The reason that a Seq is defined for only some particular values from the domain is to show that if we pass an index for which aSeq does not have a value, it will give an exception:

```
scala> aSeq(5)
java.lang.IndexOutOfBoundsException: 5
  at scala.collection.LinearSeqOptimized.apply(LinearSeqOptimized.scala:63)
  at
scala.collection.LinearSeqOptimized.apply$(LinearSeqOptimized.scala:61)
  at scala.collection.immutable.List.apply(List.scala:86)
  ... 29 elided
```

A Seq, being a PartialFunction, can prove a boon for us as developers, as there are many instances where very complex logic can become so easy to implement. There's also a method, isDefinedAt. As you may be aware, we can use it to check whether the partial function is defined for the value. A sequence is said to have a length, and encompasses two variants, named IndexedSeq and LinearSeq. These names imply most of what these collections are there for. An indexed sequence is recommended to use when we access them via indexing; in other words, by calling the length or apply methods. A linear sequence, however, is used where the performance of a subsection of a collection is important. It means that calling a method on a collection and breaking it into sub-sequences is important. Now, after knowing all this, let's take a look at the categories of operations that can be performed on these sequences:

- **Length and indexing**: Methods that depend on the length of the sequence, mainly via index or size:
    - For example, xs.apply(1), xs.length, xs.indices, and xs.indexWhere(predicate)

- **Additions**: Methods that add an element at the beginning or at the end of a sequence:
    - For example, `x+:(xs)` and `xs.:+(x)`
- **Updates**: Methods that update an element in a sequence:
    - For example, `xs(1) = 12` and `xs updated (1, 12)`
- **Sorting**: Methods that sort a given sequence:
    - For example, `xs.sorted` and `xs sortWith op`
- **Reversing**: Methods that reverse a sequence:
    - For example, `xs.reverse`, and so on
- **Comparisons and checks**: Methods that reverse a sequence:
    - For example, `xs.contains(x)` and `xs.endsWith(x)`
- **Multi-set operations**: Methods that results based on some set operations like union and distinct:
    - For example, `xs.union(ys)` and `xs.distinct`

We'll go through the implementation details of these methods in subsequent sections. Now, let's take a look at different variants of sequences:

Scala's mutable Sequences	*Scala's immutable Sequences*

Linear sequences
  • **MutableList**
  • **LinkedList**
  • **DoubleLinkedList**
 	
Indexed sequences
  • **ArraySeq**
  • **StringBuilder**
  • **ArrayBuffer**
Buffer
  • **ArrayBuffer**
  • **ListBuffer**
  • **ObservableBuffer**
  • **SynchronizedBuffer**
Other sequences
  • **Stack**
  • **ArrayStack**
  • **PriorityQueue**
	Linear sequences
	  • **List**
	  • **Stream**
	  • **Queue**
	  • **Stack**
	
	Indexed sequences
	  • **Vector**
	  • **NumericRange**
	  • **String**
	  • **Range**

Sequences

There's another form of sequences, named *Buffer*, that is mutable. It allows addition, update, removal, and other mutating operations on it. These mutations are done via methods such as +=, ++=, and *insert*. There's another sub-trait of *Iterable* which is called Map. Let's go through it.

Map

A Map can be represented as a collection containing elements in the form of a key-value pair:

```
trait Map[K, +V] extends Iterable[(K, V)] with GenMap[K, V] with MapLike[K,
V, Map[K, V]]
```

As we've just shown, Map mixes in Iterable and MapLike traits, and MapLike extends the PartialFunction trait, so we can also use maps as a partial function. Also, it is worth noting the type parameters K and V. Here, type K binds a key to value V. Here's how we can define a Map:

```
scala> val aMap = Map("country" -> "capital", "Poland" -> "Warsaw")

aMap: scala.collection.immutable.Map[String, String] = Map(country ->
capital, Poland -> Warsaw)
```

The preceding code is a map of type string to string, which means it maps a string key to a string value. As for any other collection, we need a few methods to access maps. There is more than one category for doing so. Let's go through them:

- **Associations and lookups**: Methods that look up an element from a map:
  - For example, as.get(key), and as(key), as contains key
- **Additions**: Methods that adds key-value pairs to an existing map:
  - For example, as + (key -> value) and as ++ kvs
- **Removals**: Methods that remove a pair from a given map:
  - For example, as - (key)
- **Sub-collections**: Methods that return a sub-collection from a given map:
  - For example, as.keys, as.keySet, and as.values
- **Transformations**: Methods that transform a map by applying a function to each value of a given map:
  - For example, as mapValues func

A `Map` can have several different variants based on the category, whether it's mutable or immutable:

Mutable Maps	*Immutable Maps*	
• *HashMap* • *WeakHashMap* • *OpenHashMap* • *LinkedHashMap* • *ObservableMap* • *SynchronizedMap* • *ListMap* • *MultiMap* • *ImmutableMapAdaptor*	• *HashMap* • *SortedMap* • *TreeMap* • *ListMap*	

Maps

In the preceding image, we have a couple of variants of maps in Scala. Did you notice that we have the same `HashMap` available in both the versions in different packages, *mutable* as well as *immutable*? We use these different maps depending on our requirements. After `Seq` and `Map`, there's another sub-trait of `Iterable`, named `Set`.

Set

A `Set` is a collection that contains multiple elements with no duplication at all:

```
trait Set[A] extends (A) ⇒ Boolean with Iterable[A] with GenSet[A] with
GenericSetTemplate[A, Set] with SetLike[A, Set[A]]
```

As shown in the preceding code, the `Set extends (A) => Boolean` expression, which means that passing a parameter of type A to a set of type A will result in a Boolean. The Boolean result shows whether the `Set` contains the element passed as a parameter or not. Let's see this in an example:

```
scala> val aSet = Set(1,2,3,4)
aSet: scala.collection.immutable.Set[Int] = Set(1, 2, 3, 4)

scala> aSet(2)
res0: Boolean = true
```

```
scala> aSet(5)
res1: Boolean = false

scala> aSet(0)
res2: Boolean = false
```

It can be seen that the value 2 is present in `aSet`, and the values 5 and 0 are not, so therefore passing 5 or 0 results in false. Let's go through a few methods defined in `Set`:

- **Comparisons and checks**: Methods that check for a condition:
  - For example, `xs.contains(x)`, and `xs.subsetOf(x)`

- **Additions**: Methods that add an element or a collection of elements to a set:
  - For example, `xs + x` and `xs ++ ys`

- **Removals**: Methods that remove an element or collection of elements from a set:
  - For example, `xs - x` and `xs -- ys`

- **Binary operations**: Methods that perform binary operations between two different sets:
  - For example, `xs | ys`, `xs & ys`, `xs` intersect `ys`, `xs` union `ys`, and so on

A `Set` can have several different variants based on whether it's mutable or immutable:

Mutable Sets	*Immutable Sets*	
<ul><li>*HashSet*</li><li>*BitSet*</li><li>*ObservableSet*</li><li>*SynchronizedSet*</li><li>*LinkedHashSet*</li><li>*ImmutableSetAdaptor*</li></ul>	<ul><li>*HashSet*</li><li>*SortedSet*</li><li style="list-style:none"> • *TreeSet*</li><li>*BitSet*</li><li>*ListSet*</li></ul>	

Sets

A few variants of sets contain different types, such as `HashSet`, `BitSet`, and `SynchronizedSet`, and based on the need, we can utilize them.

Now that we have an idea of some top-level collection traits in Scala, let's take a look at some concrete implementations of them. We'll talk about the common collections we use in Scala, the way they can be constructed, and how Scala treats a particular collection when we add or remove an element. It'll give you a brief idea of how Scala collections behave.

Commonly used collections in Scala

Let's start by discussing a few immutable concrete collections.

List

A list is a linear sequence and can be defined simply, as follows:

```
val aList = List(1,2,3,4)
```

The syntax shown declares and instantiates the linear sequence with the elements provided. The runtime representation of the list constructed will look like this:

```
1 :: 2 :: 3 :: 4 :: Nil
```

Here, `Nil` represents the end of the list. It's normal to represent an empty list as `Nil`. The preceding representation is also a way to construct a list, and this is possible because of the "::" operator. This is called the *cons* operator, and it is used to construct a list. It's a right-associative operator:

```
scala> aList.::(5)
res2: List[Int] = List(5, 1, 2, 3, 4)
```

Calling the *cons* operator on the list results in a list with the new element added at the beginning of the list. This is equivalent to calling the same, using the following code:

```
scala> 5 :: aList
res0: List[Int] = List(5, 1, 2, 3, 4)
```

We've mentioned that operations such as adding an element to a list don't affect the list that was previously created, but it copies the same list to another, with an added element. The reason for this is that lists are immutable. A pictorial representation of how this might look will give you an insight into what is happening. So, let's take a look at this:

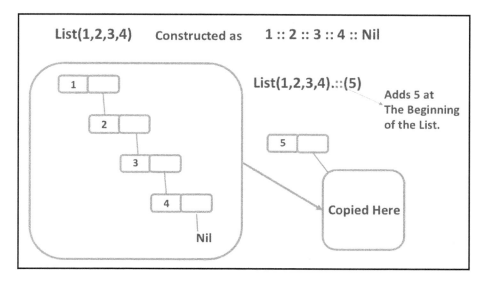

Adding an element to a List

The figure is self-explanatory, and represents the concept of adding an element to a list. Lists provide many higher-order functions, such as `map`, `flatMap`, and `filter`, which make it easy to work with. With this construction syntax and easier access to the list's head (the first element of the list) and tail (which represents every element in the list except the first), it is easy to create patterns of lists and use them in pattern matching based on your needs. Operations such as *fold* and *reduce* are also of higher importance, as they provide a mechanism to perform binary operations on elements within the sequence. These are high-performing data structures, and provide constant time access to their elements.

Map

The standard immutable map can be instantiated as easily as this:

```scala
scala> val aMap = Map(1 -> "one", 2 -> "two", 3 -> "three")
aMap: scala.collection.immutable.Map[Int,String] = Map(1 -> one, 2 -> two, 3 -> three)
```

We can provide as many key-value pairs as we want. We associate a key to its corresponding value by using the "->" operator . It can be seen that the default implementation of a map corresponds to `scala.collection.immutable.Map[Int, String]`, and it's not possible if we try to mutate the pairs. Though it's possible to add new pairs to construct another map with updated elements using the + method:

```scala
scala> aMap.+(4 -> "four")
res5: scala.collection.immutable.Map[Int, String] = Map(1 -> one, 2 -> two,
3 -> three, 4 -> four)
```

But this will not change the map we declared `aMap`:

```scala
scala> println(aMap)
Map(1 -> one, 2 -> two, 3 -> three)
```

We also discussed that map and sequences are also a `PartialFunction`, so we can check whether a value has been defined for a particular key:

```scala
scala> aMap.isDefinedAt(4)
res8: Boolean = false

scala> aMap.isDefinedAt(2)
res9: Boolean = true
```

Other versions of `Map` also exist, such as `ListMap`, and `SynchronizedMap`. These can be used if you need them. For example, you might prefer to use a `ListMap` when you need to traverse linearly on a map with better performance. Also, when mutable map implementation is needed in a thread-safe manner, one would prefer to use `SynchronizedMap`.

SortedSet

A `SortedSet` is a trait that represents a set of elements. It produces elements in a sorted manner based on ordering, because the default implementation stores elements in the form of a binary tree. One of the forms of `SortedSet` is a `TreeSet`. Creating a `TreeSet` expects you to provide an implicit `Ordering[A]` that takes care of the way elements will be ordered:

```scala
TreeSet()(implicit ordering: Ordering[A])
```

So, to create a `TreeSet`, we'll create an `Ordering` object in the current scope. Without `Ordering`, the compiler won't allow you to create a `TreeSet`:

```
package chapter5

import scala.collection.immutable.TreeSet

object TreeSetImpl extends App {

  //implicit val ordering = Ordering.fromLessThan[Int] (_ > _)

  val treeSet = new TreeSet() + (1, 3, 12, 3, 5)

  println(treeSet)
}
```

Here is the result:

```
Error:(9, 17) diverging implicit expansion for type scala.math.Ordering[T1]
starting with method Tuple9 in object Ordering
  val treeSet = new TreeSet() + (1, 3, 12, 3, 5)
Error:(9, 17) not enough arguments for constructor TreeSet: (implicit
ordering: Ordering[A])scala.collection.immutable.TreeSet[A].
Unspecified value parameter ordering.
  val treeSet = new TreeSet() + (1, 3, 12, 3, 5)
```

Uncommenting the line where we define an implicit value for `Ordering` will work fine. So, uncomment that and try running it. This will result in the following output:

```
TreeSet(12, 5, 3, 1)
```

Streams

Streams are powerful. Let's see why. Streams can be of infinite length; it may sound impractical having a sequence of infinite length, but when the computation happens lazily, this works OK. Streams serve the same purpose and the computation happens lazily. Let's see how we can create streams:

```
scala> val aStream = Stream(1,2,3,4,55,6)
aStream: scala.collection.immutable.Stream[Int] = Stream(1, ?)
```

We didn't do anything extraordinary, except replace the `List` keyword with `Stream`, but REPL gives us back something different:

```
scala.collection.immutable.Stream[Int] = Stream(1, ?)
```

You can see here that `Stream` is computed only till the very first element, because there's no need to go and compute other elements as of now. That's what we call *lazy computation*. Streams can also be constructed using *cons* like this:

```
scala> val anotherStream = 1 #:: 2 #:: 3 #:: Stream.empty
anotherStream: scala.collection.immutable.Stream[Int] = Stream(1, ?)
```

It's understandable that wherever we require our elements to compute lazily, we can use streams. One of the example use cases is when you require short-circuited evaluation from your function. You may pass a stream and evaluate. It's worth noting that a stream is not lazy with its head element, so your function will be evaluated for the first element.

Vector

The difference between the performance of a linear sequence and an indexed sequence starts to matter when our requirement is to manipulate elements in the middle of a sequence. And because of the linear performance of sequences such as a list, the performance degrades for them. Therefore, indexed sequences come to the rescue! Vector is an example of an immutable indexed sequence. The way to create a vector is to simply use the `Vector` keyword with its `apply` method, or to simply represent it as follows:

```
scala> val vector = Vector(1,2,3)
vector: scala.collection.immutable.Vector[Int] = Vector(1, 2, 3)

scala> println(vector)
Vector(1, 2, 3)
```

To add elements to `vector`, we can use methods such as ":+" and "+:":

```
scala> vector :+ 4
res12: scala.collection.immutable.Vector[Int] = Vector(1, 2, 3, 4)

scala> 4 +: vector
res15: scala.collection.immutable.Vector[Int] = Vector(4, 1, 2, 3)
```

These are indexed in order to retrieve a value by passing an index:

```
scala> vector(2)
res16: Int = 3
```

We got the value 3, because the index starts from 0. It's good that we can check whether a value is defined at a particular index, because it is a sequence:

```scala
scala> vector.isDefinedAt(5)
res17: Boolean = false
```

It's possible to update an element at a certain position by using the `updated` method:

```scala
scala> vector.updated(2,10)
res19: scala.collection.immutable.Vector[Int] = Vector(1, 2, 10)
```

A call to this `updated` method with an index and an element replaces the element at the passed index with the element passed as a parameter. The good thing about this operation is that it takes constant time and doesn't affect the original sequence. Hence, if you try to print the sequence we created, you'll get the elements unchanged:

```scala
scala> println(vector)
Vector(1, 2, 3)
```

Immutable stack

You may need a collection with *last in first out* traversal. For that, Scala provides the `stack` implementation. It's easy to create a stack, and `push` and `pop` elements in the stack:

```scala
scala> val stack = Stack(1,2,3)
stack: scala.collection.immutable.Stack[Int] = Stack(1, 2, 3)

scala> stack.pop
res24: scala.collection.immutable.Stack[Int] = Stack(2, 3)

scala> stack.push(4)
res26: scala.collection.immutable.Stack[Int] = Stack(4, 1, 2, 3)
```

Stacks are immutable, so performing any operation will not change the elements from the stack that was created previously.

Immutable queue

For those who don't know it already, a queue is *first in first out* data structure. Two helper methods to put an element into a queue and remove them are `enqueue` and `dequeue`. Let's create a queue:

```scala
scala> val queue = Queue(1,2,3)
queue: scala.collection.immutable.Queue[Int] = Queue(1, 2, 3)

scala> queue.enqueue(4)
res27: scala.collection.immutable.Queue[Int] = Queue(1, 2, 3, 4)

scala> queue.dequeue
res28: (Int, scala.collection.immutable.Queue[Int]) = (1,Queue(2, 3))
```

The preceding code is the method for enqueuing an element in a queue. It can be seen that `dequeue` returns the element removed along with the rest of the queue.

Ranges

Range describes a range of numbers. There are a few helper methods we can use to create a range in Scala. Let's take a look at them:

```scala
scala> val oneTo10 = 1 to 10
oneTo10: scala.collection.immutable.Range.Inclusive = Range 1 to 10

scala> val oneTo10By2 = 1 to 10 by 2
oneTo10By2: scala.collection.immutable.Range = inexact Range 1 to 10 by 2

scala> oneTo10 foreach println
1
2
3
4
. . . remaining elements

scala> oneTo10By2 foreach println
1
3
5
7
9
```

We created two ranges. The first one simply contains numbers ranging from 1 to 10, inclusive. Then we created numbers ranging from 1 to 10 with a step size of 2. There's also a way to create a range that does not include the last element. This can be done using the `util` method:

```
scala> val oneUntil5 = 1 until 5
oneUntil5:scala.collection.immutable.Range = Range 1 until 5

scala> oneUntil5 foreach println
1
2
3
4
```

Here, we created a range using the `Until` method containing numbers 1 to 5. Printing this range yielded the numbers from 1 to 4, because `Until` does not include the last element. `Range` is also an immutable collection. Now, after going through these immutable collections, let's take a look at few mutable concrete collections. We'll start with the most common, `ArrayBuffer`.

ArrayBuffer

`ArrayBuffer` is only available as a mutable sequence in Scala. These are efficient collections; they make it easy to add an element at the end of a collection. `ArrayBuffer` is also an indexed sequence, so retrieving an element via an index doesn't degrade the performance. Let's see how we can create and use `ArrayBuffer` in Scala:

```
scala> import scala.collection.mutable._
import scala.collection.mutable._

scala> val buff = ArrayBuffer(1,2,3)
buff: scala.collection.mutable.ArrayBuffer[Int] = ArrayBuffer(1, 2, 3)

scala> println(buff)
ArrayBuffer(1, 2, 3)
```

We can create `ArrayBuffer` by first importing
the `scala.collection.mutable` package. We can instantiate it by providing elements in
the constructor. We can add and remove elements to the buffer using methods provided for
`ArrayBuffer`:

```scala
scala> buff += 4
res35: buff.type = ArrayBuffer(1, 2, 3, 4)

scala> println(buff)
ArrayBuffer(1, 2, 3, 4)

scala> buff -= 4
res36: buff.type = ArrayBuffer(1, 2, 3)

scala> println(buff)
ArrayBuffer(1, 2, 3)
```

ListBuffer

`ArrayBuffer` uses an array to store elements internally, whereas `ListBuffer` uses a
linked list representation. Operations performed on these buffers are similar to that of
`ArrayBuffers`:

```scala
scala> val listBuffer = ListBuffer("Alex", "Bob", "Charles")
listBuffer: scala.collection.mutable.ListBuffer[String] = ListBuffer(Alex,
Bob, Charles)

scala> listBuffer += "David"
res39: listBuffer.type = ListBuffer(Alex, Bob, Charles, David)

scala> println(listBuffer)
ListBuffer(Alex, Bob, Charles, David)
```

It's worth noting that because of the internal linked list representation, it's recommended to
use `ListBuffer` instead of `ArrayBuffer` if our requirement is to convert our collection to
a list. It's applicable vice versa, if the requirement is to convert our collection to an array.

StringBuilder

StringBuilder is used to build a sequence of strings. A simple call to toString will convert it to String:

```scala
scala> val builder = new StringBuilder
builder: StringBuilder =

scala> builder ++= "aa"
res45: builder.type = aa

scala> builder ++= "b"
res46: builder.type = aab

scala> builder.toString
res48: String = aab
```

There're other mutable versions of stacks, queues, and maps. There are methods provided to update these mutable collections.

Array

Array in Scala is defined as follows; it extends the Serializable and Cloneable traits from Java. Also, it can be seen that arrays are generic:

```scala
final class Array[T] extends java.io.Serializable with java.lang.Cloneable
```

In Scala, arrays are mutable. Defining an array is simple:

```scala
scala> val array = Array("about", "to", "declare")
array: Array[String] = Array(about, to, declare)
```

Here, it's possible to perform the operations that we perform on sequences. Arrays are indexed and mutable as well:

```scala
scala> array(0) = "Where"

scala> array foreach println
Where
to
declare
```

It's also possible to perform map operations on an array, which makes Scala's arrays better than their Java counterparts.

Up to now, we have introduced all the common collections, and have a basic idea about how these collections can be declared and used. But what makes Scala collections powerful is the set of rich operations performed on these collections. There's a set of operations that can be performed using some higher-order methods available with these collections. It's time to go and take a look at those.

Rich operations performed on collections

We have quite a few methods for our collections, which we can use to simplify almost every problem regarding collections in Scala. We are going to take a look at some important methods. First, let's set the stage: so consider a scenario where you have some structured data related to football players. and you have to perform manipulations based on that. We'll perform a set of operations on the data using our collection. We'll also learn about methods, their signatures, and use cases along the way. Here's a simple code snippet that shows what we just said—nothing too interesting as of now:

```
package chapter5

object CollectionOperations extends App {

  val source = io.Source.fromFile("../src/chapter5/football_stats.csv")
// Give pathString for the csv file

}
```

Here's the thing—we have a CSV file that contains some data as comma-separated values. We can read the data in our program as a `BufferedSource`:

```
io.Source.fromFile("filePath")
```

This will load the CSV file's contents. The first thing we can do is to convert the data into a readable format so that it gets easier for us to perform any operation on it. For that, we have a case class, `Player`:

```
case class Player(name: String, nationality: String, age: String, club:
String, domesticLeague: String, rawTotal: String, finalScore: String,
ranking2016: String, ranking2015: String)
```

We'll try to read the content from the file and create a collection of players. The following expression reads from the buffered source, and converts each line to an element in a `List`:

```
source.getLines().toList
```

Here, the `getLines` method converts the buffered source to an `Iterator` object of string type. A call to the `toXXX` form of the method can be used to convert between *traversables*. We've made a call to the `toList` method on our `Iterator` object. This converts the *Iterable* of type string to a list of strings. There are other versions such as `toIterable`, `toSeq`, `toIndexedSeq`, `toBuffer`, `toSet`, and `toVector`. All these methods reside in a trait named `TraversableOnce`.

We can use the `toXXX` method to convert into another Traversable of type XXX, where XXX is a placeholder for `Set`, `Vector`, `Buffer`, and so on.

After reading the content from the CSV file, we now have a list of strings, with each string containing information about a player in the following format:

```
2016,Up/down,2015,2014,2013,Name,Nationality, Club at Dec 20 2016,Domestic
league, Age at 20 Dec 2016,RAW TOTAL,HIGHEST SCORE REMOVED,FINAL
SCORE,VOTES CAST,No1 PICK
```

Each line has information such as the ranking of the player in the past few years, his/her name, nationality, club, points scored, and age. We'll parse the string and map all the information to our `Player` object. Let's do it:

```
def giveMePlayers(list: List[String]): List[Player] = list match {
    case head :: tail => tail map {line =>
      val columns = line.split((",")).map(_.trim)
      Player(columns(5),columns(6),columns(9),columns(7),
        columns(8),columns(10), columns(12), columns(0),columns(2))
    }
    case Nil => List[Player]()
  }
```

In this method, we see one important method that works for collections. Our `giveMePlayers` function parses the list of string, and as its name suggests, it returns a list of players. The function performs a pattern match on the list of strings. We have matched the list as `head :: tail`; it treats the head as the first element of the list, and the tail as the rest of the elements. It can also be seen that the list can be empty; in that case, the second scenario will be executed, and the function will return an empty list. As we know from the CSV, the first line contains the meta-information about the rest of the file. So we omit the `head` and perform a `map` operation on `tail`, that is, the rest of the list. The `map` method basically performs the given operation on each element and returns the collection with the resulting values. In our case, we're splitting the comma-separated values from each line and converting values to the `Player` object. At the end of the call to the `map` method, we'll get a list of players.

The `map` method composes another collection, applying an operation passed to it.

The definition of the `map` method looks as follows:

```
def map[B](f: (A) ⇒ B): Traversable[B]
```

The `map` method takes a function that converts type `A` to type `B`, and performs that operation to each element of the collection, and finally returns a collection of type B. In our case, types A and B were `String` and `Player`.

At this point, our code looks like this:

```
package chapter5

object CollectionOperations extends App {

  val source =
io.Source.fromFile("/Users/vika/Documents/LSProg/LSPWorkspace/FirstProject/
src/chapter5/football_stats.csv")
  val bufferedSourceToList: List[String] = {
    val list = source.getLines().toList
    source.close()
    list
  }

  def giveMePlayers(list: List[String]): List[Player] = list match {
      case head :: tail => tail map {line =>
        val columns = line.split((",")).map(_.trim)
        Player(columns(5),columns(6),columns(9),columns(7),
          columns(8),columns(10), columns(12), columns(0),columns(2))
      }
      case Nil => List[Player]()
  }

  val players = giveMePlayers(bufferedSourceToList) }

case class Player(name: String, nationality: String, age:String, club:
String, domesticLeague: String, rawTotal: String, finalScore: String,
ranking2016: String, ranking2015: String)
```

Now, we have a fully formed collection of `Players`, thanks to our `map` method. We can perform lots and lots of different operations. We can make a list of top 10 players. How can this be done? By using our `filter` method:

```
val filterTop10 = players filter(_.ranking2016.toInt < 11)
```

This is simple; it's just a call to filter, then we tell it what predicate to filter elements upon. It'll do the filtering for you. We have checked the ranking for each player and preserved those for whom the value is less than 11:

- The `filter` method filters the collection elements that satisfy the predicate
- The `filterNot` method filters the collection elements that do not satisfy the predicate

The signature of the `filter` method looks as follows:

```
def filter(p: A => Boolean): Repr
```

This `filter` method takes a predicate, based on the predicate. The method filters out the Traversable. Here, `Repr` is a type parameter for the collection, and our Traversable collection looks like `TraversableLike[+A, +Repr]`.

To check whether the method filters out the right players, you may want to print it and see. Why not print our players in some structured way? Take a look at the following code:

```
def showPlayers(players: List[Player]) = players.foreach{p =>
  println(s"""Player: ${p.name}    Country: ${p.nationality}    Ranking
2016: ${p.ranking2016}

***** Other Information *****
Age: ${p.age}  |  Club: ${p.club}  |  Domestic League: ${p.domesticLeague}
Raw Total: ${p.rawTotal}  |  Final Score: ${p.finalScore}  |  Ranking 2015:
${p.ranking2015}
#################################################################""")
  }
```

We have defined the `showPlayers` function, which takes a list and prints player information in the following manner:

```
Player: Cristiano Ronaldo  Country: Portugal        Ranking 2016: 1

***** Other Information *****
Age: 32  |  Club: Real Madrid  |  Domestic League: Spain
Raw Total: 4829  |  Final Score: 4789  |  Ranking 2015: 2
#########################################################
```

I think you're keen enough to see that the filter traverses through the whole list to check whether the ranking is less than 11, bravo! Also, understand that this is not the way we would do this to our collection if the list were sorted. In that case, we've a few other methods, and one of them is takeWhile:

```
val takeTop10 = players takeWhile(_.ranking2016.toInt < 11)
```

This takeWhile method also takes a predicate, the same in our case, and returns a list of elements for which the predicate is true. In our case, it works, and we get the top 10 players:

- The takeWhile method takes the longest sub-collection of elements that satisfies the predicate
- The dropWhile method drops the longest sub-collection of elements that satisfies the predicate

The signature looks almost exactly like our filter method. It takes a predicate, and returns a Traversable:

```
def takeWhile(p: (A) ⇒ Boolean): Traversable[A]

def dropWhile(p: (A) ⇒ Boolean): Traversable[A]
```

There's also a dropWhile version of the method. Its intent is almost the same as takeWhile; the only thing that differs is that it drops those elements that satisfy the predicate. There can be more of this sort of method, based on the requirements we can use. One of them is the partition method, which splits apart our list into a tuple of two lists: one that satisfies the predicate, and other that doesn't. Take a look at the following code snippet:

```
val first50Players = players take 50
val (top20,least30) = first50Players partition(_.ranking2016.toInt < 21)
showPlayers(top20)
```

First, the take method selects 50 players from our list of *players*. Then, we call the partition method on our first 50 players, which splits our list into two sub-lists based on the predicate we pass. Here, we want to divide the first 50 players into two separate collections of 20 and 30 players. After calling this function, we get two new values, top20 and least30, which have the top 20 players and the bottom 30 players out of the first 50.

A simple one-liner can do this much with the collection of elements; that's the power of Scala collections:

- The `take` method selects the first n elements from the collection
- The `drop` method drops the first n elements from the collection
- The `partition` method drops the first n elements from the collection

The signatures of these methods are simple:

```
def drop(n: Int): Traversable[A]

def take(n: Int): Traversable[A]

def partition(p: (A) ⇒ Boolean): (Traversable[A], Traversable[A])
```

The `take` and `drop` methods take the number of elements to select or drop. The other method, `partition`, expects a predicate, splits the collection into two sub-collections, and returns a tuple of those two sub-collections. There are a few more of these methods; let's take a look at them:

- The `slice` method selects an interval of elements
- The `span` method splits the collection into two collections based on the predicate, where the order of elements is not preserved
- The `splitAt` method splits a collection at a given position

These methods are simple, as they do exactly what their description implies. Their description also explains the same:

```
def slice(from: Int, until: Int): Traversable[A]

def span(p: (A) ⇒ Boolean): (Traversable[A], Traversable[A])

def splitAt(n: Int): (Traversable[A], Traversable[A])
```

The `slice` method takes the initial and last index, and returns that number of elements as a collection. The second method, `span`, works exactly the same as the `partition` method. It takes a predicate and returns a pair of collections: the first satisfies the predicate, and second does not. It's possible that the order of elements has not been preserved.

The last of the three, `splitAt`, takes a value n and returns a pair of sub-collections, split at n. These methods make it easy to implement scenarios such as this:

```
Select Players from Germany who have ranking in Top 50.

first50Players filter(_.nationality.equals("Germany"))
```

Let's take a look at one more set of methods, using which we can check for a predicate in our collection:

- The `count` method counts the number of elements that satisfy a given predicate
- The `exists` method checks whether a predicate holds true for even a single element in a given collection
- The `forAll` method checks whether a predicate holds true for all elements in a given collection
- The `find` method finds the first element that satisfies a predicate

We can count the number of players from a particular country like this:

```
val isGermanPlayer: (Player => Boolean) =
_.nationality.equalsIgnoreCase("Germany")

val numberOfGermanPlayers = players count isGermanPlayer
println(s"German Players: $numberOfGermanPlayers")

Run:
German Players: 17
```

The partial function `isGermanPlayer` checks for a player's nationality. We then passed this partial function as a predicate to the `count` method, which gives the number of players. We may also want to check whether there are any players with an age above 45, and we may check that using the `exists` method:

```
val isAnyPlayerAbove45 = players exists(p => p.age.toInt > 40)
println(s"isAnyPlayerAbove45: $isAnyPlayerAbove45")

Run:
isAnyPlayerAbove45: false
```

The are two other methods, `forAll` and `find`. We'll check the top player with an age of more than 35 years:

```
val topPlayerWithAge35plus = players find(p => p.age.toInt > 35)
printPlayer(topPlayerWithAge35plus.get)

Run:
Player: Zlatan Ibrahimovic        Country: Sweden    Ranking 2016: 20

***** Other Information *****
Age: 36  |  Club: Manchester United  |  Domestic League: England
Raw Total: 1845  |  Final Score: 1809  |  Ranking 2015: 7
#######################################################
```

These methods are simple yet powerful, and composing them can bring down our solution approach to easy. Let's find the top 5 players by ranking, with ages over 35:

```
val top5PlayerWithAge35plus = players filter isAge35plus take 5
showPlayers(top5PlayerWithAge35plus)

Run:
Player: Zlatan Ibrahimovic        Country: Sweden    Ranking 2016: 20

***** Other Information *****
Age: 36  |  Club: Manchester United  |  Domestic League: England
Raw Total: 1845  |  Final Score: 1809  |  Ranking 2015: 7
#######################################################
. . . and next 4 player information
```

One of the examples is where we first called the `filter` method on our list of players, then called take 5 to select first 5 from results. We've seen these examples, so let's take a look at the definitions of these methods:

```
def find(p: (A) ⇒ Boolean): Option[A]

def count(p: (A) ⇒ Boolean): Int

def exists(p: (A) ⇒ Boolean): Boolean

def forall(p: (A) ⇒ Boolean): Boolean
```

All methods take a predicate and respond differently. The `find` method selects the very first element from a collection for which the predicate is satisfied. The next ones, `count` and `exists`, check for the total number of elements that satisfy the predicate, and whether any single element for which the predicate is satisfied exists, respectively.

Finally, the `forAll` method checks whether the predicate is satisfied for all elements in the collection. We can also call for a check if there's any element in our list using `isEmpty`, because it's obvious your filter on a collection results is an empty list. There're few methods to use to check information about the list:

- The `isEmpty` method counts the number of elements that satisfy a given predicate
- The `hasDefiniteSize` method checks whether a predicate holds true for even a single element in a given collection
- The `size` method checks whether a predicate holds true for all elements in a given collection

These methods, as their names suggest, are simple to use and clear to understand as well. You remember we did a pattern match on a list using `head :: tail`? Well, we can also call these methods on our collection in the same way. There exists a few more utility methods to access list elements:

- The `head` method returns the head element of the collection
- The `tail` method returns all elements except the head element
- The `init` method returns all but the last element
- The `last` method returns the last element of the collection
- The `reverse` method returns the list in reverse

We can use these methods while doing a pattern match, or whenever we may have to retrieve the first or last elements. Using the `init` or `tail` methods recursively is also a way to utilize list elements. Finally, one of the most important operations we can perform on a list of elements is to fold or reduce the list into a value—a single value. So, we can fold our list of players and construct another list of country names from that. How we can do this? Let's take a look at how we can use `fold` operations:

- The `fold` method folds collections using a binary associative operation
- The `foldLeft` method folds collections by applying a binary operation to the initial, and then each element going from left to right
- The `foldRight` method folds collections by applying a binary operation to the initial, and then each element going from right to left

Suppose we want to construct a list of country names from our top 20 players' information. We can do this as follows:

```
val Top20Countries = top20.foldLeft(List[String]())((b,a) => a.nationality
:: b)
```

We'll get the following on running the code:

```
List(Sweden, England, Germany, France, France, Spain, Argentina, Belgium,
Croatia, Argentina, Algeria, Chile, Gabon, Poland, Wales, Brazil, France,
Uruguay, Argentina, Portugal)
```

This can also be done by going from right to left through the list:

```
val top20Countries = top20.foldRight(List[String]())((b,a) => b.nationality
:: a)
```

We'll get the following on running the code:

```
List(Portugal, Argentina, Uruguay, France, Brazil, Wales, Poland, Gabon,
Chile, Algeria, Argentina, Croatia, Belgium, Argentina, Spain, France,
France, Germany, England, Sweden)
```

The definition of the `fold` methods look as follows:

```
def foldLeft[B](z: B)(op: (B, A) ⇒ B): B

def foldRight[B](z: B)(op: (A, B) => B): B
```

The method takes an initial value; in our case, it's a list. Then we pass a function that works on each element from our collection, and the value passed works as a seed to our operator function. The `foldLeft` and `foldRight` methods perform a binary operation on these two elements until it processes the last element in the collection, thus producing the final value for us. If you take a look at both of these methods, you'll be able to see that the order of parameters has changed. Also, the signatures of these `foldLeft` and `foldRight` methods are curried. The first curried parameter is the initial element, which works as an accumulator as we traverse through or fold our collection. The second parameter, which is a binary function, takes place and is applied to collection elements. This `fold` function results in one value over a collection that's an accumulated response for the whole collection.

After working with all these methods that make it easier to work with collections, let's take a look at a method that can convert our collection to a parallel collection, which can be processed in parallel. The method is `par`: when you call the method on our collection, it returns a `ParSeq`, that is, a parallel sequence. This parallel sequence is a parallel equivalent of our collection.

If you try to print the elements from this sequence quite a few times, the order will not be preserved, because of the parallel nature of the sequence:

```
top20Countries.par map(println(_))
```

We'll get the following on running the code:

```
Wales
Portugal
Argentina
France
Croatia
Argentina
Poland
France
Uruguay
. .. remaining elements
```

Now that we know we can convert our collections into their parallel equivalents, there should be other ways to build parallel collections. Let's go through parallel collections in Scala.

Parallel collections in Scala

It's obvious that if the number of elements in a collection is very large, then you would want to minimize the time it takes to manipulate the collection data. That's where breaking down the tasks and executing them parallel is an option, and a good one. Scala provides parallelism in the form of parallel collections, which works like a charm in scenarios where we have to deal with a big chunk of data. The good thing is that our `par` method can easily convert a normal sequential collection to its parallel counterpart implicitly, and the `map`, `fold`, and `filter` methods work great with parallel collections as well.

Understanding the architecture of parallel collections, or how these work on JVM, is out of the scope of this book. We'll keep our discussion limited to concrete implementations of parallel collections, and how we can use them in Scala. If you're into understanding parallel collections, Scala's documentation gives a brief overview at http://docs.scala-lang.org/ overviews/parallel-collections/overview. Another resource is the book *Learning Concurrent Programming in Scala* by Aleksandar Prokopec. For now, let's start with the concrete implementations of parallel collections in Scala. There are a few parallel collection classes, such as `ParArray`, `ParVector`, and `ParRange`, and also a few `set` and `map` implementations such as `ParHashMap` and `ParHashSet`.

ParArray

The `ParArray` constructor is the parallel implementation of `ArraySeq`, and holds elements in a linear fashion. It resides in the `scala.collection.parallel.mutable` package. To create a parallel array, we can import this package as follows:

```
scala> import scala.collection.parallel.mutable._
import scala.collection.parallel.mutable._

scala> val pararr = ParArray(1,2,3,4,5,6,7,8,9,10)
pararr: scala.collection.parallel.mutable.ParArray[Int] = ParArray(1, 2, 3,
4, 5, 6, 7, 8, 9, 10)
```

Here, we have created a parallel array named `pararr` by simply using the `ParArray` constructor, with elements passed as arguments. For demonstration purposes, we're using a limited number of elements in our implementation, but it's obvious we would like parallel abstractions to contain a higher number of elements to really work effectively. It's also possible to convert a parallel collection into its sequential counterpart using the `seq` method:

```
scala> pararr.seq
res1: scala.collection.mutable.ArraySeq[Int] = ArraySeq(1, 2, 3, 4, 5, 6,
7, 8, 9, 10)
```

A parallel array is a parallel mutable collection. We also have immutable versions of parallel collections. `ParVector` is one of them.

ParVector

`ParVector` is an immutable parallel sequence. We can create a parallel vector in a similar fashion to how we created a parallel array:

```
scala> val parvec = Vector(1,2,3,4,5,6,7,8,9,10)
parvec: scala.collection.immutable.Vector[Int] = Vector(1, 2, 3, 4, 5, 6,
7, 8, 9, 10)
```

We can perform the same operations using methods such as `map`, which we can use from its sequential counterpart. Let's take integers that are greater than 5 from our `parvec` parallel vector:

```
scala> parvec.filter(_ > 5)
res0: scala.collection.immutable.Vector[Int] = Vector(6, 7, 8, 9, 10)

And yes we can anytime convert our collection to it's sequential version
```

```
using seq method.

scala> parvec.seq
res1: scala.collection.immutable.IndexedSeq[Int] = Vector(1, 2, 3, 4, 5, 6,
7, 8, 9, 10)
```

In a similar fashion, we can also create `ParHashSet` and `ParHashMap`. These are immutable parallel collections. `ParHashMap` avoids collision internally by using a chaining mechanism.

It's worth knowing that the basic idea of parallelizing a collection is to split it into smaller parts using algorithms such as Divide and Conquer. These smaller parts are then operated upon using multiple tasks. Scala's parallel collection does this task scheduling through a `scala.collection.parallel.TaskSupport` object that is configurable. Also one should keep in mind that *side-effecting* operations are unpredictable, and when executed in parallel, they can produce deadlocks or race conditions. So as programmers, it's our responsibility to write code in a manner that avoids these race conditions. Parallel collections make it easier to solve problems where large amounts of data are to be processed. They make collections more powerful in Scala. You may also want to utilize this power when you use any Java collection from a library; in that case, you may want to read the next section.

Converting a Java collection into a Scala collection

Scala interoperates with a lot of Java libraries, so you may have to deal with Java code as well. It's possible for you to encounter a situation where you've a Java collection and you're expected to convert it into Scala. With this idea of converting a collection from Java to Scala, it may look a little bit scary that we've got to traverse through elements from Java's collection, and then append them to a Scala collection. But here's the catch: there're already ways you can do this. It's easy: we've a `JavaConverters` object in the `scala.collection` package, which takes care of this conversion. Actually, what happens behind the scenes when you call these conversion methods is that the implicit conversion takes place. Why not take a look at an example:

```
package chapter5

import java.time.LocalDate
import scala.collection.JavaConverters._

object CollectionConvertors extends App {
    /*
        We'll create a java collection of a couple of days and convert it to
```

```
Scala Collection
    */
    val aJavaList = new java.util.ArrayList[LocalDate]()
    aJavaList.add(LocalDate.now())
    aJavaList.add(aJavaList.get(0).plusDays(1))

    println(s"Java List of today and tomorrow: $aJavaList")

    val scalaDates = aJavaList.asScala
    scalaDates map { date =>
      println(s"Date :: $date")
    }

    val backToJavaList = scalaDates.asJavaCollection
    println(backToJavaList)
}
```

The following is the result:

```
Java List of today and tomorrow: [2017-10-01, 2017-10-02]
Date :: 2017-10-01
Date :: 2017-10-02
[2017-10-01, 2017-10-02]
```

Here's the program. We've a Java list named `aJavaList`, which is a list of dates with a few date objects in it. Yes, it's not a complex problem; what we simply have to do is to convert this list into a Scala collection so that we can perform our higher order operations such as `map` or `flatMap`. For that, as we can see, we imported the `scala.collection.JavaConvertors` object. After importing this object, we now have access to a converter method, `asScala`, which converts your Java collection to a Scala counterpart, which internally checks for the suitable collection to convert in, and the conversion happens implicitly. Finally, after conversion, we're able to use the `map` function on the `scalaDates` object, which is not a Scala collection.

It's also possible to convert a Scala collection to a Java counterpart using `asJava`. So it'll be totally fine to write something like this:

```
val backToJavaList = scalaDates.asJava
println(backToJavaList)
```

It'll convert the Scala collection into a Java collection. It's good that when you perform one conversion from the source collection to the target collection and then reconvert it, you actually get the main real object. Now that you've seen all the collections from Scala, and also have an idea that Java collections can also be converted to Scala collections, you've so many options to choose from for any requirement.

Choosing a collection

Here's the problem: after learning so many ways to make a collection of elements in Scala, it appears that we've got a big dilemma. We have quite a few options to choose from. Almost every collection has higher order functions to operate with. These are high-performing, type parameterized, and immutable collections. So how do we decide which collection to use? Now, we've the answer for that. And the answer is, it depends. Yes, it depends on multiple factors; for example, in which format would you like to have the data. Is it a simple sequence or in pair format? It's obvious that we've been talking about sequences, and maps up to now. In the majority of situations, we come up with Map, Set, List, ArrayBuffer, or a Vector. Let's talk about the factors that matter:

- If the requirement is to have a key-value lookup, we use Maps.
- We use HashMap when order is of no importance, and ListMap when we want to store the key-value pairs in a sequence. ListMap operations take linear time, as the number of elements increases. So using a Map is recommended in normal cases; if, somehow, the requirement is that we've got to operate on the first of a few collection elements, then ListMap can become a better choice.
- Sets, as you know already, contain no duplicate elements, so to remove duplicates we may choose to use a Set, or convert our collection to a Set. In Scala, a Set also extends (A) ⇒ Boolean, and this means that we may use a set to check the presence of an element in our collection. So it's simple: if you're required to check the presence of an element often, or to remove duplicates, use a Set.
- If you need to store finite elements, traverse through them, or perform some operation on them, please choose a List. An ArrayBuffer is also a good choice in case you need it to be mutable. A List is a linear sequence, so performing operations is costly when the number of elements increases due to linear performance.
- If the requirement is random access, and traversal is not of much importance, an indexed sequence is recommended, so please give ArrayBuffer a chance.
- If you want faster random access and a persistent sequence, use Vector. And yes, Vector is persistent, because it preserves the previous version of itself. That's not possible with an ArrayBuffer, because of mutability.

- Lazy evaluation can be an asset when working with Streams. It's a wise choice when the requirement is to evaluate a collection element on a need basis. We've seen how the `Stream` is represented, because of elements being lazily computed.
- Finally, the immutables. We can create a *Range* on the go with some collection's size, or something of that sort. It's easy to create a `Range` with `in`, `until`, and `by` methods.

So, it mostly all depends on what are we going to do with our collection elements. Of course, performance is of the utmost importance to us, because collections take up a big part of writing logic into our programs. We can start with a wrong choice of collection, then based on the need, we can convert those. It may look easy, but it's going to impact performance for sure. For example, it's wise to use a `ListBuffer` if later in the program you decide to convert it into a list. The reason is that a `ListBuffer` stores elements internally in a linked list format. So it's easy to convert to a list, rather than an array. Different operations, from instantiating a collection to updating, appending, or calling head or tail on your collection, all take different amounts of time, and thus can make your code less performant. So the idea is to choose wisely, based on what's of importance to your program. So why not compare the performance of several collections?

Collection performance

What are all the things you can do with a collection? Let's think of some use cases:

- First, create a collection object
- Insert an element
- Perform an operation on each element of a collection, which is only possible when you access each element
- Traverse through the collection
- Break it down into parts, perhaps one part with a single first element, and another with the rest of the collection (which are `head` and `tail`, obviously)
- Randomly seek out a particular element
- Update an element
- Reverse the collection

So, this covers pretty much everything you can do with a collection. The good thing is that if you're sure about the kinds of operations you're going to perform on your collection, you can make a performant program. The bad news is we hardly think about the operations we're going to perform later in programs, unless you're fortunate. But we've got an idea about all the collections and their performance. You may want to refer to the performance characteristics table in Scala's official documentation at
`http://docs.scala-lang.org/overviews/collections/performance-characteristics.html`.

The following observations will help with the idea of calling `apply`, `append`, `head`, or `tail` operations on a collection:

- **List:** List is a linear sequence, so methods such as `apply` and `append` take more time as the number of elements increases. But accessing `head` and `tail` elements takes a fixed amount of time:

apply => Linear	append => Linear	head => Constant	tail => Constant

   - The same goes for a `Stream` as well.

  - **Vector:** Vector is more performant than a list on a few grounds, and `apply` and `append` operations are definitely more performant than a list.

apply => Effectively Constant	append => Effectively Constant
head => Effectively Constant	Tail => Effectively Constant

  - **Range**: Range is a good option for those going for constant time access to `apply`, `head`, or `tail` operations.

apply => Constant	head => Constant	tail => Constant

  - **String**: String and Array work well for `apply` and `head` operations with a constant time response, but `tail` is a costly operation for these.

apply => Constant	head => Constant	tail => Linear

- **Maps**: Maps are used to do value lookups based on keys or add/remove key-value pairs. `HashMap` effectively provides constant time for these operations.

lookup => Effectively Constant	add => Effectively Constant	remove => Effectively Constant

Knowing the structure of a collection provides almost all the information about its performance. We now have an idea about all the collections in Scala, so it's time for you to practice more and experiment more with these collections.

Summary

This chapter was an introduction to the implementation of Scala's collections. We started learning about immutable and mutable collections. After that, we discussed Scala's collection hierarchy, where we learned about various super traits such as `Traversable` and `Iterable`. We also talked about three abstract collection types: `Seq`, `Set`, and `Map`. Then we took a look at the most commonly used collections in Scala. After that, we went the extra mile to learn about all the important functions used to work with collections. Then we learned about how we can convert collections from Java to Scala and vice versa, and found out that it was easy. After that, we discussed which collection to choose from all these options, which led us to consider the performance characteristics of collections.

With this, we've come to the end of part 1. In the next part, we'll start with the object-oriented and functional constructs provided by Scala. The next chapter is about the basics of object-oriented constructs in Scala, such as classes, traits, and objects. Learning them will enable us to utilize functional constructs efficiently in later parts of this book.

6
Object-Oriented Scala Basics

"There is a central quality which is the root criterion of life and spirit of a man, a town, a building, or a wilderness. This quality is subjective and precise."

- The Timeless Way of Building

Scala is an obvious choice for many programmers because of the goodies it contains. It's a language that's functional as well as object-oriented, which means a lot to programmers. It gives us a way of building our applications in a modular and meaningful fashion. It's important to know that Scala's functional concepts are essential, powerful, and at the core of our programs. There is no doubt that algebraic data types have provided the essential abstractions and immutable data structures that have allowed the code to work in a concurrent environment. But real-world applications could need much more than that. Often, the amount of code we write makes it essential to have a way of managing it. That's where object-oriented abstractions come to the rescue. It's great to learn that we now have classes and objects that provide a way to create manageable code. In the next few chapters, we'll equip ourselves with these object-oriented concepts in Scala, and they will help us later when we'll start to use functional concepts and abstractions more and more.

You're probably familiar with object-oriented basics if you're coming from Java or any other object-oriented language background. If not, we'll discuss the concepts as we go along. Mainly, when we discuss object-oriented principles, we come up with four core principles, namely: *abstraction, encapsulation, inheritance,* and *polymorphism*. They work as their names suggest. For example, *abstraction* is basically hiding the concrete or internal processing of a task or process, in simpler words, making something abstract. In Scala, we have abstract classes, traits, and a few other concepts, which provide abstraction. *Classes* and *objects* are a way to provide *encapsulation*, basically encapsulating a meaningful piece of code in a unit.

There's a way we can inherit members and their behaviors from parent classes and put them into other classes known as child classes. This property is known as *inheritance*. Finally, *polymorphism*, as the name suggests, means different ways to define and perform one operation. One of the examples of polymorphism is method overriding.

This chapter is a basic introduction to classes and objects in Scala. To make our agenda clear, we'll mainly go through three topics in this chapter:

- Classes
- Objects
- Case classes

Classes

To understand classes in Scala, let's make it clear that classes don't just do one thing for us. Classes work as a container for members in our programs, and as in any other object-oriented language, we can create instances of our class constructs and reuse them. By members we mean the variables and methods defined within. Why not take a look at a simple Scala class?

```scala
class Country(var name: String, var capital: String)
```

Yes, the preceding code is a class that we defined named `Country`. It has two members named `name` and `capital`. Let's create a new country instance and print its values:

```scala
object CountryApp extends App {
  val country = new Country("France", "Paris")
  println(s"Country Name: ${country.name} and Capital: ${country.capital}")
}
```

On running the preceding code, we get the following result:

```
Country Name: France and Capital: Paris
```

Now, believe me, it's going to be hard to resist Scala once I tell you that a class in Java with the same capabilities would need a few more lines. Take a look at the following code:

```java
public class CountryJava {
    private String name;
    private String capital;

    public CountryJava(String name, String capital){
        this.name = name;
```

```
        this.capital = capital;
    }

    public void setName(String name){this.name = name;}
    public String getName(){return this.name;}

    public void setCapital(String capital){this.capital = capital;}
    public String getCapital(){return this.capital;}
}
```

This still isn't finished. We'll now create an instance and print the country object:

```
class CountryJavaApp {
    public static void main(String[] args) {
        CountryJava country = new CountryJava("France", "Paris");
        System.out.println("Country Name: "+ country.getName() + " and
Capital: "+ country.getCapital());
    }
}
```

The following is the output:

```
Country Name: France and Capital: Paris
```

The reason why we're differentiating based on the way we define classes is to see the conciseness. A lot of unnecessary or boilerplate code has been omitted. Accessors for our members such as name and capital are still there due to the var keyword we added while defining our class.

Let's try to omit the var or val keyword as part of the class constructor:

```
class Country(name: String, capital: String)
```

These two, name and capital, will remain as class constructor arguments. Their scope will be limited; it won't be possible to use these arguments outside the class scope. To understand better, think of a class constructor as a method with some parameters. While calling the method, we pass a certain number of arguments and their scope is limited to the definition of the function. The same happens with Scala classes. You can think of some use cases when it comes to using class constructor arguments:

```
println(s"Country Name: ${country.name} and Capital: ${country.capital}")
```

The compiler will not let you access name and capital members.

When we use the `var` keyword as a modifier of our constructor arguments, we get access to these arguments. So, if you instantiate your `Country` object outside this class, you'll get a reference to these two fields and you can access them. Adding `var` as a prefix lets you reassign the parameter's value; that's not a good idea though. The following code snippet does the same:

```
object CountryApp extends App {
  val country = new Country("France", "Paris")
  country.name = "Germany"
  country.capital = "Berlin"
  println(s"Country Name: ${country.name} and Capital: ${country.capital}")
}
```

The following is the output:

```
Country Name: Germany and Capital: Berlin
```

The same happens with the `val` keyword. The only difference is that `val` parameters can only be read and not mutated. So in other words, your members become immutable:

```
class Country(val name: String, val capital: String)
```

The preceding definition lets you access the members named `name` and `capital` but it won't let you change the value of `name` and `capital` once an instance is instantiated:

```
country.name = "Germany"
country.capital = "Berlin"
```

If you try to do this, the compiler will come up with an error stating, `reassignment to val`. There's another construct that lets you do this, which means you don't actually put `val` in constructor arguments, but use a `case` class instead. Defining a `case` class is as easy as defining any other class:

```
case class Country(name: String, capital: String)
```

Writing a `case` class with arguments by default means it takes them as immutable parameters; there is no need to explicitly make them a `val`. We'll learn more about case classes in subsequent topics. We can also declare some methods in our classes, and those methods are going to be specific to the instance of our classes. For example, let's add a method that gives the population for a given year. To make it work, we'll add a map with the year and population in millions. The following is just for illustration purposes:

```
class Country(val name: String, val capital: String){
  var populationMap = scala.collection.mutable.Map[String, Double]()
  def getPopulation(year: String): Double = populationMap(year) //In
```

```
Million
}

object CountryApp extends App {
   val country = new Country("France", "Paris")
   country.populationMap += ("2015" -> 64.39) += ("2016" -> 64.67) +=
("2017" -> 64.93)
   println(s"Country Name: ${country.name} and Population 2017:
${country.getPopulation("2017")} million")
}
```

The following is the output:

```
Country Name: France and Population 2017: 64.93 million
```

In the preceding class definition, we have defined a mutable map for population that stores the population of a country based on the year as a key. Passing a year will return the population in millions for that year. Now, every instance of the country class is going to contain a separate reference to these members. You can picture it as a separate name, capital, populationMap, and getPopulation method for each instance that we create. Then, values that we give to these members are also separate from each other. It's possible, though, that we have two separate references pointing to the same value in cases where we have different values for our instance members pointing to different value objects. Let's take a look at the following figure to make it clearer:

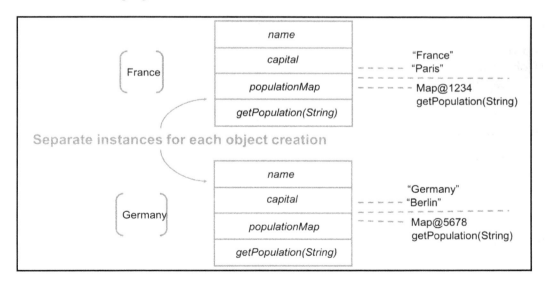

Class instances

It's important to know that when we compile our classes, they get converted to their Java equivalent code. A class with `var` constructor parameters when converted to the Java equivalent looks as follows:

```
public class chapter6.Country {
    public java.lang.String name();
    public void name_$eq(java.lang.String);
    public java.lang.String capital();
    public void capital_$eq(java.lang.String);
    public chapter6.Country(java.lang.String, java.lang.String);
}
```

The preceding methods, `name()` and `capital()`, work as *getters* and return the values for these two fields. The other two are methods named `name_$eq` and `capital_$eq`. We can use these methods to assign values:

```
object CountryApp extends App {
  val country = new Country("France", "Paris")
  country.name_=("Germany")
  country.capital_=("Berlin")
  println(s"Country Name: ${country.name} and
                  capital: ${country.capital}")
}
```

The following is the output:

```
Country Name: Germany and capital: Berlin
```

It shows that we don't explicitly create these mutator methods, but the Scala compiler does this job for us. Note, `name_$eq` represents `name_=` and nothing more. Finally, the last method represented in the compiled form is actually a constructor for our `Country` class.

Class constructors where we use `val` don't get access to mutator methods. It means that the compiled form of the class does not contain mutator methods:

```
public class chapter6.Country {
    public java.lang.String name();
    public java.lang.String capital();
    public chapter6.Country(java.lang.String, java.lang.String);
}
```

The preceding code is the compiled form of our `Country` class with `val` arguments. Here, we have access to only accessor methods and not mutators.

By default, all the members that we define work as public members. This means it's possible to access them outside the class. We can make them private just by adding a `private` modifier:

```
private def getPopulation(year: String): Double = populationMap(year)
//In Million
```

To illustrate this, let's make our `getPopulation(year: String)` method private. After that, we won't be able to perform this operation outside this class, even with an instance of the `Country` class:

```
println(s"Country Name: ${country.name} and Population 2017:
${country.getPopulation("2017")} million")
```

The Scala compiler won't let you perform this operation. Another thing to note about classes in Scala is that you have to define `toString`, `equals`, and `hashCode` implementation for your classes. These methods are essential if you want Scala to print your class instance in some particular format or perform equality operations. To remove this boilerplate, it's recommended to use case classes. Without defining these methods, try running the following:

```
val country = new Country("France", "Paris")
println(country)
```

Scala will print the runtime instance as it is, that is, `Country@2d209079`. To make this meaningful, we can override the `toString` method and give its definition:

```
class Country(val name: String, val capital: String){
   override def toString: String = s"Country($name, $capital)"
}
```

Now, if you try printing an instance of `Country`, it will print in the preceding format:

```
val country = new Country("France", "Paris")
println(country)
```

The following is the result:

```
Country(France, Paris)
```

Sometimes we want to create classes that are abstract, contain nothing but the class name, and indicate a type that some subsequent classes do want to inherit. We declare these as abstract classes.

Abstract classes

We can define abstract classes using the `abstract` keyword:

```
abstract class Person
class Customer extends Person
class Employee extends Person
```

Here, what we wanted was two subclasses that can also be treated as instances of a superclass, in our case, `Person`. For now, we have not shown any behavior in our abstract class. But, there are times when we want to imply some behaviors in our abstract classes that subsequent subclasses can inherit and define for themselves:

```
abstract class Person(category: String) {
  val idPrefix: String
}

class Customer extends Person("External") {
  override val idPrefix: String = "CUST"
}

class Employee extends Person("Internal") {
  override val idPrefix: String = "EMP"
}
```

Our intention to use abstract classes is clearer now. We may want a set of classes that inherit methods or values from a particular class. When we extend classes, we can use the `override` modifier in our definition. This kind of behavior is likely to present itself in one more concept we have in Scala, that is, a trait.

Abstract classes and traits

It's possible for you to declare things like the following:

```
trait Person {
  val category: String
  val idPrefix: String
}

class Customer extends Person {
  override val category: String = "External"
  override val idPrefix: String = "CUST"
}
```

```
class Employee extends Person {
  override val category: String = "Internal"
  override val idPrefix: String = "EMP"
}
```

Here, we used a trait. We'll learn more about traits in the next chapter. For now, let's see how they are different to abstract classes. We may be able to see that we've provided constructor parameters in abstract classes; this is not possible with traits:

```
abstract class Person(category: String) //can give cons params

trait Person(category: String) //can't give cons params
```

We cannot give constructor parameters for traits. However, we can, give a definition of methods in both abstract classes and traits. This is not the only way we may want to use classes. It's also possible that you don't want any other class to inherit from your classes. In those scenarios, we may declare the class using the `final` keyword.

The final classes

If you're coming from a Java background, you may have this idea of a `String` class:

```
public final class String extends Object
```

The `final` keyword tells you that you can't inherit from the `String` class. In the same way, we can also use this `final` keyword to make classes with behaviors that can't be modified or inherited by any other classes. You've got the idea. If you make our `Person` class final then you won't be able to inherit it. It's weird though, in Scala you can declare a class as final as well as `abstract`. Yes, it's possible in the following way:

```
scala> abstract final class Person
defined class Person

scala> class Employee extends Person
<console>:12: error: illegal inheritance from final class Person
       class Employee extends Person
```

Thankfully, the compiler doesn't let us inherit from abstract final classes. It would be great if you could find use cases though. For instant gratification, you may want to search for phantom types in Scala and think of use cases for our, can't instantiate or inherit abstract classes.

Also, if you're coming from an object-oriented programming background, or have an idea about `static` members in Java, you may be thinking, how do we achieve that in Scala? The basic usage of a static class or static member is that, for those that have only one instance, that particular member will be the same for all instances of a particular class. If you change the value of a static member, it'll be changed for all instances. You'll be getting more of an idea of what we're talking about in the next topic that we're going to discuss.

Objects as singletons

There are no static members or classes in Scala. Once you feel the need to create a static member, for example a static method or a class that is going to have only one instance, you should create an object. Yes, up until now, almost all the time we have been creating an object that extends the `App` trait so that we don't have to define the `main` method. This is the entry point to our application. So, it's also obvious that when we mention `object`, we don't mean an instance of any class; rather, an `object` in Scala has a different meaning.

An object, just like classes, is a container for functions and values. The reason why we may want to declare an object is so we can define utility methods for any particular type, or sometimes define JSON formatters and similar use cases. Let's take another look at how we can define an object:

```
object CountryUtil {
}
```

Looks like we just created an object. Nothing fancy, just an `object` keyword along with the name of the object. We know that objects are singletons, hence it does not make any sense to pass arguments in the constructor and therefore, Scala doesn't allow you to do so. That's it. Why not use your `CountryUtil` object to define some utility methods such as a method that takes a sequence of populations and returns the average of them? Let's try that in the following code:

```
object CountryUtil {
  /*
  * Function takes a sequence of population per million and returns
  average.
  * */
  def populationAverage(pops: Seq[Double]) = pops.sum / pops.length
}

object CountryApp extends App {
  val country = new Country("France", "Paris")
  country.populationMap += ("2015" -> 64.39) += ("2016" -> 64.67) +=
```

```
("2017" -> 64.93)

  println(s"Country Name: ${country.name} and Population 2017:
${country.getPopulation("2017")} million")

  println(s"${country.name}'s average population:
${CountryUtil.populationAverage(country.populationMap.values.toSeq)}")
}
```

The following is the output:

```
Country Name: France and Population 2017: 64.93 million
France's average population: 64.66333333333334
```

And here we are, with the average population of France for the years we wanted. We achieved this by passing the map to our utility function named `populationAverage` that takes a sequence of population values in millions. The idea here was to present a container that can contain utility methods for a class, and that's why we have objects.

In case you're wondering, if it's possible to extend from an object:

```
class WeCant extends CountryUtil {
}
// Sorry we can't extend from an object
```

No, we cannot. The first reason is that it's unintended. Secondly, the Scala compiler creates a compiled Java version of our objects, which is a `final` class. What happens when we create an *object* and it gets compiled? Scala creates a few class files based on the modifiers you choose. In our case, if you compile the `CountryUtil` object, the compiler creates `CountryUtil.class` and `CountryUtil$.class`, and these are final by nature. Let's take a look at these.

The following is an implementation of the `CountryUtil.class` class:

```
public final class chapter6.CountryUtil {
  public static double
populationAverage(scala.collection.Seq<java.lang.Object>);
}
```

The following is an implementation of the `CountryUtil$.class` class:

```
public final class chapter6.CountryUtil$ {
  public static chapter6.CountryUtil$ MODULE$;
  public static {};
  public double populationAverage(scala.collection.Seq<java.lang.Object>);
}
```

Yes, this is quite some Java code. You may not be very interested in the details right now, but two things to look out for are the keywords `static` and `final`. First, these two classes are `final`, as we discussed, and the utility method is `static`. Thus, you may get an idea of what the Scala compiler is cooking in the background. Great. Also, this does not stop you from extending a class or trait from an object. Hence, writing something like the following is possible:

```
class Continent

object CountryUtil extends Continent {
    //some code here
}
```

Well, that said, let's discuss more use cases of objects in Scala. We all know that we can define utility methods for a particular class in Scala objects. Using them is also easy, plus these utility methods can be used from anywhere. All you need to do is to add an `import` statement:

```
import java.time.LocalDate
import java.time.format.{DateTimeFormatter, TextStyle}
import java.util.Locale
import scala.util.{Failure, Success, Try}

object DateUtil {
  /*
   * Just pass a date with format DD/MM/YYYY, get back DAY_OF_WEEK
   * */
  def dayOfWeek(date: String): Option[String] = Try{
      LocalDate.parse(date,
DateTimeFormatter.ofPattern("dd/MM/yyyy")).getDayOfWeek
    } match {
      case Success(dayOfWeek) =>
Some(dayOfWeek.getDisplayName(TextStyle.FULL, Locale.ENGLISH))
      case Failure(exp) => exp.printStackTrace; None
    }
}

object TestDateUtil extends App {
  import DateUtil._

  val date = "01/01/1992"

  dayOfWeek(date) match {
      case Some(dow) => println(s"It was $dow on $date")
      case None => println(s"Something went wrong!")
```

```
    }

}
```

The following is the output:

```
It was Wednesday on 01/01/1992
```

We defined a `DateUtil` object with a utility `dayOfWeek(date: String)` function. This tells us the day of the week when we pass a date to it in a certain format. We also created an app which imports this `DateUtilobject` and from that, we get access to all functions inside that object. With this, we were able to directly make a call to our function and get the result.

This is a fair pattern where we define a class and then create some functions that are not instance-specific but can be used from instances, such as the example we had for the `Country` class and its utility object named `CountryUtil`. The language creators knew it well, and introduced the concept of what we call companion objects. That's what we're going to learn about next.

Companion objects

Companion objects are not very different to what we have already seen when we discussed objects. One specific difference is that we name those the same as our class names. It means that instead of defining `CountryUtil`, we can give this object the same name as our `Country` class and call it our companion object:

```
class Country(val name: String, val capital: String){
    var populationMap = scala.collection.mutable.Map[String, Double]()
    def getPopulation(year: String): Double = populationMap(year) //In
Million

    override def toString: String = s"Country($name,$capital)"
}

object Country {
    /*
    * Function takes a sequence of population per million and returns
average.
    * */
    def populationAverage(pops: Seq[Double]) = pops.sum / pops.length
}

object CountryApp extends App {
```

```
  val country = new Country("France", "Paris")
  country.populationMap += ("2015" -> 64.39) += ("2016" -> 64.67) +=
("2017" -> 64.93)

  println(s"Country Name: ${country.name} and Population 2017:
${country.getPopulation("2017")} million")

  println(s"${country.name}'s average population:
${Country.populationAverage(country.populationMap.values.toSeq)}")
}
```

The preceding code does what we had said earlier. We named our object the same as our `Country` class. This is how we define companion objects. This structures your code in a nice manner as well, as it provides you with the ability to make your types do something. It's handy to know that, to make your objects a *companion* you must define them in the same source file.

If, by chance, you find yourself trying that in the Scala REPL it should be done in paste mode (`:paste`). Let's see what we mean by that. So, open the Scala REPL and try creating a class and its companion object. The REPL will show a warning: *previously defined class is not a companion to object. Companions must be defined together; you may wish to use :paste mode for this.*

So we do as suggested. We give the `:paste` command in the REPL, which will enable paste mode, and then write our class with companion mode. Then everything seems good.

These are useful constructs that we've used in various places already. When we use `case` *classes* or typeclass (we'll learn about typeclasses in Chapter 10, *Advanced Functional Programming*) implementation, we'll be searching for companion objects for them. In fact, whenever we see our class has a particular thing to do, we have this nice way of building its companion object with the `apply` method. Take a look at the following example:

```
import java.time.LocalDate
import java.time.format.DateTimeFormatter

class Date(val dateStr: String) {
  override def toString: String = s"Date(${this.dateStr})"
}

object Date{
  def apply(str: String): Date = {
    val dater = LocalDate.parse(str,
DateTimeFormatter.ofPattern("dd/MM/yyyy"))
    new Date(s"${dater.getDayOfWeek} ${dater.getDayOfMonth}-
${dater.getMonth}-${dater.getYear}")
```

```
    }
}

object DateApp extends App {
  val date = Date("01/01/1992")
  println(date)
  }
```

The following is the result:

```
Date(WEDNESDAY 1-JANUARY-1992)
```

This example is for illustration purposes. There were different ways we could have achieved what we did here, but to understand *companion objects* with `apply` methods is simpler this way. So, what's different in the preceding example? Is it the way we used our `DateApp` application? Yes, when we define the `apply` method in the companion object the Scala compiler lets us use it without an explicit call to itself. That's what we did here:

```
val date = Date("01/01/1992")
```

We defined a class named `Date`, and along with that we created its companion with the `apply` method. It gives us the advantage of manipulating the instance into giving us something back. In our case, we retrieved some more information to make the instances of `Date` more meaningful, and instantiated `Date` with more information. Users of `Date` will get more information than we give. This seems interesting. However, the actual implementation needs to take care of exceptional scenarios as well. For example, what if, while parsing the date, we encounter an exception? We won't go into detail right now, as our motto was to understand this pattern and find uses for it.

Think of simpler scenarios where we want to omit the unnecessary boilerplate code that we have to write when we create a simple class, such as this:

```
class Country(val name: String, val capital: String) {

  override def toString: String = s"Country($name,$capital)"

  override def equals(obj: scala.Any): Boolean = ???

  override def hashCode(): Int = ???

}
```

Here, we have our simple `Country` class where, thanks to Scala, we don't have to define accessors and mutators for our class. However, this is not so great. We still have to define methods such as `toString`, `equals`, or `hashCode`. What if Scala could does it for you, along with the removal of extra keywords that we have to write such as `new`, `val`, and so on?

And yes, the entire point of mentioning all these is to affirm that we can do a lot in Scala using case classes, which we are going to discuss in the next section.

Case classes

What are case classes, why do we have them, and how do we use them? These are a few questions you may want an answer to. So, in simpler words, a case class can omit the amount of code we may have to write to achieve this:

```scala
class Country(val name: String, val capital: String) {

  override def toString: String = s"Country($name,$capital)"

  override def equals(obj: scala.Any): Boolean = ???

  override def hashCode(): Int = ???

}
```

Instead of declaring `Country` as we do in the preceding code, we would prefer to do the following:

```scala
case class Country(name: String, capital: String)
```

And our case class `Country` definition takes care of the rest. We have accessor methods for our `name` and `capital` members. We have our `toString` and `equals` methods defined by the Scala compiler, or let's say, auto-generated for us:

```scala
case class Country(name: String, capital: String)

object CountryUtil extends App {
  val country = Country("France", "Paris")
  println(s"Our country is: $country")

  println(s"Equality => ${country == country}")

  println(s"HashCode for country instance: ${country.hashCode()}")
}
```

The following is the output:

```
Our country is: Country(France,Paris)
Equality => true
HashCode for country instance: -66065175
```

Now, the preceding code snippet shows what we mentioned. We did not explicitly define `toString`, `equals`, or `hashCode` methods for the `Country` class. Still, we were able to perform these operations for the case class instance of the Country class. Why so? This happens because when we define a case class in Scala, the compiler automatically creates its companion object with a few methods, such as apply, unapply, and so on. During compilation, whenever the Scala compiler finds a case class, it converts the class files from Scala to Java; in our case, we'll get Country$.class and Country.class. The body of these files tells you a lot about what's happening in the background:

The following is an instance of the `Country$.class` class:

```
public final class chapter6.Country$ extends
scala.runtime.AbstractFunction2<java.lang.String, java.lang.String,
chapter6.Country> implements scala.Serializable {
  public static chapter6.Country$ MODULE$;
  public static {};
  public final java.lang.String toString();
  public chapter6.Country apply(java.lang.String, java.lang.String);
  public scala.Option<scala.Tuple2<java.lang.String, java.lang.String>>
unapply(chapter6.Country);
  public java.lang.Object apply(java.lang.Object, java.lang.Object);
}
```

The following is an instance of the `Country.class` class:

```
public class chapter6.Country implements scala.Product,scala.Serializable {
  public static scala.Option<scala.Tuple2<java.lang.String,
java.lang.String>> unapply(chapter6.Country);
  public static chapter6.Country apply(java.lang.String, java.lang.String);
  public static scala.Function1<scala.Tuple2<java.lang.String,
java.lang.String>, chapter6.Country> tupled();
  public static scala.Function1<java.lang.String,
scala.Function1<java.lang.String, chapter6.Country>> curried();
  public java.lang.String name();
  public java.lang.String capital();
  public chapter6.Country copy(java.lang.String, java.lang.String);
  public java.lang.String copy$default$1();
  public java.lang.String copy$default$2();
  public java.lang.String productPrefix();
  public int productArity();
  public java.lang.Object productElement(int);
```

```
public scala.collection.Iterator<java.lang.Object> productIterator();
public boolean canEqual(java.lang.Object);
public int hashCode();
public java.lang.String toString();
public boolean equals(java.lang.Object);
public chapter6.Country(java.lang.String, java.lang.String);
}
```

A lot of interesting things are going on in the background. The Scala compiler creates and defines all the necessary methods for our case class and making our life easy. All these conciseness is because of the compiler's ability to remove all the boilerplate that we may have to write. A few important methods that the compiler defines for us are:

- apply
- unapply
- copy
- canEqual
- hashCode
- equals
- toString

Along with these, the compiler also creates the constructor along with immutable fields, as well as accessors for those fields and a few utility methods such as productArity, productPrefix, and productElement. It's worth noting that a few methods such as the apply and unapply methods are declared static in compiled form. It means that these can be called in the form of Country.apply(...) or Country.unapply(...), but others can be called upon instances of the case class. It won't be possible to call Country.copy(...), as the compiler will not allow us to perform this operation. Speaking of all these, let's try them for our example Country case class:

```
package chapter6

object CountryUtil extends App {
  case class Country(name: String, capital: String)
  val country = Country("France", "Paris")
  println(s"Country: => $country")
  println(s"Equality: => ${country == country}")
  println(s"HashCode: => ${country.hashCode()}")

  println(s"Unapply: => ${Country.unapply(country)}")
  println(s"apply: => ${Country.apply("Germany","Berlin")}")

  println(s"copy: => ${country.copy("Germany","Berlin")}")
```

```
println(s"copyName: => ${country.copy(name="Germany")}")
println(s"copyCapital: => ${country.copy(capital="Berlin")}")

println(s"productArity: => ${country.productArity}")
println(s"productPrefix: => ${country.productPrefix}")
println(s"productElement(0): => ${country.productElement(0)}")
println(s"productElement(1): => ${country.productElement(1)}")
}
```

The following is the result:

```
Country: => Country(France,Paris)
Equality: => true
HashCode: => -66065175
Unapply: => Some((France,Paris))
apply: => Country(Germany,Berlin)
copy: => Country(Germany,Berlin)
copyName: => Country(Germany,Paris)
copyCapital: => Country(France,Berlin)
productArity: => 2
productPrefix: => Country
productElement(0): => France
productElement(1): => Paris
```

We saw all the methods applied in the preceding code. It's worth noting that these methods are useful and provide more information about the class instance along with the basic behavior. That was our intention of creating a companion object. Remember, we created our Date class with a companion object, whose instance happened to be more meaningful than the information provided at declaration time.

There are more than one reason to prefer using case classes over usual classes in Scala. It's obvious that case classes are concise and yet give us more than we may get by writing our own. Due to that reason, we have more information about these case classes and their members. For example, the unapply method gives us information that you may need when inspecting an instance. We can use these in pattern matching and it's also recommended to do so:

```
case class Country(name: String, capital: String)
val country = Country("France", "Paris")

country match {
  case Country("Germany", _) => println(s"It's Germany")
  case Country("France", _) => println(s"It's France")
  case Country(_, _) => println(s"It's some country")
}
```

This may look simple, but it's a powerful construct and used heavily. No wonder you also find yourself matching case class instances more often. It's simple to do so and, according to our snippet, it'll print the following:

```
It's France
```

It does this as expected due to the `unapply` method; pattern matching worked on our case class instance. It is also worth knowing that you can't declare a case class along with a class with the same name. Scala won't allow you to declare a class and case class with the same name in the same scope. By same scope, what we mean is that if you declare a case class, let's say country with the same name as a Country class in the same compilation unit, it's fair enough, because those belong to different scopes. To make the statement clear, look at an example:

```
package chapter6

object CountryUtil extends App {
  case class Country(name: String, capital: String)
  val country = Country("France", "Paris")
}

class Country(name: String, capital: String)
```

The preceding code is totally fine to declare, but if we try to put our class inside `CountryUtil` or take our case class outside of `CountryUtil`, the compiler will not let us do this:

```
package chapter6
case class Country(name: String, capital: String)

object CountryUtil extends App {
  val country = Country("France", "Paris")
}

class Country(name: String, capital: String)
```

The Scala compiler will not let you do so, saying the following:

```
Country is already defined in scope
```

Well, you may not want to do such a thing anyway. In case you're wondering whether it's possible to extend from a case class or not, it's possible to do the following with case classes:

```
abstract class Continent
case class Country(name: String, capital: String) extends Continent
```

We'll learn more about inheritance in the next chapter. For now, we've seen enough to be prepared for what comes next. It's time to summarize what we've learned in this chapter.

Summary

This chapter was interesting because we learned the details of Scala classes and object implementation. We started with what classes means in Scala, how we can declare them, and use them. Then we talked about objects as singleton instances in Scala. We then talked about interesting companion objects, which led us to case classes. We learned that case classes not only give us the conciseness we want but can also be very useful in scenarios where we may want to do pattern matching over instances. Finally, we discussed all the methods and goodies that case classes provide.

In the next chapter, we'll take our knowledge of object-oriented Scala to the next level and talk more about traits, inheritance, and a lot more.

7
Next Steps in Object-Oriented Scala

"I was born not knowing and have only had a little time to change that here and there."

– Richard Feynman

The idea of companion objects gave us the feeling that it's important to know how your programming language treats the constructs you write. Suppose you were given a task to generate a `case` class with some sensitive parameters (by sensitive, we mean when trying to print that class, those sensitive fields should print some dummy values). What you are going to do in order to achieve that entirely depends on your knowledge of how Scala treats the `case` classes, and we learned that in the previous chapter. So, what now? Now it's time to do some composition as well as use inheritance. Remember, we talked about how we should think of a class as a type that we can define? It's a really useful and fun task to mix these types all together and try to make sense out of them and at the same time, add functionalities. That's why we have static typing, isn't it? Let me tell you, it's fun to learn composition while mixing in those types, creating more than one way to access such constructs. And that's what we're going to do in this chapter. We'll have fun and learn. So, this is how we are going to proceed:

- Composition versus inheritance
- Class inheritance
- Default and parameterized constructors
- Traits

- Traits as mix-ins
- Linearization
- Packaging and importing
- Visibility rules
- Sealed traits

Before we move forward I want to clear this up. The terms *composition* and *inheritance* will be used in this chapter a lot. It's better if we differentiate these two up front.

Composition and inheritance

In programming terms, to inherit or extend our classes we use the `extends` or `with` keywords. These are essential for the relationship between two or more classes or similar constructs. This association or relation between two classes or similar constructs can be in the form of inheritance (Is-A) or composition (Has-A). They are two different notions but they converge to some extent. In simple words, **inheritance** is a superclass-subclass relationship where the subclass inherits the implementation of the superclass, whereas **composition** is when a class depends on another object to provide some or all functionality. With an inheritance relationship, you can use the subclass object wherever superclass is expected. Think of it as this relationship between a `Dictionary` and a `Book` class:

```
class Book(val title: String)
class Dictionary(name: String) extends Book(name) {
  // data and behavior
}
```

We can picture the **Book** and **Dictionary** relationship as shown in the following figure:

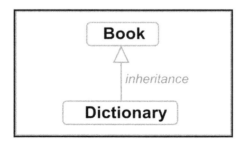

Here, a `Dictionary` class is inheriting from a `Book` class, so it means that:

- `Dictionary` is a subclass of `Book`. It can be used as a `Book` type wherever required.
- Dictionary has access to all the fields (data) and member functions (behavior) of the `Book` class. This means that you're allowed to override the behavior of a particular function from the superclass, as well as define your own functions in terms of behavior from superclass functions.

These points in a way make it easier to understand the inheritance relationship and help you to form a good object-oriented design. However, sometimes you as a developer feel duty-bound to change the behavior of the superclass as it's now a dependency for other subtypes as well.

Composition also may look similar when implemented (in case of traits mix-ins) but it's different in nature. As the name suggests, composition actually makes the whole out of parts. It's easier to understand with the help of an example:

```
class Book(val title: String) {
  val chapters = scala.collection.mutable.Set[Chapter]()
  def addChapter(chapter: Chapter) = chapters.add(chapter)
  def pages = chapters.foldLeft(0)((b, c) => b + c.noOfPages)
}

case class Chapter(name: String, sn: Int, noOfPages: Int)

object BookApp extends App {
  val book = new Book("The New Book")
  book.addChapter(Chapter("Chapter1", 1, 15))
  book.addChapter(Chapter("Chapter2", 2, 13))
  book.addChapter(Chapter("Chapter3", 3, 17))

  println(book.title)
  println(book.pages)
}
```

In the preceding code, we have shown a `Book` class that consists of a set of chapters. Each chapter is represented by a `Chapter` class. This is a *Has-a* relationship between the `Book` and `Chapter` classes. This relationship is also called **aggregation**. And as a special form of aggregation, our topic of interest for now is composition. There's a field named `chapters` in the `Book` class that is composed of `chapters`. Without the `Chapter` construct, there's no possibility of forming a book object that makes sense.

This is composition and it's directional. The following figure will help us to understand the concept:

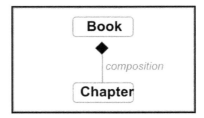

Composition relationship between a Book and Chapter

With the `Set` object in `chapters`, we can extend some functionalities that can only be performed on `Chapter` objects. I bet you get the idea of composition. The reason why we're discussing this is because we'll be doing that using mix-ins of traits in Scala, and it looks almost like we're extending them as part of inheritance, but that's not the case. So the idea is clear:

- Composition is not just code reuse but also making a whole out of parts. The existence of `Book` is unclear without a `Chapter` object.
- Composition also adds up functionalities to our already defined class constructs (we'll see this when we talk about *traits as mix-ins* later in the chapter).

It's important to know the difference between these two. You may only have a vague idea of how to implement inheritance or composition in Scala for now, but the terms and their meaning are clear. It's going to make the way clear for us to move forward and discuss how we can implement class inheritance in Scala.

Class inheritance

You already know that inheritance plays an important role in good object-oriented design. We are lucky enough to have constructs such as classes with names, and we can increase the possibility of relating those with other classes by using inheritance. Inheritance is about forming a meaningful hierarchy of classes to solve the purpose of code reuse. And mark my words, I mentioned *meaningful hierarchies*. I'll justify my words later. Let's take a look at how we can extend classes to make a hierarchy.

Extending classes

We use the `extend` keyword to inherit a class. Let's see our `Book` example to understand this:

```
class Book(val title: String){
  // data and behaviour for Book
}

class Dictionary(name: String) extends Book(name) {
  // data and behaviour for dictionary
}

object BookApp extends App {
  val dictionary = new Dictionary("Collins")
  println(dictionary.title)
}
```

The result is as follows:

```
Collins
```

We can see that `Dictionary` inherits from `Book` or `Dictionary` and is a subclass of the `Book` superclass. It's important to know that all classes, regardless of using the `extends` keyword, explicitly inherit `Any` in Scala. It means that our `Book` class inherits `Any`. Now with the establishment of this relationship, if you try to create an instance of `Dictionary`, you'll have access to all non-private members of the superclass. That's the reason we're able to print the title of our dictionary. That's code reuse. If you don't want to allow a particular member to be accessible from outside, you may make it `private`, an access modifier. We'll learn about access levels later in this chapter. With this inheritance relationship, it's possible to use a `Dictionary` instance wherever a `Book` instance is expected. The reason for this is that `dictionary` is a subtype of the `Book` type. To make things clearer, let's talk about subtyping and subclassing.

Subtyping versus subclassing

Classes are not types in Scala. When we inherit from a class, we form a superclass-subclass relationship between the two. And for most cases, the notion of subclassing and subtyping are the same. But in cases where *variance* (inheritance behavior under parameterized classes) plays its part, things become different. Under variance, subclassing doesn't guarantee subtyping as well.

We will take a look at both cases, positive and negative. Let's say a dictionary inherits from book, and it makes sense to say that a stack of dictionaries is a stack of books. This is the positive scenario, where subclassing and subtyping are similar in nature. But what about the second scenario? Suppose the `Keyboard` class extends from the `Button` class. `Button` has a value and also the functionality. So, while forming a meaningful keyboard object, we used the `Button` class. But do you think a stack of keyboards is the same as a stack of buttons? No! Hence here, the subclassing is perfect between `Keyboard` and `Button` classes, but we're not allowed to say that the `Keyboard` is a subtype of `Button`. I think you get the idea of subtyping and subclassing and their differences. Still, in programming terms, let's see it this way: if `Dictionary` is a subtype of `Book`, then `List[Dictionary]` is going to be a subtype of `List[Book]`. We call this property **covariance**. In the other case, `Keyboard` subclasses `Button` but it's not a subtype of `Button`. Let's visualize what we just tried to understand:

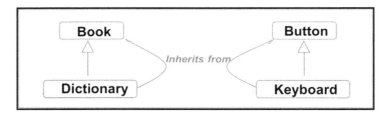

Sub-classing

This relationship speaks for itself. In the case of keyboard and buttons, it's better to choose composition instead of inheritance. But that's a different perspective. For now, it has become clear we should differentiate between subtyping and subclassing. So now, let's go over one more interesting topic—overriding the behavior of superclasses. Yes, it's possible for us to override the functions defined in a superclass.

Overriding data and behavior

We know that subclasses have access to all non-private members of a superclass, hence we can call or invoke functions from a superclass to show some behavior. If we want to manipulate the behavior, it's possible in Scala to override any function or value from a superclass. Let's see how we can do that. We'll refer to our previously mentioned `Book` and `Dictionary` example. Suppose in the `Book` class we have a function named `cover` that for demonstration purposes simply takes a `String` object as `cover`.

We inherit from `Book` and create a `Dictionary` class that wants to override the functionality of this function named `cover`:

```
class Book(val title: String){
  def cover(cover: String): String = "Paperback_" + cover
}

class Dictionary(name: String) extends Book(name){
  // wants to define its own version of cover method
}
```

We can `override` the definition of the `cover` method by simply adding the modifier keyword named `override`:

```
class Dictionary(name: String) extends Book(name){
  override def cover(cover: String): String = "Hardcover_" + cover
}

object BookApp extends App {
  val dictionary = new Dictionary("Collins")
  println(dictionary.title)
  println(dictionary.cover("The Collins Dictionary"))
}
```

The result is as follows:

```
Collins
Hardcover_The Collins Dictionary
```

As you can see in the preceding example, we've overridden the `cover` method. What if we don't use this keyword named `override`? In that case, the Scala compiler will give us an error stating the following:

```
Error:(18, 7) overriding method cover in class Book of type (cover:
String)String;
 method cover needs `override' modifier
 def cover(cover: String): String = "Hardcover_" + cover
```

The `cover` method needs the `override` modifier. Method overriding works if we've kept the signature in the subclass intact. If you try to change the signature, the compiler will give you an error stating that the `cover` method overrides nothing:

```
Error:(18, 16) method cover overrides nothing.
Note: the super classes of class Dictionary contain the following, non-
final members named cover:
def cover(cover: String): String
override def cover(cover: Cover): String = "Hardcover_" + cover
```

So it's important to keep the method signature as it is in the subclass to override it. Scala requires you to provide the `override` keyword whenever you try reusing the same method in a subclass. In Java, the `override` keyword is optional. This causes problems in real-time scenarios when writing code. Let's suppose you want to change the behavior in the `Book` superclass to support the newly introduced `Cover` class as a parameter in the `cover` method, and you have overridden this `cover` method in a few places, such as the `Dictionary` class. What happens in scenarios where the `override` keyword is not mandatory? you may ask. Hence, Scala requires you to add it. So at compile time, you're going to get an error that the `cover` method in `Dictionary` overrides nothing, and you can change the definition as needed.

One more important thing to know: for understanding overriding behaviors thoroughly we must understand the scope of them. It's possible to override a non-parameter `def` member with a `val` field. What do we mean by this? Let's take a look:

```
class Book(val title: String){
  def coverType: String = "Paperback"
  def cover(cover: String): String = coverType + "_" + cover
}

class Dictionary(name: String) extends Book(name){
  override val coverType: String = "Hardcover"
}
```

This example shows you that a non-parameter method named `coverType` in `Book` can be overridden in the `Dictionary` subclass with a `val` object. It's perfectly legal to perform such overriding operations. If you try to do this the other way around, it's not possible. The Scala compiler will not allow you to perform such an operation stating that the `coverType` method needs to be a stable, immutable value:

```
Error:(19, 16) overriding value coverType in class Book of type String;
  method coverType needs to be a stable, immutable value
    override def coverType: String = "Hardcover"
```

It's logical; what you're trying to do here is to make something mutable, a definition is mutable. This shouldn't be allowed and the Scala compiler is intelligent enough to tell you this. Suppose you want a particular member of your superclass to be intact, and not changeable. You want to restrict following subclasses from overriding behavior of the superclass, what'll you do in that case? That's what we'll learn next.

Restricting inheritance – final keyword

If you want to restrict subclasses from overriding a particular behavior or some data, you may use the `final` keyword to do so:

```
class Book(val title: String){
  final val coverType: String = "Paperback"
  def cover(cover: String): String = coverType + "_" + cover
}
```

Here, we have declared our `coverType` value as `final`. If you try to override this, the Scala compiler will throw an error stating the value cannot override the `final` member:

```
Error:(19, 16) overriding value coverType in class Book of type String;
  value coverType cannot override final member
  override val coverType: String = "Hardcover"
```

It's useful for when there's some data you want to remain intact and still have this superclass-subclass relationship working. With this overriding of behaviors in several related classes, there comes confusion when you try to invoke a particular method that's in a superclass as well as subclasses. That confusion is solved using the concept of dynamic binding. So, let's explain where dynamic binding is used before we learn how it works in detail. Dynamic binding is used to resolve which member function will get invoked when classes are in an inheritance relationship. This is resolved on the basis of objects at runtime. Let's talk in detail about it.

Dynamic binding in function invocation

We talked about the dynamic binding of objects to their references and invocation of methods. The invocation takes place based on the type of object on which that method is called. This is easier to understand with an example. Take a look at the following example:

```
class Book(val title: String){
  val coverType: String = "Paperback"
  def cover(cover: String): String = coverType + "_" + cover
}

class Dictionary(name: String) extends Book(name){
  override val coverType: String = "Hardcover"
}

class Encyclopedia(name: String) extends Book(name){
  override val coverType: String = "Blue_Hardcover"
}
```

```
object BookApp extends App {
  val dictionary: Book = new Dictionary("Collins")
  val encyclopedia: Book = new Encyclopedia ("Britannica")
  val theBoringBook: Book = new Book("TheBoringBook")

  println(s"${dictionary.title} has cover ${dictionary.cover("The Collins
Dictionary")}")
  println(s"${encyclopedia.title} has cover
${encyclopedia.cover("Britannica")}")
  println(s"${theBoringBook.title} has cover ${theBoringBook.cover("Some
Book")}")
}
```

The result is as follows:

```
Collins has cover Hardcover_The Collins Dictionary
Britannica has cover Blue_Hardcover_Britannica
TheBoringBook has cover Paperback_Some Book
```

Take a closer look at the following:

```
val dictionary: Book = new Dictionary("Collins")
val encyclopedia: Book = new Encyclopedia ("Britannica")
val theBoringBook: Book = new Book("TheBoringBook")
```

Here, we have created three different objects with the same return types, `Book`. The first thing to notice is that the class on the left-hand side of the equals operator will always be higher in the inheritance hierarchy. Secondly, all three are different instances. So, when you try to invoke a member function named `cover` from all these instances, you may observe different behavior in all three cases and see that the invocation is done based on the runtime type of the class. What do we mean by the runtime type of the class? It means that at compile time, all three expressions were of the same type, `Book`, but at runtime, things are different. Invocation of `Dictionary`, `Encyclopedia`, and `Book` takes place resulting in invocation of their respective versions of the cover method. In our case, the result that gets printed out shows the expected behavior. This behavior is termed **dynamic binding** in object-oriented languages.

By now, I'm sure that you're pretty well-versed in the concept of inheritance, and are ready to take this characteristic into account when designing models for your next application, right? Well to make it clearer, we'll think of inheritance as a concept that solves the issue of code duplication, by code reuse. But it's our responsibility to keep in mind that with the relationship that these classes form using inheritance, they also transmit some significant semantic information. What do we mean by that? We mean that it's important to understand that when we inherit from some superclass, it becomes a public interface/construct representing our subclass.

Hence, when inheriting dictionary from book, if it also keeps semantic information about whether the book is going to have a title, pages, cover, author, or other information, then its subclass is also expected to have this information available. The reason for this is that a `Book` is a public interface for a `dictionary` because of the inheritance relationship. And that's where sometimes we find ourselves using inheritance in the wrong way. Let's discuss this in brief.

Misusing inheritance

Take a look at this example:

```
class CustomStack extends util.ArrayList[String] {
  def push(value: String) = ???
  def pop = ???
}
```

Here, a class named `CustomStack` is inheriting from `ArrayList[String]`. What you see here is a semantic code smell. Just because your `CustomStack` class has extended from `ArrayList` means that you have access to all of its public members. Anyone with a stack object is not only going to have access to `push` or `pop`, but a whole set of methods like `get`, `set`, `add`, `remove`, and so on. This is wrong; you're allowed to use an array list object internally to form a stack object but the public interface should have nothing to do with it. In our case, our code shows that if you have access to `CustomStack`, you have access to all those methods. You should avoid using this in the `Stack` construct. The reality is that both of these are different concepts altogether so we should avoid using such types of modeling where it is semantically wrong. Although it may be a design choice, still we should keep in mind a few points when making these decisions:

- Check for Is-A relationship, if it holds true.
- Check if rules for encapsulation, such as data hiding, hold true. You should never expose internal implementation details to the outer world. In our case, `Stack` should've implemented the array list internally instead of inheriting from it.
- We should check for domains of each construct, the cross domain inheritance model is not a good choice, for sure. `Stack` and `ArrayList` are different conceptually. One can be composed using the other but should not inherit the other.

If you follow these points, you'll make a better design choice for modeling inheritance relationships.

Well, you remember we learned about `case` classes and the way we used to instantiate them without the `new` keywords? That makes me wonder, what if we want to have more than one way to construct new objects of such a `case` class? If you're also thinking the same; good! It's possible to have parameterized constructors in Scala. Let's talk about them.

Default and parameterized constructors

The primary constructor for any class defined in Scala is the body itself. It means that whatever you declare and define inside a class body gets instantiated when you make an instance of it. There are other ways to define secondary/auxiliary constructors as well. Take a look at the following `case` classes:

```
import java.time.LocalDate

case class Employee(name: String, id: String, contact: String, email:
String)

case class StartUp(name: String, founder: Employee, coFounders:
Option[Set[Employee]], members: Option[List[Employee]], foundingDate:
Option[LocalDate])
```

We can see two `case` classes named `Employee` and `StartUp`. You may wonder why `Employee` is specific to our `StartUp` class. The `StartUp` case class takes a few attributes such as `founder`, `coFounder`, `members`, and `foundingDate`. So, for creating instances of these `case` classes, we have to provide values for each member. In this case, if someone on the client side wants to use this `case` class and does not want to provide `members` or `coFounder` information, they still have to give dummy values. Now, the solution to this could be to construct auxiliary constructors for our client's sake. This can be done if we provide alternative invocation strategies for the `StartUp` case class. Let's do that:

```
case class StartUp(name: String, founder: Employee, coFounders:
Option[Set[Employee]], members: Option[List[Employee]], foundingDate:
Option[LocalDate]){

  //founder | name
  def this(name: String, founder: Employee) = this(name, founder, None,
None, None)


  //founder | foundingDate
  def this(name: String, founder: Employee, foundingDate: LocalDate) =
this(name, founder, None, None, Some(foundingDate))
```

```
//founder | coFounders
def this(name: String, founder: Employee, coFounders: Set[Employee]) =
this(name, founder, Some(coFounders), None, None)

//founder | coFounders | members
def this(name: String, founder: Employee, coFounders: Set[Employee],
members: List[Employee]) = this(name, founder, Some(coFounders),
Some(members), None)

//founder | coFounders | foundingDate
def this(name: String, founder: Employee, coFounders: Set[Employee],
foundingDate: LocalDate) = this(name, founder, Some(coFounders), None,
Some(foundingDate))

//founder | members   | foundingDate
def this(name: String, founder: Employee, members: List[Employee],
foundingDate: LocalDate) = this(name, founder, None, Some(members),
Some(foundingDate))

}
```

A few points to note here. Firstly, we can define overloaded versions of `this` method that work as auxiliary constructors. Secondly, in each definition, we're making a call to the main constructor with some other values. This practice can be done on either of these sides. By this we mean that passing optional values can be done either at the time of declaring these `case` classes or on the client side where we use these. We've done it while declaring these classes. Now let's use them in our `StartUpApp`:

```
object StartUpApp extends App {

  val startUpWithFoundingDate = new StartUp("WSup", Employee("Rahul
Sharma", "RH_ID_1", "9090000321", "rahul_sharma@abc.com"), LocalDate.now())

  println(s"${startUpWithFoundingDate.name} founded on
${startUpWithFoundingDate.foundingDate.get} by
${startUpWithFoundingDate.founder.name}")

  val startUp = new StartUp("Taken", Employee("David Barbara", "DB_ID_1",
"9090654321", "david_b@abc.com"))

  println(s"${startUp.name} founded by ${startUp.founder.name}")
}
```

The result is as follows:

```
WSup founded on Sun Jun 13 20:29:00 IST 2016 by Rahul Sharma
Taken founded by David Barbara
```

It was easy to use these auxiliary constructor versions of the `StartUp` case class. We can see that we only passed the needed parameters, and if the version was available to us, we were able to create an instance for it. But wait a second, we had these case classes and yet still we used the `new` keyword to create an instance for the `StartUp` class. What if we try to create an instance without using the `new` keyword? Let's try that:

```
object StartUpApp extends App {
  val startUp = StartUp("Taken", Employee("David Barbara", "DB_ID_1",
"9090654321", "david_b@abc.com"))
  println(s"${startUp.name} founded by ${startUp.founder.name}")
}
```

If you try to do so, the Scala compiler will throw an error stating the following:

```
Error:(30, 24) not enough arguments for method apply: (name: String,
founder: chapter7.Employee, coFounders: Option[Set[chapter7.Employee]],
members: Option[List[chapter7.Employee]], foundingDate:
Option[java.util.Date])chapter7.StartUp in object StartUp.
Unspecified value parameters coFounders, members, foundingDate.
val startUp = StartUp("Taken", Employee("David Barbara", "DB_ID_1",
"9090654321", "david_b@abc.com"))
```

This happens because when you declare `case` classes, the compiler generates a companion object with the `apply` method for it and the `apply` method takes all the parameters of the `case` class definition. When we define auxiliary constructors, we don't really overload the `apply` method defined in companion objects. Hence, when we try to use `case` class instantiation without the `new` keyword, the Scala compiler is not able to find a corresponding `apply` method version and gives an error. If you really want to use it that way, you can define overloaded versions of the `apply` method in companion objects. We'll try to overload an implementation with only two parameters, `name` and `founder`. Let's do this:

```
object StartUp {

  def apply(name: String, founder: Employee): StartUp = new StartUp(name,
founder, None, None, None)
}
```

It's easy to do. Defining an `apply` method that takes only `name` and `founder` gives us the option to create an instance of our `StartUp` object without using the `new` keyword:

```
object StartUpApp extends App {

  val startUp = StartUp("Taken", Employee("David Barbara", "DB_ID_1",
"9090654321", "david_b@abc.com"))

  println(s"${startUp.name} founded by ${startUp.founder.name}")
}
```

The result is as follows:

```
Taken founded by David Barbara
```

These are just a few ways; we can make the client's life easier by providing a variety of options to construct new objects. Now that we have seen how we can define various options for a class construct and also how inheritance can be effective if used properly, we can make our constructs more powerful by using traits in Scala. That's what we're going to explore next.

Traits

What are traits? For those coming from a Java background, it's tempting to see them as interfaces, but in reality they are something different. **Trait** constructs may look similar but are of a different nature to interfaces in Java. The meaning of the word trait is: a distinguishing quality or characteristic, typically one belonging to a person. One of the purposes of traits is the same. What if you want to add a particular characteristic to our hierarchy of classes or a single class? You can do this by extending or mixing in a trait. It's easier to say that we mix-in traits rather than extend from them. How are these two different? We'll talk about this as we go along but for now, let's take a look at how we define a `trait` in Scala:

```
trait Socialize {
  //people who socialise, greets.
  def greet(name: String) = "Hello " + name
}
```

Look at it this way. One of the qualities of people who tend to socialize well is that they greet you wholeheartedly when they meet you. In programming terms, you want to make a class named `Person` social. You can create a `trait` named `Socialize`, which for now just defines a method `greet`. This is simple: by defining a `trait`, we use the keyword `trait` and give it a name. We'll talk about this as we go along but for now, let's take a look at how we define a `trait` in Scala:

```
case class Person(val name: String)

object SocializeApp extends App {
  val person = Person("Victor Mark")
  val employee = new Employee("David Barbara") with Socialize

  println(employee.greet(person.name))

  class Employee(fullName: String) extends Person(fullName)
}
```

The result is as follows:

```
Hello Victor Mark
```

In the preceding code snippet, we defined an `Employee` class that extends `Person` in the inheritance hierarchy. While instantiating the `Employee` object, we're able to extend an employee's characteristic of socializing through a mix-in. Also, we have access to the `greet` method from our `trait`. This happened on the go, we didn't specify `Employee` to have this characteristic statically, but dynamically. When instantiating, we extended the possibilities and characteristics of `Employee`. That's why traits are powerful. A few points to note about traits are as follows:

- Traits do not take parameters
- Traits can also form an inheritance hierarchy, a trait can mix-in another trait
- You can't have a class and trait with the same name in the same scope
- The order in which we mix-in traits matters and can affect the behavior of your implementation

We can define traits by observing the previous points, but it's also good to know how Scala treats traits at compile time. To understand this, we can use the `javap` command on our `Socialize` class. It's going to show the compiled form of our trait:

```
public interface chapter7.Socialize {
  public static java.lang.String greet$(chapter7.Socialize,
java.lang.String);
  public java.lang.String greet(java.lang.String);
```

```
public static void $init$(chapter7.Socialize);
}
```

In the preceding snippet, you can see the compiled version of the `Socialize` trait. The Scala compiler compiles down a trait to its Java counterpart, `interface` (this happens in Scala version 2.12 and later. In previous versions, traits were also compiled to a set of classes). Here, the `greet` method is available as a static and a non-static member. It's possible for us to include an abstract, as well as concrete, method of a trait. For example, take a look at the following:

```
trait Socialize {

  def greet(name: String) = "Hello " + name

  val socialNetworks = Set("Facebook", "LinkedIn", "Twitter", "Instagram",
"Youtube")

  def linkToSocialNetwork(network: String, uri: String)
}

object SocializeApp extends App {

  val employee = new Employee("David Barbara")
  employee.linkToSocialNetwork("LinkedIn",
"www.linkedin.com/profiles/david_b")

  println(employee.mapOfSocialNetwork)

}

class Employee(fullName: String) extends Person(fullName) with Socialize {

  var mapOfSocialNetwork = new scala.collection.mutable.HashMap[String,
String]()

  override val socialNetworks = Set("LinkedIn", "Twitter", "Youtube")
  override def linkToSocialNetwork(network: String, uri: String): Unit = if
(socialNetworks contains network) mapOfSocialNetwork.put(network, uri)
}
```

The result is as follows:

```
Map(LinkedIn -> www.linkedin.com/profiles/david_b)
```

The preceding example shows that we can have abstract, as well as concrete members, as part of our traits. Here we have just declared our `linkToSocialNetwork` method without definition and also our previous method, named `greet`, that has its definition:

```
def linkToSocialNetwork(network: String, uri: String)
```

We have given its implementation in the `Employee` class, which mixes in this trait. With this abstraction, we now can compare traits to abstract classes in Scala. What's the distinction between these two? First, you may see that we can't pass constructor parameters to our traits. Second, as constructs, traits are heavier than abstract classes. So it's a matter of choice for you to decide between these two. The recommendation is to select a trait if you're extending any functionality, or if only as a class hierarchy, then an abstract class could be a good choice. One more aspect of a trait is that it's stackable. This means it's obvious you can mix-in more than one and its effect can be used in a stackable manner. Let's take a look at how traits can be used to showcase stackable behavior.

Traits as mix-ins

The way we do trait mix-ins is no different than inheriting any class in Scala; the only difference is that you can mix-in more than one trait and for that we have this nice keyword called `with`. Why do we call it mix-in? We could have called it something else. Well, yes but this explains almost everything you can do with traits. It's easy to modify or add up behaviors to an already existing functionality or construct without affecting already existing behavior. We'll see that in a bit. Traits can be used in a variety of use cases such as:

- Composable mix-ins; to make already existing interfaces richer
- Stackable modifications

Traits as composable mix-ins

By **composable mix-ins** we mean that we can create an instance of a particular type, with mix-ins of a trait, that can have certain additive functionalities. If you're thinking why would we want to do that, then the answer is maybe you want to add some particular behavior that makes sense to your functionality and you want it to behave as if it has come from the library itself. As a client of such constructs or libraries, we want them to feel as natural as they are. Traits help us add certain functions, keeping the real library intact.

We can understand this better with the help of an example. So, suppose you have an already existing `CreditCard` functionality. For demonstration purposes, we'll limit our expectations from this `CreditCard` functionality. This class has a certain way of generating credit card numbers for each subscriber. This is a thing of the past. Now, in the future, let's say in the next few days, we want to introduce certain new `CreditCard` subscriptions with more offers (conditions apply). Also, we want to have our own way of generating `CreditCard` numbers, without affecting the already existing functionalities or the business. The reality might be different, but for learning purposes it's fine to generate credit card numbers ourselves, isn't it? So, now that you have this picture in mind. Let's see what we already have:

```scala
package chapter7


case class Amount(amt: Double, currency: String){
  override def toString: String = s"$amt ${currency.toUpperCase}"
}

abstract class CreditCard {
  val ccType = "Default"
  def creditLimit(x: Double) : Amount
  //legacy creditCardNumberGeneratorLogic
  val ccNum = scala.util.Random.nextInt(1000000000).toString
  //other methods
}

object CCApp extends App {
  val basicCreditCard = new CreditCard {
    override def creditLimit(x: Double): Amount = Amount(x, "USD")
  }

  val limit = basicCreditCard.creditLimit(1000)
  println(s"CreditCardNumber ${basicCreditCard.ccNum} with limit: $limit")
}
```

The result is as follows:

```
CreditCardNumber 44539599 with limit: 1000.0 USD
```

Now, we can see how this `CreditCard` abstract class is defined, and our client `CCApp` is accessing that to create a new credit card account with a certain amount. Also, if you take a closer look, we didn't try to define isolated concrete classes that extend our abstract class named `CreditCard`, but we directly instantiated `CreditCard`, which is only possible because Scala generates and instantiates an anonymous class for us and expects us to define the abstract method, in our case `creditLimit`. Now, our requirement is that without playing with the already available code, we want to have our own version of the `creditCardNumber` generator that generates the credit card number for us. Let's do that then. But think about it, how are we going to do that and make it look natural? We want to do it this way:

```
val basicCreditCard = // Some Credit Card impl
basicCreditCard.ccNumber
```

For this, we can define a `trait`, let's say `CreditCardOps`, that's going to define the functionality with which we can refer to the new logic without affecting the logic previously implemented. And for the clients it's going to be natural. Let's take a look at the implementation:

```
trait CreditCardOps {
    self: CreditCard =>
    val ccNumber: String = ccType match {
      case "BASIC" => "BC" + ccNum
      case _ => "DC" + ccNum
    }
}

object CCApp extends App {
  val basicCreditCard = new CreditCard with CreditCardOps {
    override def creditLimit(x: Double): Amount = Amount(x, "USD")
  }

  val limit = basicCreditCard.creditLimit(1000)
  println(s"CreditCardNumber ${basicCreditCard.ccNumber} with limit:
$limit")
}
```

The result is as follows:

```
CreditCardNumber DC896146072 with limit: 1000.0 USD
```

The usage didn't change too much, and we also achieved what we intended. The only new thing we introduced was a `trait` named `CreditCardOps`. This `trait` has defined the new logic that we wanted. A few points to note about this implementation:

- First, we need to mix-in this `trait` to our `CreditCard` implementations whenever we want this synthetic behavior.
- We also may want to ensure that this `trait` is specific to `CreditCard` types, hence any other traits or classes should not be allowed to mix-in this. We have eventually ensured that too. If you try to do something like the following:

  ```
  class DebitCard
  val someDebitCard = new DebitCard with CreditCardOps
  ```

- The Scala compiler will not allow us to do this; the reason being that the syntax we choose to write while defining our trait is as follows:

  ```
  self: CreditCard =>
  ```

- This syntax gives a bit of information to the Scala compiler about upcoming statements in the current scope, as well as also limiting the trait's availability for certain types. Because of this syntax, we're only allowed to mix-in the `CreditCardOps` trait to `CreditCard` types.

- Look at the following implementation:

  ```
  trait CreditCardOps {
    self: CreditCard =>
    val ccNumber: String = ccType match {
      case "BASIC" => "BC" + ccNum
      case _ => "DC" + ccNum
    }
  }
  ```

  We are able to refer to `ccType` and `ccNum`, members of the `CreditCard` class, only because of this `self` type declaration. This declaration gives us access to members of the type specified.

- We've just modified the logic for `ccNum` and consumed the previous logic to create the new one. This was possible because of mix-ins.

- Also, one constraint that we faced is that you may have wanted to `override` the value, `ccNum`, so that the clients of your `CreditCard` object, when accessing `ccNum`, could get the value based on the new logic, something similar to the following:

```
trait CreditCardOps {

  self: CreditCard =>
  val ccNumber: String = ccType match {
    case "BASIC" => "BC" + ccNum
    case _ => "DC" + ccNum
  }
  override val ccNum = ccNumber // will be null
}
```

But, that's not possible. The compiler will let you do so but at runtime, the value will be null. A closer look will tell you that `self` is just a reference to the `CreditCard` type, hence you'll be able to refer to members, like we did while doing pattern matching, but if you try to `override`, it won't show the expected behavior. One reason for that is traits evaluate at runtime.

With this, we are finally able to get add-on behavior for only `CreditCard` types. This is the way we can make already existing constructs more powerful and can also modify them to suite our specific needs. We have a term for this process, we call it making thin interfaces rich through composable mix-ins. Why rich? Because of additive or selective modifications. There's more to traits based on our own use-cases. It's natural for an entity to have more than one trait, isn't it? Also, its understood if two or more composable behaviors are applied together, they'll both have their impact. It's an interesting topic; the way these behaviors are implemented. One of the ways these can be implemented is as *stackable modifications.*

Traits as stackable modifications

Before we learn about **stackable modifications,** we should know why we may need them, shouldn't we? Yes, so the best way to understand that is by using an example. Suppose there's a consumer of a service. He can pay to subscribe to a particular service. That service, for example your DTH TV subscription service, includes several channel packages. Now, what's of interest to us here is that we may want to implement this service. For implementation, we want to have a list of channels or packages the consumer is subscribed to. At the beginning of the month, he subscribed to a particular package, let's say `BasicPackage`. So we said the following:

```
new Service with BasicPackage
```

This, in fact is self-explanatory. We created a `Service` with `BasicPackage`. Thinking programmatically, we can assume that we've a particular value in our `Service` class that has the list of packages/channels listed in a certain package. So with this declaration, that attribute must've been updated with the value. Up till now, everything has been fine. What if the consumer wants to subscribe to one more package? And we don't want to have a mechanism that explicitly modifies the list of channels for us, but it should happen by default. This is like a behavior that's getting modified as we keep adding different packages. This kind of situation gets you to the concept of stackable modifications:

```
new Service with BasicPackage with DiamondPackage
```

With each added package, a list of channels/packages is going to update. We'll see in a bit how the implementation implicitly stacks modifications as we add more packages. These modifications can be done on some data structure, where we can pipeline operations on data, or scenarios like we just mentioned. A sequence of operations/modifications in terms of traits can be added. Let's take another example and work on it. For that we'll take our `CreditCard` abstract class and modify it to suit our newly introduced `GoldCreditCard` and `PlatinumCreditCard`. These new card subscriptions have a lot to offer to consumers along with an increased limit. Subscribers to the gold card will get a credit limit of 10% more than the standard/basic credit card. The increased limit amount for a platinum card is 25% more than a standard card, apart from the other goodies that they bring. A consumer who is adventurous enough may want to opt for both subscriptions together. So how do you think we can implement this? One hint, we may be using stackable modifications, which we just discussed. So, let's take a look what we already have:

```
abstract class CreditCard {
  val ccType = "Default"
  def creditLimit(x: Double) : Amount

  //legacy creditCardNumberGeneratorLogic
  val ccNum = scala.util.Random.nextInt(1000000000).toString

  //other methods}
```

Nothing different here. We have our old abstract `CreditCard` class. We may want to create a standard/basic credit card:

```
class BasicCreditCard extends CreditCard {
  override def creditLimit(x: Double): Amount = Amount(x,"USD")
}
```

This isn't alien code, it's easy to understand. We created a `BasicCreditCard` class extending `CreditCard` and we are overriding the `creditLimit` method. This method is simply returning the `Amount` object for the limit amount. Now, let's take a look at the implementation of other subscription types:

```
trait GoldSubscription extends CreditCard {
    abstract override def creditLimit(x: Double): Amount =
super.creditLimit(x * 1.10)
}

trait PlatinumSubscription extends CreditCard {
    abstract override def creditLimit(x: Double): Amount =
super.creditLimit(x * 1.25)
}
```

Two more types named `GoldSubscription` and `PlatinumSubscription` as we discussed in terms of traits are added. What's different here? Syntactical analysis will say that this has an `abstract override` modifier, but how? How can you have these two together? We declare something `abstract` if we are not willing to provide its definition and use `override` to redefine something already in scope. So, the thing is, both of these are conflicting. However, Scala, as we already know, is intelligent enough to know that this is done in the context of a trait, which gets evaluated at runtime, and when you try to create an instance of such a trait or mix-in with some already created concrete class, it's going to override the particular definition. See the following:

```
abstract override def creditLimit(x: Double): Amount = //super call
```

Here, we are going to expect a concrete implementation of `CreditCard` to mix-in this trait. Let's take a look at the implementation `CCApp` to understand better:

```
object CCApp extends App {
  val basicCreditCard = new BasicCreditCard()
  println(basicCreditCard.creditLimit(15000))

  val goldCreditCard = new BasicCreditCard() with GoldSubscription
  println(goldCreditCard.creditLimit(15000))

  val platinumCreditCard = new BasicCreditCard() with PlatinumSubscription
  println(platinumCreditCard.creditLimit(15000))

  val gpluspCreditCard = new BasicCreditCard() with GoldSubscription with
PlatinumSubscription
  println(gpluspCreditCard.creditLimit(15000))
}
```

The result is as follows:

```
15000.0 USD
16500.0 USD
18750.0 USD
20625.0 USD
```

In the preceding code is the implementation of the solution we came up with for our problem using stackable modifications. A few points to note here are as follows:

- Consider the following code snippet:

```
trait GoldSubscription extends CreditCard {
  abstract override def creditLimit(x: Double): Amount =
super.creditLimit(x * 1.10)
}
```

We didn't try to define some explicit logic implementation but made a *super* call to an already defined method with certain *additions/limitations/modifications* in a parameter value.

- With this, we're allowed to pass the same type of parameter and as it is composed, the value we'll get will be modified.
- We can apply as many `CreditCard` subscriptions as we want and based on the logic, we'll get the expected value for `creditLimit`. That's why we were able to call the following:

```
val gpluspCreditCard = new BasicCreditCard() with GoldSubscription
with PlatinumSubscription

println(gpluspCreditCard.creditLimit(15000))
                  and we got the desired result: 20625.0 USD
```

- Last but not least, we mix-in the traits to concrete classes with overridden implementations for our abstract method, that's why `abstract override` worked here.

This was interesting, you know. We passed a `creditLimit` value of `15000` for all the different instances and we got corresponding values. All of this is due to trait's use of stackable modifications.

Linearization

The reason why multiple inheritances become a burden when we try to implement them is due to *the diamond problem*. Take a look at the following image:

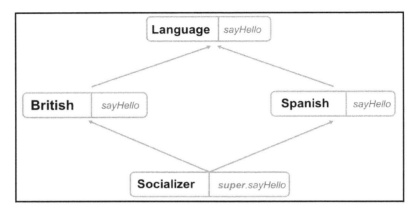

Diamond problem

Here, suppose we have an abstract class named `Language`, that has a method named `sayHello`. Two traits, named `British` and `Spanish`, extend the abstract `Language` class and define their own implementation of the `sayHello` method. Then we create a trait, named `Socializer`, that mixes in the other two traits with a `super` call to the `sayHello` method implementation. Now, confusion occurs as to which implementation of `sayHello` is getting called when we invoke this method. The primary reason for this problem is there's no multiple inheritance in Java, but Scala supports a form of multiple inheritance through *trait mix-in*. The concept Scala uses to resolve the problem of super calls is linearization. Let's first code for the problem and see it's behavior, then we'll understand linearization and the rules that justify the behavior we are going to see.

Suppose we code for the problem shown in the preceding image. It's going to look as follows:

```
abstract class Language {
  def sayHello: String
}

trait British extends Language {
  override def sayHello: String = "Hello"
}

trait Spanish extends Language {
```

```
    override def sayHello: String = "Hola"
  }

  class Socializer extends British with Spanish {
    override def sayHello: String = super.sayHello
  }

  object Linearization extends App {

    class Person(val name: String)

    val albert = new Person("Alberto")
    val socializer = new Socializer()

    println(s"${socializer.sayHello} ${albert.name}")
  }
```

The result is as follows:

```
Hola Alberto
```

Did you expect this result? We had declared our class `Socializer`:

```
class Socializer extends British with Spanish {
  override def sayHello: String = super.sayHello
}
```

The result shows that the call made to `super.sayHello` invoked `sayHello` from the `Spanish` trait. Well, such behavior is due to linearization. But how does it work? The rules for linearization are as follows:

1. We'll start with the very first extended trait/class and think of the hierarchy. We'll consider `AnyRef` and `Any` are also part of the inheritance hierarchy.

    This is going to give us the following result:

    ```
    British -> AnyRef -> Any
    ```

    Let's call this a **linearized hierarchy** for now.

2. Take the next trait/class and write a hierarchy down for it:

    ```
    Spanish -> AnyRef -> Any
    ```

Remove the traits/classes from this hierarchy that already exist in the linearized hierarchy.

So we'll remove `AnyRef -> Any`. Remaining syntax will be:

```
Spanish ->
```

Add the remaining traits/classes to the bottom of the already available linearized hierarchy.

```
Spanish -> British -> AnyRef -> Any
```

3. Repeat *step 2* for all traits/classes.
4. Finally, place the trait/class at the very first position from the left:

```
Socializer -> Spanish -> British -> AnyRef -> Any
```

The direction of super calls is going to be from *left* to *right*. And for our implementation, where we extended from `Spanish` with `British`, we now know that the `super` call invoked is on the `Spanish` trait due to linearization. The result was from the `Spanish` trait.

The result is as follows:

```
Hola Alberto
```

This understanding can help us a lot to learn the usual behavior of trait mix-ins and inheritance. Knowing how linearization works is essential to understanding already written code and creating a good design yourself. Now that you know how linearization works, why not learn another important concept in object-oriented programming?

Packaging and importing

One of the important aspects of object-oriented programs is how we define modular, reusable, and hierarchical structures. We're allowed to put all the code that we write, constructs like classes, traits, and objects, in some particular package. By using *packaging* and *visibility* rules, we can make our code more to reason about, means to expose some method to other classes or and we get structured and modular code as an added advantage. There are a couple of ways you're allowed to write package statements in Scala; we'll take a look at those.

Package statements

We can write package statements at the beginning of the file. One of the simplest examples is as follows:

```
package country

class Country(val name: String) {
  import Country._

  val populationsMap  = scala.collection.mutable.Map[Int, Double]()

  def showAveragePopulation() =
println(averagePopulation(this.populationsMap.values))
  }

object Country {
    def averagePopulation(populations: Iterable[Double]) = populations.sum /
populations.size

  }
```

Here, we defined the package name as country. Now, whatever we define in the corresponding file is going to stay within the scope of this country package. This is the reason why, when we wanted to use a function in the Country companion object, we did not need to explicitly put the following:

```
import country.Country._
```

The ending _ underscore symbol, is Scala's ways of doing a wildcard import. It means that non-private members are going to be accessible within the current scope.

Multiple package statements in a file

Scala also allows us to put multiple package declarations and nested package declarations. First let's take a look at how:

```
import country.Country
import customutil.Util.averagePopulation

package country {

  class Country(val name: String) {

    val populationsMap  = scala.collection.mutable.Map[Int, Double]()
```

```scala
    def showAveragePopulation() =
println(averagePopulation(this.populationsMap.values))
    }
}

package state {

  class State(val name: String) {

    val populationsMap  = scala.collection.mutable.Map[Int, Double]()

    def showAveragePopulation() =
println(averagePopulation(this.populationsMap.values))
    }

  }

package customutil {
  object Util {

    def averagePopulation(populations: Iterable[Double]) = populations.sum
/ populations.size

  }
}
```

In the preceding code we see how we can define multiple package statements within a file. A thing worth noticing is the way we did this. We used curly parentheses along with a `package` keyword to tell the Scala compiler that here's our package. Whatever we write inside this is going to reside in that package. Here, we defined three packages. One is `country`, to define country-specific constructs, another one is `state`, to define state specific constructs. The last one is a `customutil` package, which, as the name tells us, is to define utility functions for all the country/state functionalities. The `averagePopulation` function is not specific to country or state but can be used in both cases, hence it is defined in separate packages and imported globally at the top. With that import, we've gotten access for `customutil` to the scope of the whole compilation unit. One more thing we could have done is to declare package `state` as a nested package to `country`, because it's obvious multiple `country` constructs and members should be directly accessible to `state` constructs as well. Let's see how it's going to look.

Nested package statements

We know there might be times when we need some `country` package constructs directly available to the `state` package. In those scenarios we can define the `state` package as a nested package inside `country`. Let's write that as follows:

```
import country.Country

package country {
  import customutil.Util.averagePopulation

  abstract class Region
  class Country(val name: String) extends Region{

    val populationsMap  = scala.collection.mutable.Map[Int, Double]()

    def showAveragePopulation() =
println(averagePopulation(this.populationsMap.values))

  }

  package state {

    class State(val name: String) extends Region {

      val populationsMap  = scala.collection.mutable.Map[Int, Double]()

      def showAveragePopulation() =
println(averagePopulation(this.populationsMap.values))
    }

  }
}

package customutil {
  object Util {

    def averagePopulation(populations: Iterable[Double]) = populations.sum
/ populations.size

  }
}
```

Here, we have a package `state` declaration nested inside a `country` package declaration. What this does is to avoid making explicit mentions to the full package declaration while importing. Also, it makes code easier to understand and more structured. It shows that it's OK to expect a country to be a `Region`, and a state can also be treated as a region. Thus, nesting of packages is also a good way to document your code. It shows an understanding of the structure.

Chaining package statements

There's another way we can put up these package declarations, and that is by chaining the declarations of packages. How can we do this?

```
package country
package state

class State(val name: String) extends Region {

  val populationsMap   = scala.collection.mutable.Map[Int, Double]()

  def showAveragePopulation =
println(averagePopulation(this.populationsMap.values))
  }
```

By keeping the `Region` class in the `country` package, if we declare the `State` class with the preceding syntax, things will work out fine, and your class `State` is going to reside in package `country.state`. That means `state` is going to be a nested package. This way of writing package names is widely used in several libraries, you may find this out when you explore some of them.

These are all ways you can declare package names, and now you also know the reasoning behind it. Just because of the fact that we have the license to declare multiple package names, means it's easier for us to separate constructs based on their usage. For example, it's perfectly fine to declare a package for a `TestSuite` for your classes in the same file with a different package name. Everyone has their ways of writing and structuring package names. With these, declarations, we also have more than one way of importing these constructs in other scopes. Importing packages in Scala can also be done in some interesting ways; why not take a dig at that.

Importing packages

In simpler scenarios, just to bring some objects into scope, we put an `import` statement before it. This is how importing can be done:

```scala
object CountryApp extends App {
  import customutil.Util.averagePopulation
  val aCountry = new Country("France")
  aCountry.populationsMap.put(2017, 64.94)
  aCountry.populationsMap.put(2016, 64.66)
  aCountry.populationsMap.put(2015, 64.395)

  println(averagePopulation(aCountry.populationsMap.values))
}
```

The result is as follows:

```
64.66499999999999
```

We use an `import` keyword and give the name of the import. A few points to note down while using `import` in Scala:

- We are allowed to use imports anywhere in the file
- In instances where two imports collide, we have the right to hide one over the other
- We can also rename some imports

With this, we get flexibility while importing packages. Let's take a look at some of these:

```scala
package country {
  abstract class Region

  import customutil.{Util => u}

  class Country(val name: String) extends Region {

    val populationsMap  = scala.collection.mutable.Map[Int, Double]()

    def showAveragePopulation =
println(u.averagePopulation(this.populationsMap.values))
  }

  package state {

    class State(val name: String) extends Region {
```

```
import u.{averagePopulation => ap}

val populationsMap  = scala.collection.mutable.Map[Int, Double]()

def showAveragePopulation = println(ap(this.populationsMap.values))
    }

  }
}

package customutil {
  object Util {

    def averagePopulation(populations: Iterable[Double]) = populations.sum
/ populations.size

  }
}
```

In the preceding examples, we declared an `import` statement just before we wanted to use it. Also, see the following statement:

```
import customutil.{Util => u}
```

This allowed us to use `u` in place of the `Util` object:

```
println(u.averagePopulation(this.populationsMap.values))
```

Using these depends on the scenario; most often we need to take care of code readability. For example, renaming `scala.collection.mutable` to something shorter is a good thing to do—developers following the code are going to find it easier to understand. Also, if you take a closer look, we renamed the object `Util`, so it's proven that Scala allows us to import as well as rename objects. Moreover, Scala is capable enough of renaming the function names, and why not? Those are members that we are importing. We did just that in the following:

```
import u.{averagePopulation => ap}
```

We renamed the `averagePopulation` function to `ap`, and used that in the following:

```
println(ap(this.populationsMap.values))
```

We may need to keep in mind the same point: we may be renaming whenever it makes sense to do so—in our example, it doesn't. But for demonstration purposes, it's OK to consider that it does. Scala's extensive ways for packaging and importing makes things easier for us. In namespace collision scenarios, we've ways to hide a definition over the other. That can be done with the following syntax:

```
import package1.{Member => _}
```

You see? The declaration is self-explanatory. We renamed a particular package/member to a wildcard. It no longer provides any means to using this particular Member in the current scope and hides it. This is Scala's way of hiding a particular package/member.

These multiple ways of packaging and importing make our code easy to understand, but this is not all. We can also provide a few modifiers to control access to our members. We can make them private, protected, or by default public. Let's discuss them.

Visibility rules

There are times when we don't want to let another class or similar construct use a few members. Here, we can use Scala's provided access modifiers. How we achieve control over the accessibility of members of our classes/traits/objects is through private, public, or protected access modifiers. Take a look at the following example:

```
package restaurant

package privaterestaurant {

  case class Dish(name: String)

  trait Kitchen {
    self: PrivateRestaurant =>

    private val secret = "Secret to tasty dish" //Think of a secret logical
  evaluation resulting in value, we don't want to expose.

    def cookMyDish: Option[Dish] = Some(Dish(secret))

  }

  class PrivateRestaurant extends Kitchen {

    def serveDishWithSecret = Dish(secret) // Symbol secret is inaccessible
  from this place.
```

```
      def serveDish = cookMyDish // Works fine
    }

  }
```

Here, we have some trait named `Kitchen`. It has a secret way of cooking a really tasty dish, but only for `PrivateRestaurant` types. The secret cannot be shared outside the kitchen. In those scenarios, we can keep the secret as it is by declaring it with a modifier named `private`. With this, when we try to access the secret recipe, we are not able to do that. The Scala compiler gives an error stating: *Symbol secret is inaccessible from this place.* With that we were able to keep our secret intact. But what if you want to let your private restaurant access the secret and no one else. In that case you can make it `protected`.

After making our secret protected, we can get access to it only if `PrivateRestaurant` extends `Kitchen`. If you remember, this is doing composition and thus we'll have access to the secret by just changing the `private` modifier to `protected`:

```
protected val secret = "Secret to tasty dish" //Think of a secret logical
evaluation resulting in value, we don't want to expose.
```

We should know, for `protected` to work, it's a must to inherit the member class/trait. What we mean by this is the following:

```
class PrivateRestaurant extends Kitchen {

  def serveDishWithSecret = Dish(secret) // Works fine
  def serveDish = cookMyDish // Works fine
}
```

As you can see, we have this mix-in. That's the reason why, after applying the `protected` modifier, we got access to the secret recipe. By the way, when we don't specify any access modifiers, Scala treats the members as `public` and those members can be accessed if in scope. When it comes to controlling the access levels, Scala has more to offer than what we just learnt. We can also specify the scope of protection. By scope of protection we mean that the particular member is visible up to a certain level. Here, it depends on us what level we define. Let's look at an example to understand this:

```
case class Dish(name: String)

class Restaurant

package privaterestaurant{
   trait Kitchen {
     self: Restaurant =>
```

```
    private[privaterestaurant]  val secret = "Secret to tasty dish" //Think
of a secret logical evaluation resulting in value, we don't want to expose.

    def cookMyDish: Option[Dish] = Some(Dish(secret))

  }

  class  PrivateRestaurant  extends Restaurant with Kitchen  {

    def serveDishWithSecret = Dish(secret) // Symbol secret is inaccessible
from this place.

    def serveDish = cookMyDish // Works fine
  }

}

package  protectedrestaurant {

  import restaurant.privaterestaurant.Kitchen

  class ProtectedRestaurant extends Restaurant with Kitchen {

    def serveDishWithSecret = Dish(secret) // Symbol secret is inaccessible
from this place.

    def serveDish = cookMyDish // Works fine
  }
}
```

With a proper look at the code, there are some points that we can consider:

- In the following declaration, it makes it clear that the secret value is going to be privately accessible within this package named privaterestaurant:

    ```
    private[privaterestaurant] val secret = "Secret to tasty dish"
    //Think of a secret logical evaluation resulting in value,
    //we don't want to expose
    ```

- Also, the Scala compiler is not going to complain about the way you used these scopes, but at runtime you can expect an exception if your scope is not within the package. It means that for our following declaration:

    ```
    private[privaterestaurant] val secret
    ```

For it to work properly, we need to be part of this package. That's logically correct, otherwise it's not wise to apply privacy to something that's not ours.

- Similar to `private[X]`, we can also define `protected[Y]` and so on. Defining `protected` for some package is going to make it available to classes in the inheritance tree.
- There's another level of protection, that is, `private[this]`. It's going to make a particular member available to an instance of the same class.

It's really important to control the access level. With it we can have fine-grain scope for every construct. This keeps the client away from unnecessary details that you might not want them to access. This is all about limiting the scope for members. There are a few more construct such as `sealedtraits`, that help us structure the code in a good way, but that's just one thing about them. There's much more to know about.

Sealed traits

One good thing about **sealed traits** is that standard Scala library uses these constructs a lot, and you've also seen them many times so far. It's time to learn about them. We'll start with an example:

```
sealed trait Season

case object Autumn extends Season
case object Winter extends Season
case object Spring extends Season
case object Summer extends Season
case object Monsoon extends Season

object SealedApp extends App {
  def season(season: Season) = season match {
    case Autumn => println(s"It's Autumn :)")
    case Winter => println(s"It's Winter, Xmas time!")
    case Spring => println(s"It's Spring!!")
    case Summer => println(s"It's summer, who likes summer anyway!")
    case Monsoon => println(s"It's Monsoon!!")
  }
  season(Spring)
}
```

The result is as follows:

```
It's Spring!!"
```

Here, we defined a sealed trait named `Season`. Then there're a few child season case objects extending from the `sealed trait Season`. By the way, case objects are like `case` classes with the difference being that these are only instances with already available names, unlike the `case` classes. There're a few points to note about the preceding implementation of the sealed trait named `Season`.

- All children extending the `Season` trait should be defined in the same file.
- Constructs such as sealed traits come with a license to perform pattern matching. This is good for design constructs.
- Also, when we perform *pattern matching* on sealed traits, we need to take care of all the possibilities. Otherwise, as we know, the Scala compiler is intelligent enough to come up with a warning about the remaining scenarios whenever it sees that the pattern match is on a sealed trait.

A few good and known examples of sealed traits are `Option` type to two children named `Some` and `None`. Then, `List` is also defined as a sealed trait. This was a short introduction to sealed traits with the license for you to experiment with the construct. With sealed traits we have come to the end of the chapter. Let's summarize what we have learnt so far.

Summary

This chapter was more exciting. We learnt about inheritance in Scala and discussed composition and inheritance. It's really going to help us when we take design decisions about our implementation. Then we learnt about this amazing construct named traits and we tried various ways of using traits. Then we learnt about the concept of linearization which it helped us understand how super calls are resolved. Then we talked about packaging and importing which was exciting as Scala provides different ways to use them. Finally, we learnt about *visibility rules* and *sealed traits*. And after going through all these concepts, we can say with confidence that we now understand the object-oriented concepts in Scala. So, it's time for us to do some real functional programming. In the next few chapters our focus will be on using functions in Scala.

8
More on Functions

"The problems are solved, not by giving new information, but by arranging what we have known since long."

– Ludwig Wittgenstein

One of the reasons we choose to write a function is because it can make our code more readable and look more concise. It's also better, when providing a solution, to break our problem statements down into components/actions and form corresponding functions for them. In this manner, it's going to be easier to solve problems with any programming language that provides function constructs (almost all languages provide such constructs because they are important). Scala provides a variety of ways in which we can write functions to achieve things. Our intention in this chapter is to learn *how*. If you remember correctly, we touched upon functions in Scala in `Chapter 4`, *Giving Meaning to Programs with Functions*. We discussed how we can declare functions and call them using different sets of parameters. We've already learned about function evaluation strategies and the important concepts of function literals and partial functions, and these concepts will help us better understand what we're going to learn in this chapter. Let's take a look. We'll continue with function literals then discuss the following:

- Methods
- Functions versus methods
- Closures
- Higher-order functions
- Partially applied functions
- Currying

Higher-order functions take you to a new universe where it's fun to use functions, return functions, and find other ways we can use those functions. We'll end up our discussion in this chapter with higher-order functions. For now, let's continue our understanding of function literals.

Function literals

A function literal, in simple terms, is a representation of an action that can be performed to specify the input and output parameter types:

```
(value1: Int, value2: Int) => Int
```

This line represents a function literal, which is easily readable. It displays a function that takes two values, `value1` and `value2` of type `Int`, and returns another, `Int`. We've seen some examples of it, such as our `ColorPrinter` example where we were simply able to print color as well as simple black and white pages using just one function named `printPages`:

```
def printPages(doc: Document, lastIndex: Int, print: (Int) => Unit) =
if(lastIndex <= doc.numOfPages) for(i <- 1 to lastIndex) print(i)

val colorPrint = (index: Int) => println(s"Printing Color Page $index.")
val simplePrint = (index: Int) => println(s"Printing Simple Page $index.")

println("---------Method V1----------")
printPages(Document(15, "DOCX"), 5, colorPrint)

println("---------Method V2----------")
printPages(Document(15, "DOCX"), 2, simplePrint)
```

Our `colorPrint` and `simplePrint` values are examples of function literals of the following type:

```
(index: Int) => Unit
```

The `Unit` type here represents the absence of a return type. In other words, don't expect any output from the function literal. We discussed this concept in `Chapter 4`, *Giving Meaning to Programs with Functions*, where we answered the *what* and *how* of function literals. So now, let's answer the *why*, and by *why* we mean the problem it solves. We'll take the preceding example of it. Take a closer look and you'll see that we abstracted the problem statement. If we had declared specific functions for simple and color pages, they would have spoken for themselves, such as in the following example.

Here's a `printColorPages` function, which takes a `Document`, `lastIndex` page number, `startIndex` page number, and then prints color pages. The same goes for `printSimplePages`:

```
def printColorPages(doc: Document, lastIndex: Int, startIndex: Int) =
if(lastIndex <= doc.numOfPages) for(i <- startIndex to lastIndex)
colorPrint(i)

def printSimplePages(doc: Document, lastIndex: Int, startIndex: Int) =
if(lastIndex <= doc.numOfPages) for(i <- startIndex to lastIndex)
simplePrint(i)
```

There are code smells here and they are as follows:

- In both of these functions only the implementation part varies, that is, `colorPrint` and `simplePrint`
- In both of the implementations, input and output parameters do not vary
- Let's take both implementations out and pass them as parameters. It's going to be a function literal of the same form as the function:

```
(index: Int) => Unit
```

By answering these kinds of questions we get to our end function. It looks as follows:

```
def printPages(doc: Document, lastIndex: Int, print: (Int) => Unit) =
if(lastIndex <= doc.numOfPages) for(i <- 1 to lastIndex) print(i)
```

I hope it's now clear how we go through this kind of refactoring. The best thing about it is that it will all come easily to you once you write the code yourself. One more thing we would like to know about the representation is that when you specify these literals and assign them to a value, you should know how they differ. The following representation is going to help you do that. Let's take a look at the following figure:

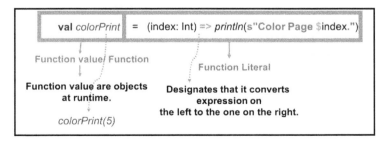

Function values and function literals

In the preceding figure, we can see two forms. The one on the left is called a function value and the one on the right is a function literal. Function values are runtime objects. The question arises, *runtime objects of which type*? The answer is a `Function1` type, which is a trait in Scala and declared in the following form:

```
trait Function1[-T1, +R] extends AnyRef
```

In brackets, [], we have specified the type parameters; we'll learn about these in `Chapter 10`, *Advanced Functional Programming*. For now, just understand that these two specify that our implementation of `Function1` is going to take an input parameter of the first type `T1` and the output will be of type `R`. Basically, our literal representation is just an anonymous instantiation of this trait and we can verify how the compiled version of it looks. The `javap` representation of the previous function literal looks as follows:

```
public static scala.Function1<java.lang.Object, scala.runtime.BoxedUnit>
colorPrint()

public static void printPages(chapter4.Document, int,
scala.Function1<java.lang.Object, scala.runtime.BoxedUnit>,
scala.Function0<java.lang.Object>)
```

The preceding representation means that the following are equivalent:

Literal syntax	FunctionX syntax
val *colorPrint* = (index: Int) => *println*(s"Printing Color Page $index.")	**val** *colrPrintV2* = **new** Function1[Int, Unit]{ **override def** apply(index: Int): Unit = *println*(s"Printing Color Page $index.") }

Here, on the right-hand side, we override the `apply` method for the `Function1` trait. Does it look more concise written in a literal way? Yes! That's why Scala has this syntax. Also, it means that a function value of this type is going to support all methods defined in `Function1`. We know that the trait has an `apply` method that's an abstract member from the trait. We also have a few concrete members such as the following:

```
def andThen[A](g: (R) ⇒ A): (T1) ⇒ A

def compose[A](g: (A) ⇒ T1): (A) ⇒ R
```

We'll try to understand these method implementations using an example. Take a look at the following code snippet. We have two function literals, `incrementByOne` and `isEven`, and we want to form another method that performs these two operations in sequence. We can use `andThen` for this. Check out our implementation of `incrementAndCheckForEven`. It looks like plain English, telling the Scala compiler, "I'll provide you with an integer, please first execute the `incrementByOne` function and then check for even numbers.":

```
val incrementByOne = (num: Int) => num + 1

val isEven = (num: Int) => num % 2 == 0

val incrementAndCheckForEven = incrementByOne andThen isEven

println(s"Representing andThen function ${incrementAndCheckForEven(1)}")
```

Take a look at the following for a better understanding:

```
def andThen[A](g: (R) => A): (T1) => A
```

This tells us that `isEven` is the function literal g, that is, of form `(R) => A`. The type R for our implementation is `Int` and X is `Boolean`. The return type of `andThen` is `g(apply(x))`.

In the same manner, we can also find use cases for our `compose` function. The difference between `andThen` and `compose` can be understood with the help of two example functions—f and g:

- In case of `andThen(g)`: `f(x) == g(apply(x))`
- In case of `compose(g)`: `f(x) == apply(g(x))`

You can do the remaining mathematics, but it's fun forming such a pipeline of operations using literals because they are readable and easy to implement. This example brings our discussion of function literals to an end but believe me, we'll be using these a lot in practice.

Up till now, we've been using the terms method and function interchangeably but the reality is a bit different. These two are different. The question is *how*, so let's start by talking about the methods to learn more.

Methods

We've already seen Scala methods and used them many times so far. However, to differentiate between methods and functions, we'll take a look at the Scala methods once again. What are methods in Scala? Throughout our discussion of methods, we'll look at several definitions of what a method is. Let's start with what a method may contain:

```
annotations(Optional) def methodName(parameter: ParameterType): returnType(Optional) = {
    // method definition
}

One of the often used Example for Annotations for methods:       Mandatory for recursive
                                                                 methods.
    @Override def toString(str: String) ={"I'ma: "+str}
```

Method signature

As you can see, we start our method with a few modifiers such as annotations, or keywords such as `final` and so on. This is followed by a `def` keyword, method name, parameter list, and then a return type that is optional. Scala methods are intelligent enough to infer the return type. Usually, a return type for a method is what the last expression evaluates to. Check out the following example:

```
object Methods {

  def filePrinter() = {
    println("Version 0")
    val filesHere = (new File(".")).listFiles()
    for(file <- filesHere)
      println(file)
  }

  def main(args: Array[String]): Unit = {
    filePrinter()
  }

}
```

The result is as follows:

```
Version 0
./.idea
./FirstProject.iml
./out
./src
```

In the preceding example, we have a method named `filePrinter`, which does nothing but print the filenames in the current directory one by one. It's worth noticing a few things. We have used a `def` keyword, an assignment operator, and braces. We've preferred to omit specifying the return type, that is, `Unit` in our case. Methods which do not return any specific type except `Unit` can also be written in procedure syntax. In procedure syntax, we omit the assignment operator and directly define the method instead:

```
def filePrinterV2() {
  println("Version 2")
  val filesHere = (new File(".")).listFiles()
  for(file <- filesHere)
    println(file)
}
```

In the preceding code, we wrote a method that prints all the filenames from the current directory. Now, take a look at the following:

```
import java.io.File

object Methods {

  def filePrinter() = {
    println("Version 0")
    val filesHere = (new File(".")).listFiles()
    for(file <- filesHere)
      println(file)
  }

  def filePrinterV1()
  {
    println("Version 1")
    val filesHere = (new File(".")).listFiles()
    for(file <- filesHere)
      println(file)
  }

  def filePrinterV2() {
    println("Version 2")
    val filesHere = (new File(".")).listFiles()
    for(file <- filesHere)
      println(file)
  }

  def filePrinterV3() = println("Version 3")
    val filesHere = (new File(".")).listFiles()
    for(file <- filesHere)
```

```
        println(file)

  def main(args: Array[String]): Unit = {
    filePrinter()
    filePrinterV1()
    filePrinterV2()
    filePrinterV3()
  }

}
```

We have four representations for our `filePrinter` method in the form of different versions, from V0 to V3. Our intention is the same for all four methods. We want to print the filenames in the current directory. Can you guess which ones will work?

If you're done with guessing, let's take a look at the output:

```
./.idea
./FirstProject.iml
./out
./src
Version 0
./.idea
./FirstProject.iml
./out
./src
Version 1
./.idea
./FirstProject.iml
./out
./src
Version 2
./.idea
./FirstProject.iml
./out
./src
Version 3
```

Here's the output of our file printers. By taking a closer look, you'll see that for `filePrinter` versions V0, V1, and V2, the output is correct but for version V3, it's not. Plus, the sequence of evaluation tells us that from somewhere in our code, we're printing filenames. You might realize that it's because of the way we tried to define version v3 of our method. The `filePrinterV3` method defines only a simple `println`. The Scala compiler treats subsequent statements outside the scope of our method. Well, we can ensure these kind of mistakes don't happen.

We can do this by explicitly specifying the return type of our methods. Specifying the return type makes the Scala compiler take care of such mistakes and then notifies you at compile time.

A thing to note about methods in Scala is that they are **non-value** types. This means no instance or no object at runtime. This notion causes us to investigate what we mean by this and how it works. This statement also provides a major difference between functions and methods. Let's investigate the difference.

Functions versus methods

At the beginning of the chapter, we mentioned that we usually use the terms **function** and **method** interchangeably. But the reality is different. In Scala, these two are different concepts altogether. We'll use several examples to help understand this.

We'll take a look at all the differences, from syntactical differences to semantic differences. We'll also look at when to use what: a function or a method. For now, let's use a previous example. For the colorPrinter function, in both versions, we'll define a method and give it the name, colorPrintV3:

```
val colorPrint = (index: Int) => println(s"Printing Color Page $index.")
```

```
val colorPrintV2 = new Function1[Int, Unit]{
  override def apply(index: Int): Unit =
    println(s"Printing Color Page $index.")
}
```

```
def colorPrintV3(index: Int) = println(s"Printing Color Page $index.")
```

The way we can call these is similar. Syntactically there's no difference:

```
println("---------Function V1-----------")
printPages(Document(15, "DOCX"), 2, colorPrint)

println("---------Function V2-----------")
printPages(Document(15, "DOCX"), 2, colorPrintV2)

println("---------Method V3-----------")
printPages(Document(15, "DOCX"), 2, colorPrintV3)
```

Here, `colorPrint` and `colorPrintV2` are functions and `colorPrintV3` is a method. In the preceding use case, we passed all these as literals. This looks similar, and it also works in a similar way. It also provides output:

```
---------Function V1-----------
Printing Color Page 1.
Printing Color Page 2.
---------Function V2-----------
Printing Color Page 1.
Printing Color Page 2.
---------Method V3-----------
Printing Color Page 1.
Printing Color Page 2.
```

We said that methods and functions in Scala are different, but the way we use them and the results are similar. This happens because the compiler helps to convert a method into a function dynamically when it sees the possibility of doing it. So this is our counter-statement to this conflicting situation. We better investigate this.

We'll check class files generated by the compiler. Our intention is to investigate these three:

- `colorPrint`
- `colorPrintV2`
- `colorPrintV3`

The files generated by the compiler is as follows:

```
:> javap ColorPrinter.class
Compiled from "FuncLiterals.scala"
public final class chapter4.ColorPrinter {
  public static void main(java.lang.String[]);
  public static void delayedInit(scala.Function0<scala.runtime.BoxedUnit>);
  public static void delayedEndpoint$chapter4$ColorPrinter$1();
  public static long executionStart();

  public static void colorPrintV3(int);

  public static scala.Function1<java.lang.Object, scala.runtime.BoxedUnit>
colorPrintV2();

  public static scala.Function1<java.lang.Object, scala.runtime.BoxedUnit>
colorPrint();

  public static void printPages(chapter4.Document, int,
scala.Function1<java.lang.Object, scala.runtime.BoxedUnit>,
```

```
scala.Function0<java.lang.Object>);

    public static boolean printerSwitch();
}
```

When we observe the preceding compiled class representation of the `colorPrint` series of functions, it becomes clear that the way Scala treats them internally is different. The takeaway points from this are:

- Scala function literals are compiled down to the form of a FunctionX trait (X here, is a placeholder for a number, meaning, the number of parameters this function is going to support). We've already seen that this FunctionX trait comes with more methods such as `apply`, `andThen`, and `compose`.
- Scala methods are compiled down to normal Java methods.
- Finally, methods suited to the context of an object, for example, the `apply` method from the FunctionX trait, only get called on anonymous instances of FunctionX, so the following makes sense for the `apply` method:

```
colorPrintV2(3)
```

The preceding code is equivalent to the following:

```
new Function1[Int, Unit]().apply(3)
```

This tells us that Scala does some magic with the function syntax at compile time. Also, we know that our literals are *Ffunction objects* so we can perform operations like `toString`, as well as equality operations on them. Hence, the following is valid:

```
colorPrint == colorPrintV2 //false
```

However, the compiler won't let you perform the following:

```
colorPrint == colorPrintV3 //Compile Time Error
```

The reason for this is that `colorPrintV3` is a method and not a value type. Also if you try to call `toString` on `colorPrintV3`, the compiler will complain about it and won't let you perform such operations on a method type. The Scala compiler automatically converts a method to its literal equivalent and provides a way to explicitly perform it. We use the following syntax for that:

```
val colorPrintV4 = colorPrintV3 _
```

Take a look at the trailing underscore. This syntactic sugar is enough to tell the Scala compiler to convert the method to a function. Now, you may call `toString`, create a function pipeline, or use `andThen` or `compose` methods on `colorPrintV4`. We can even perform equality methods on it. So that's how methods and functions are different in Scala, but now the question arises when to choose what?

Methods or functions?

Now that you have an idea about the difference between a method and a function, you might be wondering where and when to use what. Should I prefer a function over a method or the opposite? Earlier, we defined a `colorPrinterV3` method and passed that to our higher-order `printPages` function (we'll talk about higher-order functions in later sections). Now that you know that the compiler has to put some extra effort into converting the method into its function equivalent, it becomes obvious that in use cases where we're depending upon higher-order functions, it's a good choice to have functions in scope so that we can communicate properly. Apart from that, it's also obvious that defining a function instead of a method gives us more functionality options. We've seen examples of methods such as `andThen` and `compose`. These methods let us enhance the functionality. Performance-wise, there's not much of a difference in the usage. There are a few scenarios where only methods are the solution:

- We can provide default values for method parameters, but that's not possible for functions.
- In a parent-child class relationship, when we override a method from a superclass, we can still access the parent class version of that method using a `super` call. However, once you override a function, you can't make a super call and are stuck with the implementation.

So it's wise to choose which one to use depending on the requirements you have. Functions provide us with more chaining capabilities. We may choose to use whichever suits us the best.

For now, let's again take a look at the snippet we have, and see if we can make some more modifications:

```
object ColorPrinter extends App {

  val printerSwitch = false

  def printPages(doc: Document, lastIndex: Int, print: (Int) => Unit,
  isPrinterOn: => Boolean) = {
```

```
    if(lastIndex <= doc.numOfPages && isPrinterOn) for(i <- 1 to lastIndex)
print(i)

  }

  val colorPrint = (index: Int) => println(s"Printing Color Page $index.")

  val colorPrintV2 = new Function1[Int, Unit]{
    override def apply(index: Int): Unit =
      println(s"Printing Color Page $index.")
  }

  println("---------Function V1-----------")
  printPages(Document(15, "DOCX"), 2, colorPrint, !printerSwitch)
  println("---------Function V2-----------")
  printPages(Document(15, "DOCX"), 2, colorPrintV2, !printerSwitch)
}

case class Document(numOfPages: Int, typeOfDoc: String)
```

I'm using this `Printer` example because it's easy to understand and we've already seen bits and pieces of it. So, when taking a look at the calling of the `printPages` function, we may want to do some refactoring. First, we know the logic that checks if the printer is ON or OFF by checking `printerSwitch` value. Moreover, every time we call `printPages`, we have to pass the `!printerSwitch` parameter. We want to omit this extra burden of telling the printer to check if it's on or not. We want the printer to already know that, that's what we're going to do. But in a programming context, is it possible to refer to `printerSwitch` from the inner scope of the `printPages` function? Yes, it's possible if we choose to use a closure. Let's discuss closures and how we can define them in Scala.

What are closures?

We'll solve the problem in the previous section using closures. But first, let's explain the concept of a **closure**. In programming terminology, a closure has more than one definition:

- A closure is simply a function value that gets created at runtime and encompasses a reference to a free variable that's not in the local scope
- A closure in practical terms is a function that you can pass around that retains the same scope and values as the ones it had at the time of creation

What do we mean by these statements? Let's check that using a very simple, but a fun example:

```
object AClosure extends App {

  var advertisement = "Buy an IPhone7"

  val playingShow = (showName: String) => println(s"Playing $showName.
Here's the advertisement: $advertisement")

  playingShow("GOT")
  advertisement = "Buy an IPhone8"

  playingShow("GOF")

}
```

The result is as follows:

```
Playing GOT. Here's the advertisement: Buy an IPhone7
Playing GOF. Here's the advertisement: Buy an IPhone8
```

So, you're getting it, aren't you? Here, we created a function that expects a `showName` and plays it. That doesn't go so smoothly and we get to watch some advertisements. That's what is happening in the preceding code. It's obvious that the use case is not practical, but it's easy to understand the concept. We're trying to refer to a variable that's not in the local scope of our `playingShow` function. When we tried using this function for the first time, the runtime representation of `playingShow` was referring to the iPhone 7 advertisement. Then we time travel, and the second time we called `playingShow`, we watched an advertisement that was different from the previous one. The point to take away is the runtime representation of our `playingShow` is called a closure. Some terminology included with a closure are *open terms* and *closed terms*. Here, in our example, `advertisement` is called a free variable because it doesn't reside in the local scope of our *function/closure* whereas the `showName` parameter, which we explicitly referred to, is called a *bound* variable. When we try to form a function literal with only bound variables, it's called a closed term. And the other way around, when you include a free variable, it makes an open term.

A closed term example is as follows:

```
(showName: String) => println(s"Playing $showName. No Advertisement")
```

An open term example is as follows:

```
(showName: String) => println(s"Playing $showName. Here's the
advertisement: $advertisement")
```

One more thing to note is that a closure only keeps the reference to the free variables. That's the reason we were able to detect the change in the value of advertisement.

Now that you've some idea about closures, let's get back to the refactoring of the printPages function. Our intended behavior was that the printer should already know how to switch before printing. We can omit the function literal specified in printPages. Then there are two possible solutions:

```
val printerSwitch = false

def printPages(doc: Document, lastIndex: Int, print: (Int) => Unit) = {

   if(lastIndex <= doc.numOfPages) for(i <- 1 to lastIndex) print(i)

}

val colorPrint = (index: Int) => if(!printerSwitch) println(s"Printing
Color Page $index.")

val colorPrintV2 = new Function1[Int, Unit]{
   override def apply(index: Int): Unit =
      if(!printerSwitch) println(s"Printing Color Page $index.")
}
```

In the preceding snippet, we've removed the isPrinterOn function literal and added the explicit printerSwitch check in two functions, colorPrint and colorPrintV2. This is possible because we were sure about the printer functionality driven by the switch. Also, we removed the extra burden of passing this function literal each time we call for a print. This is a fine and acceptable solution to our problem and the reason we're trying out this example is that it's using a closure in the solution. When we include printerSwitch, which is not in the local scope of our colorPrint function literal, we make it a closure. Then, as with our last example, the runtime representation of our colorPrint is going to keep the reference of our printerSwitch forming a closure. The refactor seems fine, but it can be enhanced, let's check out the second solution:

```
val printerSwitch = false

def printPages(doc: Document, lastIndex: Int, print: (Int) => Unit) = {

   if(lastIndex <= doc.numOfPages && !printerSwitch) for(i <- 1 to
lastIndex) print(i)

}

val colorPrint = (index: Int) => println(s"Printing Color Page $index.")
```

```
val colorPrintV2 = new Function1[Int, Unit]{
  override def apply(index: Int): Unit =
    println(s"Printing Color Page $index.")
}
```

What we've done in the second solution is we removed `isPrinterOn` from our `printPages` function's parameter list and put the implementation with `!printerSwitch`. This makes our `printPages` function a closure and somehow we were able to reduce code duplication in `colorPrint` and `colorPrintV2`. So this is another alternative we have to our solution.

I hope you get the idea of what a closure is and how it can be used. We also learned that closures don't solve any problems that can't be solved without them. They are just an alternative to getting things done in a concise manner. We also saw a closure carry state with them; this is a concept defined in many languages and in languages where there's no state present such as **Haskell**, hence these are used to carry *immutable state*. However, these are an essential and fun alternative to solving a particular problem. In Scala, there are several such tool type constructs available, using which we can make our code smell good, a closure is one of them.

We've talked a lot about functions, methods, and closures. During which we've come up with various higher-order functions. So now, we're kind of comfortable with the concept of higher-order functions. When we see one, it doesn't feel odd or doesn't make us feel uncomfortable. Great, then let's discuss them in detail. You already have some idea about the power of them in a functional programming context. We'll explore them more.

Higher-order functions

We know that we can only pass a first-class value object as an argument to a method or a function. For example, take this simple method:

```
def sum(a: Int, b: Int) = a + b
```

This is a method named `sum` and declares two parameters `a` and `b`. Now, to use this method, we will pass arguments. In the argument list, it's obvious we'll have to pass values of the integer type. It's clear that any type, if it's a value, can be declared as a function parameter and can be used as an argument while calling a function.

In Scala, function literals are nothing more than function trait objects, hence it's obvious that we can declare them as parameters and use them as arguments. This gives rise to functions which contain functions as parameters, and function calls which contain function literals as arguments. These types of functions are called **higher-order functions** (**HOF**). Using higher-order functions has its own advantages. We've already seen a couple of those. Wherever we define abstract syntax in libraries, frameworks, or code, higher-order functions are used at large. If you think about how these behaviors/functions can be used in higher orders, you'll come up with a few of the following scenarios:

- Function as an output
- Function as an input
- Function as a parameter

The preceding scenarios specify three conditions where we can use function literals as higher-order functions. Take a look at the following figure to get a clear picture:

input	*form*	*output*
int	*int -> (int -> int)*	*as output* *int -> int*
as input *int -> int*	*(int -> int) -> int*	*int*
int	*as parameter* *int -> int*	*int*

A few forms of higher-order functions

As shown in the table, we have used a function literal of form int => int, which means a function that takes an integer as an input and gives back another integer after performing some operation on it. The first form in the figure takes an integer as an input parameter and returns a function literal of form int -> int. In the second form, we are taking a function literal of form int -> int, and giving an integer as an output. In the final form, we are expecting an integer and a function literal of the same form int -> int as a parameter. Let's see a few examples to see things clearer:

```
object HOFs extends App {

    def multiplier10(x : Int): Int => Int = x => x * 10     //functionAsOutput

    def intOpPerformer(g: Int => Int) : Int = g(5)          //functionAsInput
```

```
    def multiplicator(x: Int)(g: Int => Int): Int = g(x)
//functionAsParameter

    println(s"functionAsInput Result: ${intOpPerformer(multiplier10(5))}")

    println(s"functionAsParameter Result:
${multiplicator(5)(multiplier10(5))}")

    }
```

The result is as follows:

```
functionAsInput Result: 50
functionAsParameter Result: 50
```

In the preceding code, we defined all three forms. The first gives a function as an output, named `multiplier10`, the form itself is explanatory. It takes an integer and returns a function literal that is a multiplier of 10.

The second one is a higher-order method which takes a function literal as input and outputs an integer as a result. The `intOpPerformer` method, as the name suggests, performs an operation of type `Int => Int`, be it a multiplication operation or any other operation. Whichever we pass, it's going to be used and the output will be an integer as mentioned in the signature. We can call the function by providing an input function literal:

```
intOpPerformer(multiplier10(5))
```

So this is another way we can utilize the higher-order nature of a function. There's one more, the third version, where we pass this function literal as part of the parameter list and it applies the first parameter value to the second parameter function and gives an integer result. The `multiplicator` function is an example of such a construct. We have used the curried form of the function. We'll learn about currying in subsequent sections:

```
multiplicator(5)(multiplier10(5))
```

These are the ways we can incorporate higher-order functions and all of them solve certain problems. By removing code duplication, we can abstract out the pattern and make a higher-order version of our function. That's how we use them.

Our famous `ColorPrinter` example also uses higher-order functions:

```
def printPages(doc: Document, lastIndex: Int, print: (Int) => Unit,
isPrinterOn: => Boolean) = {

    if(lastIndex <= doc.numOfPages && isPrinterOn) for(i <- 1 to lastIndex)
print(i)

    }
```

Here, `print` is a higher-order function that we are passing as a parameter. A close look will explain it better. The `colorPrint` argument itself is a function literal:

```
printPages(Document(15, "DOCX"), 2, colorPrint, !printerSwitch)

val colorPrint = (index: Int) => println(s"Printing Color Page $index.")
```

This is possible just because `colorPrint` is a value object. While we are on the subject, sometimes you may read: "Functional languages treat functions as first class values." What do we mean by *first class values*? It means that the way we declare an integer or string value and use them as parameters. In the same way, we can declare a function literal and use it as a parameter in other functions.

Higher-order functions make it a lot easier to compose functions or chains of functions to perform a complex task in an easy and readable manner. Needless to say, utility functions such as `map`, `flatmap`, `filter`, `fold`, and so on are all higher-order functions. In Scala or any other programming language, functions such as `map`, `filter`, or `flatmap` are a result of trying to solve a particular pattern of problem. Hence, it's obvious that we take a part of a certain pattern from our functions and replace it with a higher-order function. The idea for this action is to abstract out the implementation in the form of a function literal.

A simple example, to get a better understanding, is a simple mathematical operation for two integers. Take a look at the following:

```
def add(a: Int, b: Int) = a + b

def multiply(a: Int, b: Int) = a * b

def subtract(a: Int, b: Int) = a - b

def modulus(a: Int, b: Int) = a % b
```

In the preceding code are a few methods that take two input parameters and perform a particular operation. Using these is also pretty easy:

```
add(10, 5)
subtract(10, 5)
multiply(10, 5)
modulus(10, 5)
```

But as good programmers, it's our duty to check the implementation details, even if the solution is working. When you do that, you get to see that all four implementations have many things in common. All four methods have two parameters but the definition proves to be different as each method is performing a different operation. In a sense, we know we can abstract out the signature and implementation details in the form of function literals and form a higher-order function. So we take steps for that.

- First, we create function literal versions of all four implementations, which have a form of `(Int, Int) => Int` and we come up with something like the following:

```
val add = (a: Int, b: Int) => a + b
val multiply = (a: Int, b: Int) => a * b
val subtract = (a: Int, b: Int) => a - b
val modulus = (a: Int, b: Int) => a % b
```

This ensures that we can pass these literals without worrying about internal dynamic conversions.

- Then, we write the abstracted out method that takes one such function literal and two integer parameters to perform the operation on. The result looks something like the following:

```
def operation(op: (Int, Int) => Int, a: Int, b: Int) : Int = op(a, b)
```

Here, `operation` is the higher-order method which takes a function literal and two parameters and calls the function passed with the other parameters.

Now, using the higher-order method is as easy as calling any other function:

```
operation(add, 10, 5)
operation(subtract, 10, 5)
operation(multiply, 10, 5)
operation(modulus, 10, 5)
```

You may ask whether this makes sense. We still wrote the same (with a couple of extra) lines of code. So let's remove the literals we wrote, as those are just literals we named. We can directly use the functionality by providing what you intend to do dynamically to our operation function. Our code looks like the following after the final implementation:

```
object HOFs extends App {
    def operation(op: (Int, Int) => Int, a: Int, b: Int) : Int = op(a,b)

    println(operation((a, b) => a + b, 10, 5))
    println(operation((a, b) => a * b, 10, 5))
    println(operation((a, b) => a - b, 10, 5))
    println(operation((a, b) => a % b, 10, 5))

}
```

The result is as follows:

```
15
50
5
0
```

The real function required is just a one-liner, the operation higher-order function. The next few lines are the calls to the previous operation function. One thing to note, on the calling side of the operation function we didn't provide the a and b type of parameters. That's because Scala is powerful enough to understand that an operation functions first parameter expects the same type as we are providing.

I hope this example helps you to understand the concept of higher-order functions. In practice, the more you use them, the more you get to see the power of them. A couple of forms exist, using which we solve problems.

Now that we've seen more than one representation and one use case of higher-order functions, let's take a look at another way of calling functions using currying. You may have heard about currying as a concept. Here, our motto is to understand what Currying is and what purpose it solves.

Currying

Scala allows you to pass multiple parameters in functions or methods. We may want to create intermediate versions of such functions. This gives us more than one version of a single function. In other words, we can break down every function with multiple parameters into single parameter functions. Why would we want to create single parameter functions? The answer to this is, we can leverage it for function composition. For example, we can launch a website with the help of a domain name, hosting, and web platform. See the following example:

```
WebsitePlatform => DomainName => Host
```

If you have a function that takes a domain name, another function that takes a website platform, and another function that takes a hosting platform as a parameter, you can compose them together to have a full-fledged website. Functional composition is powerful because it gives you more options together with intermediate functions. A normal function would look like the following:

```
def makeWebsite(platform: WebsitePlatform, domainName: DomainName, host:
Host) = println(s"Making $domainName using $platform with hosting from
$host ")
```

This form of a method does not provide you with the same power that you have when you compose a function. As mentioned, in Scala it's possible to convert our functions to a curried form or convert functions with multiple parameters into a function with single parameters. For that Haskell Curry has provided the concept of currying. Here's an example to help us understand this. We'll take the same example of making a website. The problem statement is clear. We want to compose intermediate functions where we can pass multiple, single parameter lists. The end function should look like the following:

```
def makeWebsite(platform: WebsitePlatform)(domainName: DomainName)(host:
Host): Unit
```

Here, `WebsitePlatform`, `DomainName`, and `Host` are the types we choose to use. We can create these using Scala, providing the `type` keyword. A form of the preceding function is as follows:

```
WebsitePlatform => DomainName => Host => Unit
```

Suppose you want to have an intermediate function that does not have to deal with the website platform, and simply creates a WordPress.com platform account for the intended account. The function should return something like the following:

```
DomainName => Host => Unit
```

The same goes for the other two intermediate versions. For example, you want to create a dummy website with the default WordPress.com (`https://wordpress.com/`) platform and a dummy WordPress URL for your website. The version then looks like the following:

```
Host => Unit
```

The final version deals with all the defaults using bluehost.com as the default hosting provider and creating a website for you. An example application would look like the following:

```
object Curried extends App {

  type WebsitePlatform = String
  type DomainName = String
  type Host = String

  def makeWebsite(platform: WebsitePlatform)(domainName: DomainName)(host:
Host) =
    println(s"Making $domainName using $platform with hosting from $host ")


  val wordPress: DomainName => Host => Unit = makeWebsite("WordPress")

  val wordPressDummyDotCom : Host => Unit = wordPress("dummy123.com")

  val blueHostedWordPressDummyDotCom : Unit =
wordPressDummyDotCom("Bluehost.com")

  blueHostedWordPressDummyDotCom

}
```

The result is as follows:

```
Making dummy123.com using WordPress with hosting from Bluehost.com
```

Did you take a look at the preceding code? We used composition, step-by-step, to make a default website creator that uses WordPress.com as a website platform, bluehost.com as hosting provider, and some dummy URI as URL. Let's try to understand how this is working. The first thing that we did was just add a syntactic enhancement for a better understanding. The three types we declared using the type keywords are just strings. These strings are, of course, for demonstration purposes. They can be of different types. Then we declared the curried version of a method that takes three different single parameter lists. The definition is not very important right now, we're just printing.

Then comes the interesting part. We created an intermediate version of our function, named `wordPress`, and the return type of this function is `DomainName => Host => Unit`. In the very next step, we created another intermediate function named `wordPressDummyDotCom` that is particular to WordPress.com and uses a dummy URL. In the same way, we again composed another function that gives another default website component. The advantage of this is that we can create multiple versions with different website platforms and thus things will be easier for the client of your program, as you're providing multiple versions of default functions for almost every set of parameters. For that, we have used nothing more than the curried form of our function. It is so common to convert or write curried versions of your function in Scala, that the language has a default way of doing it. In Scala, it's possible to convert a function with multiple parameters to its curried counterpart.

Converting a function with multiple parameters to curried form

In Scala, we have a function called `curried`, using which we can convert our functions to a curried form. Let's see a simple example for a better understanding:

```
def add = (x: Int, y: Int) => x + y

val addCurried = add.curried

println(add(5,6))
println(addCurried(5)(6))
```

The result is as follows:

```
11
11
```

Here, we defined a simple two-parameter function literal named `add`. Then, we used a Scala-provided function named `curried` to convert the function to its curried form. We named the result `addCurried`. With that, we were able to call both functions and got the same result.

There's also a way to uncurry curried functions. We have this `uncurried` method, using which we can convert the curried function to uncurried form:

```
val addCurriedUncurried = Function.uncurried(addCurried)

println(addCurriedUncurried(5,6))
```

The result is as follows:

```
11
```

This is how we use currying in Scala. There are similar constructs that we can use in Scala to fulfill the same intentions, and we call them *partially applied functions*. These are different to currying. Let's discuss the topic in detail.

Partially applied functions

Partially applied functions, as the name suggests, apply the functions partially. It means that for functions with multiple parameters in a parameter list, we don't provide a value for each of the parameters. If we don't want to provide parameters we just leave them blank. Now that we know this, let's look at a similar example to the one we looked at when learning currying. With this, you'll be able to differentiate between the two.

First, take a look at the multiple parameter functions, which we'll convert to partially applied forms:

```
def makeWebsite(platform: WebsitePlatform, domainName: DomainName, host:
Host) =
    println(s"Making $domainName using $platform with hosting from $host ")
```

Here, `makeWebsite`, as we have already seen, takes three parameters, `platform`, `domainName`, and `host`. Take a look at an application we can create with various intermediate or partially applied functions:

```
object PaF extends App {

  type WebsitePlatform = String
  type DomainName = String
  type Host = String
  type Protocol = String

  def makeWebsite(platform: WebsitePlatform, domainName: DomainName, host:
Host) =
      println(s"Making $domainName using $platform with hosting from $host ")

  val wordPressSite: (DomainName, Host) => Unit = makeWebsite("WordPress",
_: DomainName, _: Host)

  val makeExampleDotCom: (WebsitePlatform, Host) => Unit = makeWebsite(_:
WebsitePlatform,
      "example.com",
```

```
        _: Host
    )

  val makeBlueHostingExampleDotCom: (WebsitePlatform) => Unit =
makeWebsite(_: WebsitePlatform,
    "example.com",
    "bluehost.com"
    )
  makeWebsite("Wordpress", "anyDomain.com", "Godaddy.com")
  wordPressSite("example.com", "Godaddy.com")
  makeExampleDotCom("Wordpress", "bluehost.com")
  makeBlueHostingExampleDotCom("Blogger")

}
```

The result is as follows:

```
Making anyDomain.com using Wordpress with hosting from Godaddy.com
Making example.com using WordPress with hosting from Godaddy.com
Making example.com using Wordpress with hosting from bluehost.com
Making example.com using Blogger with hosting from bluehost.com
```

So, here we can see three partially applied functions. Take a look at the first one:

```
val wordPressSite: (DomainName, Host) => Unit = makeWebsite("WordPress", _:
DomainName, _: Host)
```

The function name suggests what this does. We can expect this function to provide a partially applied function for `WebsitePlatform`, and that's the reason the return type of the function is of the following form:

```
(DomainName, Host) => Unit
```

To use this function, we simply provide the unapplied parameters and it works:

```
  wordPressSite("example.com", "Godaddy.com")
```

In the same way, we also described other versions, let's take a look at them. For one of them, we provided a default dummy URL for our website, the website platform, and hosting service that we can provide at the time of calling the same:

```
val makeExampleDotCom: (WebsitePlatform, Host) => Unit = makeWebsite(_:
WebsitePlatform,
    "example.com",
    _: Host
  )
```

The version returns back the type as follows:

```
(WebsitePlatform, Host) => Unit
```

When we take a look at the implementation part, we see that the unapplied parameters are replaced with an underscore. We've also provided the types explicitly with the parameters. So, in a way, *partially applied functions* solve almost the same kind of problems that currying solved for us. Also, we know that *partial functions* have a similar concept. As we've already gone through *partial functions,* we must know that they are just functions that are defined for a particular set of input values. Hence, we should be able to differentiate between these three concepts.

With this discussion of *partially applied functions,* we have come to the end of our chapter. Let's summarize what we have learned.

Summary

In this chapter, we enhanced our knowledge of functions in Scala. We started with the basic method and function definitions, investigated the difference between them, and looked at how Scala treats them. We also saw that Scala is intelligent enough to convert a method to a function whenever needed. Then we took the discussion further and talked about closures. We got to know what *closures* are and then we had a solid discussion regarding higher-order functions in Scala. That was essential as we were already using higher-order functions and we saw multiple forms of them. Afterwards, we looked at currying and talked about *partially applied functions.* We know that partially applied functions are different from *partial functions* and *currying.* So now we have a solid understanding of functions in Scala because we have investigated them thoroughly.

Now it's time to go further and learn about a few advanced functional constructs. The knowledge gained in this chapter will help us do that in the next chapter, where we'll learn about advanced functional constructs.

9
Using Powerful Functional Constructs

"We cannot solve our problems with the same thinking we used when we created them."

– *Albert Einstein*

When we try to solve problems by writing programs, our intention is to write better code. More precisely, we mean that code should be readable and efficient at compile time and runtime. Readability and efficiency are two major factors, along with other important concepts such as concurrency, asynchronous tasks, and so on. We can think of the first two as the building blocks for the next set of characteristics we want. Scala, as a multi-paradigm language, provides multiple constructs that ensure the code we write is optimized, and also provides syntactic sugar wherever required. Many of the functional constructs or concepts used in *functional programming* enable you to write *better* code that not only fulfills the first two requirements but also allows your code to run in *concurrent* and *distributed* environments.

Our intention in this chapter is to learn the ways we can make our code better. For that, we'll go through some of the syntactical constructs. Let's take a look at what we are going to go through in this chapter:

- For expressions
- Pattern matching
- Option type
- Lazy declaration

- Tail call optimization
- Combinators
- Type parameterization

All these concepts are simple but very useful for when you write Scala code. Some of them we've already gone through, such as *for expressions*. Our intention here is to compare for expressions with the available higher-order functions, such as `map`, `flatMap`, and `withFilter`.

For expressions

We would not be wrong, if we say that the `for` expressions are powerful constructs in Scala. For expressions let you traverse through any collection and perform operations such as filtering and yielding out new collections. We have already gone through this concept in `Chapter 3`, *Shaping Up our Scala Program*. Let's recall the example we saw:

```
object ForExpressions extends App {

  val person1 = Person("Albert", 21, 'm')
  val person2 = Person("Bob", 25, 'm')
  val person3 = Person("Cyril", 19, 'f')
  val persons = List(person1, person2, person3)

  val winners = for {
    person <- persons
    age = person.age
    name = person.name
    if age > 20
  } yield name

  winners.foreach(println)

}

case class Person(name: String, age: Int, gender: Char)
```

The result is as follows:

```
Albert
Bob
```

In the previous example, we have a collection of `Person` objects. We are performing a traversal on the collection and generating another collection consisting of names for all persons based on some condition. As we already know, for this we are using three constructs, or let's say expressions:

- Generator
    - `person <- persons`
- Definition
    - `age = person.age`
    - `name = person.name`
- Filter
    - `age > 20`

With these three expressions we were able to perform slightly complex logic with very little syntactical effort. We could have done a similar operation in the form of higher-order functions. Using `map` and `withFilter` we can perform such operations, let's take a look at an example:

```
val winners1 = persons withFilter(_.age > 20) map(_.name)
winners1.foreach(println)

case class Person(name: String, age: Int, gender: Char)
```

The result is as follows:

```
Albert
Bob
```

Here, we have used higher-order functions to implement the same logic we implemented using for expressions. We're already familiar with the `map` method from a collection. It's going to provide you a list of persons whose age is greater than 20. So now, we have the same logic implemented in two different ways. First, in the form of *for expressions*, and second, in the form of *higher-order functions*. So it's important for us to know how this happens. What the Scala compiler does is it internally breaks down for expressions into higher-order functions. Programmers tend to prefer using for expressions for readability but it's a matter of choice. Now that we know what happens internally, we can start thinking about the translation Scala does for slightly complex for expressions, can't we? Yes, so let's try it out.

Now, suppose we have a list of car brands, and each brand has many cars in it (in other words, each brand has a list of cars). The code will look something like the following:

```
case class Car(name: String, brandName: String)
case class Brand(name: String, cars: List[Car])

val brands = List(
Brand("Toyota", List(Car("Corolla", "Toyota"))),
Brand("Honda",  List(Car("Accord", "Honda"))),
Brand("Tesla",  List(Car("Model S", "Tesla"),
                          Car("Model 3", "Tesla"),
                          Car("Model X", "Tesla"),
                          Car("New Model", "Tesla")))))
```

You may want to yield a list of pairs for all the Tesla cars whose name starts with the `Model` keyword . You'll perform something like the following:

```
val teslaCarsStartsWithModel = for {
  brand <- brands
  car <- brand.cars
  if car.name.startsWith("Model") && brand.name == "Tesla"
} yield (brand.name, car.name)

teslaCarsStartsWithModel foreach println
```

The result is as follows:

```
(Tesla,Model S)
(Tesla,Model 3)
(Tesla,Model X)
```

We used for expressions for this task. This has two generator expressions, and we are also performing a filtering operation on it. While translating these kinds of for expressions into higher-order functions, Scala uses the `flatMap` method. Let's see how the same can be implemented using `flatMap`:

```
val teslaCarsStartsWithModel2 = brands.flatMap(brand =>
  brand.cars withFilter(_.name.startsWith("Model") && brand.name ==
  "Tesla") map(car => (brand.name, car.name)))

teslaCarsStartsWithModel2 foreach println
```

The result is as follows:

```
(Tesla,Model S)
(Tesla,Model 3)
(Tesla,Model X)
```

We got a similar result with this definition. So let's try to break this `teslaCarsStartsWithModel2` down to understand how we implemented this. First, what we had was the following:

```
For(gen1 <- list, gen2 <- gen1.list, filter1)
```

In scenarios where we have two generators, we use `flatMap` functions instead of `map`. Let's go through the translation from for expressions to higher-order functions step by step:

1. We have the following:

```
for {
  brand <- brands
  car <- brand.cars
  if car.name.startsWith("Model") && brand.name == "Tesla"
} yield (brand.name, car.name)
```

2. We first used `flatMap`:

```
brands.flatMap{ brand =>
    for{
      car <- brand.cars
      if car.name.startsWith("Model") && brand.name == "Tesla"
    } yield (brand.name, car.name)
}
```

3. Now that we've got the brand, we have access to the cars list. We can proceed with a filtering predicate as follows:

```
brands.flatMap{ brand =>
    brand.cars withFilter{ car =>
      car.name.startsWith("Model") && brand.name == "Tesla"
    } map(car => (brand.name, car.name))
}
```

This is the final version of our implementation. What we have done here is we filtered out elements from our `cars` collection and finally transformed our collection to the intended form.

So this is the way the Scala compiler does translations of our for expressions into the provided functions. As programmers, we only have to deal with the implementation part. You may want to put your logic in the for expressions instead of writing nested higher-order functions, and Scala does the rest for you.

Here, we learned how you can add your logic in different forms in detail. Similarly, you'll also find cases that we will have to go through and then execute any logic applicable. In this process of matching different cases, we can empower ourselves by matching through different patterns. For example, we may want to match our list type against the possible values. The options are going to be either an empty list or a list with certain values. Scala doesn't limit you to matching in these two ways, but you'll have more options to match against. All this is possible via a concept called *pattern matching*. The good thing is, we've already gone through the pattern matching concept so what we are going to do now is try to understand it further.

Pattern matching

We use **pattern matching** to execute code on a case-by-case basis. Take a look at the following:

```
val somelist = List(1,2,3)

somelist match {
  case Nil => Nil
  case _ => ???
}
```

By taking a look at the structure of our pattern match expression, we see a few things. First, we execute a match on some value followed by the `match` keyword and then we put cases. For each case we specify some patterns. Now, the pattern can be a constant value, a variable, or even a constructor. We'll soon have a look at all of these patterns. Pattern matching also allows us to put guards on our match in the form of a condition. In that case, the pattern will only match if the condition is applicable. If you take a look at the previous toy example about `somelist`, you'll see there's an _ underscore. It's called a **wildcard pattern**. It'll match all values or patterns against the case. Logically, you can't put another case after a wildcard. For example, the following does not make any sense and throws a warning:

```
val somelist = 1 :: 2 :: 3 :: Nil

val x = somelist match {
  case Nil => Nil
  case _ => println("anything")
  case head :: tail => println("something with a head and a tail")
}
Warning:(21, 10) patterns after a variable pattern cannot match (SLS 8.1.1)
    case _ => println("anything")
```

```
Warning:(22, 33) unreachable code due to variable pattern on line 21
    case head :: tail => println("something with a head and a tail")
Warning:(22, 33) unreachable code
    case head :: tail => println("something with a head and a tail")
```

This is a pretty basic example of pattern matching in Scala. There are more ways we can pattern match. Why not take a look at all of them?

Different ways we can pattern match

Pattern matching in Scala proves to be a very important concept. We can match on variables, constants, and even constructors. We'll take a look at all of them. Let's start with matching against a variable.

Matching a variable

At times, when we have to use the value after the pattern match is successful, we want to match against cases with variables. What this does is it assigns the value to the variable and then we can use that in our code for that particular case. It's better if we look at the following example:

```
import scala.util.control.NonFatal

def safeToInt(canBeNumber: String): Option[Int] = {
  try {
    Some(canBeNumber.toInt)
  } catch {
    case NonFatal(e) => None
  }
}

safeToInt("10") match {
  case None => println("Got nothing")
  case someValue =>  println(s"Got ${someValue.get}")
}
```

The result is as follows:

```
Got 10
```

Here, we have defined a method which tries to convert a number represented by a string to an integer. Then, we call the method with a parameter and try to match the same using a variable named `someValue`. This `someValue` variable is going to be of the same type as the value's matched type.

Matching a constant

We can also match cases against a constant, such as basic switch statements. Take a look at the following:

```
def matchAgainst(i: Int) = i match {
  case 1 => println("One")
  case 2 => println("Two")
  case 3 => println("Three")
  case 4 => println("Four")
  case _ => println("Not in Range 1 to 4")
}

matchAgainst(1)
 matchAgainst(5)
```

The result is as follows:

```
One
Not in Range 1 to 4
```

Here, we directly matched our expression against constant values. This can be any value, depending upon the type your method accepts. You are allowed to match against a Boolean, string, or any other constant value.

Matching a constructor

Okay, what does a constructor pattern look like? It's about matching a constructor against a value, or we could say, extracting values of our choice. Let's take an example:

```
def safeToInt(canBeNumber: String): Option[Int] = {
  try {
    Some(canBeNumber.toInt)
  } catch {
    case NonFatal(e) => None
  }
}
```

```
safeToInt("10") match {
  case None => println("Got nothing")
  case Some(value) =>  println(s"Got $value")
}
```

The result is as follows:

```
Got 10
```

The only difference we can see here is, instead of providing a variable, we gave a constructor pattern. `Some(value)` lets you extract the `value` out of itself. Here in the given example, the `safeToInt` method returns an `Option` type. We're going to learn about types in subsequent sections. For now, the interesting information for us is that we have two subtypes of our `Option` type named `Some` and `None`, and as the names suggest, `Some` means some value and `None` means no value. The `Some` subtype expects a particular value as its constructor parameter. Hence it's possible for us to match on that. The following line does the exact thing we just mentioned:

```
case Some(value) => println(s"Got $value")
```

With this declaration we can extract a value, in our case the extracted parameter name is also `value`, hence we used it. This is an example of using a constructor for our pattern matching. We've learned about `case` classes in Scala and also mentioned that `case` classes provide us an exact structure, using which we can directly perform pattern matching. So let's take an example:

```
trait Employee
case class ContractEmp(id: String, name: String) extends Employee
case class Developer(id: String, name: String) extends Employee
case class Consultant(id: String, name: String) extends Employee

/*
 * Process joining bonus if
 *      :> Developer has ID Starting from "DL"  JB: 1L
 *      :> Consultant has  ID Starting from "CNL":  1L
 */
def processJoiningBonus(employee: Employee, amountCTC: Double) = employee
match {
   case ContractEmp(id, _) => amountCTC
   case Developer(id, _) => if(id.startsWith("DL")) amountCTC + 10000.0
else amountCTC
   case Consultant(id, _) => if(id.startsWith("CNL")) amountCTC + 10000.0
else amountCTC
 }

val developerEmplEligibleForJB = Developer("DL0001", "Alex")
```

```
val consultantEmpEligibleForJB = Consultant("CNL0001","Henry")
val developer = Developer("DI0002", "Heith")

println(processJoiningBonus(developerEmplEligibleForJB, 55000))
println(processJoiningBonus(consultantEmpEligibleForJB, 65000))
println(processJoiningBonus(developer, 66000))
```

The result is as follows:

```
65000.0
75000.0
66000.0
```

Here in this example, we defined three categories of employees: `Developer`, `Consultant`, and `ContractEmp`. We've a problem to solve: we'll have to process the joining bonus amount for specific employees in a specific category with some conditions. The whole logic is very simple to implement in terms of `case` classes and pattern matching and that's what we have done here. Take a look at the following line from the previous solution:

```
case Developer(id, _) => if(id.startsWith("DL")) amountCTC + 10000.0 else
amountCTC
```

Here we matched against a `case` class constructor. We gave some names to the required parameters, others we replaced with the wildcard _ underscore. Here, we had to put a condition on the `id` parameter, hence we mentioned it in the constructor of the respective `case` class. You can see how `case` classes and pattern matching can make a slightly complex domain problem very easy to solve. Well, it doesn't end there, there's more. We can also put guards against our `case` expressions. Let's see the same example with guards:

```
/*
 * Process joining bonus if
 *      :> Developer has ID Starting from "DL"  JB: 1L
 *      :> Consultant has  ID Starting from "CNL":  1L
 */
def processJoiningBonus(employee: Employee, amountCTC: Double) = employee
match {
   case ContractEmp(id, _) => amountCTC
   case Developer(id, _) if id.startsWith("DL") => amountCTC + 10000.0
   case Consultant(id, _) if id.startsWith("CNL") =>  amountCTC + 10000.0
   case _ => amountCTC
}
```

The result is as follows:

```
65000.0
75000.0
66000.0
```

If we look at the following expression, we can see guards on our `case` patterns. So the value will only match if the guard allows it to:

```
case Developer(id, _) if id.startsWith("DL") => amountCTC + 10000.0
```

So, before going to the right-hand side of the execution block, this expression checks if the `id` starts with `"DL"`, and based on that, it matches. This is how we can use a constructor directly to extract parameters and use them. You can also use patterns in some more ways. For example, we can perform a match against a sequence or a tuple. It's also possible for when we have to match some nested expression, or match a `case` class that has another `case` class inside. For our code to make more sense, and for readability purposes, we can bind the nesting `case` class using the @ symbol and perform pattern matching. Let's take an example:

```
case class Car(name: String, brand: CarBrand)
case class CarBrand(name: String)

val car = Car("Model X", CarBrand("Tesla"))
val anyCar = Car("Model XYZ", CarBrand("XYZ"))

def matchCar(c: Car) = c match {
  case Car(_, brand @ CarBrand("Tesla")) => println("It's a Tesla Car!")
  case _ => println("It's just a Carrr!!")
}

matchCar(car)
matchCar(anyCar)
```

The result is as follows:

```
It's a Tesla Car!
It's just a Carrr!!
```

The preceding example is self-explanatory. We have a nested `case` class inside our `Car`, named `CarBrand`, and we performed a pattern match against that. We got access to that particular object using the @ symbol. So, these are a few ways we can use pattern matching to perform all those tasks very easily. By now, you must have an idea about pattern matching; how powerful and important it is.

While performing all these pattern matches, we felt that there are counter cases where we don't want to perform matches, and use a wildcard so that we can provide any value in return. It's possible that there's no intended value for such cases, and we just want our code to make sense and at the same time return a meaningful response. In those cases, we can use our Option type. As the name suggests, when you define a type as Option, you may get either some value or no value. To make it more clear, let's recall our safeToInt function:

```
def safeToInt(canBeNumber: String): Option[Int] = {
  try {
    Some(canBeNumber.toInt)
  } catch {
    case NonFatal(e) => None
  }
}

safeToInt("10") match {
  case None => println("Got nothing")
  case Some(value) =>  println(s"Got $value")
}
```

Here, in the definition of our safeToInt function, we defined our response type to be Option simply because we knew that it may or may not respond with a meaningful value. Now the reason for using an Option instead of using any type directly is clear, let's discuss the Option type.

Option type

Option is one of the type constructors that Scala provides. The question arises, what's a type constructor? The answer is simple; it lets you construct a type. We'll take two statements:

1. Option is a type constructor
2. Option[Int] is a type

Let's discuss these in detail. When I say Foo is a type constructor, it means that Foo expects you to provide a particular type in the form of a parameter. It looks like Foo[T], where T is an actual type. We call them **type parameters** and we'll talk about them in the following few sections.

In the second statement, we saw that we gave an `Int` type to our `Option` type constructor in brackets and it formed a type. If you try this in the Scala REPL, it'll tell you exactly the same thing we discussed:

```
scala> val a: Option = Some(1)
<console>:11: error: class Option takes type parameters
       val a: Option = Some(1)

scala> val a: Option[Int] = Some(1)
a: Option[Int] = Some(1)
```

In simple words, the `Option[T]` type represents an optional value of any given type `T`. Now `T` can be any type you pass, in the previous example it was `Int`. The `Option[T]` type has two subtypes:

- `Some(T)`
- `None`

When there's a value available, we'll get the `Some` value, otherwise `None`. The `Option` type also provides you a `map` method. The way you would want to use an option value is by calling the `map` method:

```
scala> a map println
1
```

What happens here is the `map` method gives you the respective value if it's available. Otherwise, if the optional value is `None`, it's not going to do anything. Usually, you would want to use this type as an exception handling mechanism. How can we do this? We've already seen an example of it. Recall our `safeToInt` method, without `Option` it'll look like this (maybe):

```
def safeToInt(canBeNumber: String): Int = {
  try {
    canBeNumber.toInt
  } catch {
    case NonFatal(e) => throw Exception
  }
}
```

But if you take a look at the signature, the declaration tells you that the function is going to return you an `Int` but the function, in reality, may also throw an `Exception`. That's neither intended nor correct. The function should follow its own declaration. Hence, we can use our `Option` type, which as a savior, does what our declaration says. `Option` is one of the constructs *functional programming* provides for you.

There're more of these and they provide you with some ready-to-use constructs. Some of them are the types, `Either`, `Try`, and a few more. You may refer to the Scala API documentation (`http://www.scala-lang.org/api/2.12.3/scala/util/Either.html`) for more information about these types.

Next, we'll talk about one more functional construct. It's more than just a construct, it's a scheme of evaluation. Yes, we are talking about *lazy evaluation*. Scala allows you to use this scheme in more than one way. Let's talk about the `lazy` keyword.

Lazy declaration

Before learning more about the `lazy` keyword or lazy evaluation, let's talk about why we need it and exactly what it is. Just how beneficial lazy evaluation is can be explained with a few lines, or a few pages, but for our understanding let's have a one liner.

Lazy evaluation lets you write your code in a way where the order of evaluation doesn't matter. It also saves you some time, by only evaluating expressions that you need. It's like so many complex evaluations, that exists in your code, but never evaluation dues to a certain. The last line is only possible due to the concept of lazy evaluation. In Scala, you can declare a value as `lazy`. Let's take an example. Try the following in the Scala REPL:

```
scala> lazy val v = 1
v: Int = <lazy>

scala> val z = 1
z: Int = 1
```

Here, when we assigned a value of 1 to our `val v`, the REPL gave us the `Int` type and the value as `<lazy>`, and for the `val z` we got `1`. Why this happened is because of the `lazy` declaration. In Scala, when you declare a value as lazy, the compiler evaluates the value only when we use it for the first time. With this, you free yourself from the worry of putting the `val` declaration in any order. Each `lazy` value is evaluated when it's needed.

While we're talking about making our code optimized, let's look at another concept, *tail call optimization*. We first introduced *tail call optimization* in `Chapter 3`, *Shaping Up our Scala Program* while discussing *recursion*. Let's talk about it in brief.

Tail call optimization

We are familiar with the limitations recursion brings with it. We are aware that each function call, if not tail recursive, builds a new stack frame. For scenarios where we have to deal with a large number of function calls, this could possibly result in a stack overflow, which is undesirable. So, what's suggested in this kind of scenario is to make the recursive function call the last statement in your function definition, the Scala compiler then does the rest for you. Take a look at the following:

```scala
import scala.annotation.tailrec

object TailRecursion {
  def main(args: Array[String]): Unit = {
      val list = List("Alex", "Bob", "Chris", "David", "Raven", "Stuart")
    someRecursiveMethod(list)

  }

  /*
      You have a sorted list of names of employees, within a company.
      print all names until the name "Raven" comes
  */
  @tailrec
  def someRecursiveMethod(list: List[String]): Unit = {
      list match {
        case Nil => println("Can't continue. Either printed all names or
encountered Raven")
        case head :: tail => if(head != "Raven") {
          println(s"Name: $head")
          someRecursiveMethod(tail)
        } else someRecursiveMethod(Nil)
      }
    }
  }
```

The result is as follows:

```
Name: Alex
Name: Bob
Name: Chris
Name: David
Can't continue. Either printed all names or encountered Raven
```

In the preceding example, if you take a closer look, you'll see that wherever we made a recursive call, it's the last statement in that particular scope. It means that our call to `someRecursiveMethod` is a last call and there was no other call after that. If it isn't, the Scala compiler will alert you with a message saying the recursive call is not in the tail position:

```
@tailrec
def someRecursiveMethod(list: List[String]): Unit = {
    list match {
      case Nil => println(s"Can't continue. Either printed all names or
encountered Raven")
      case head :: tail => if(head != "Raven") {
        println(s"Name: $head")
        someRecursiveMethod(tail)
        println("Won't happen")
      } else someRecursiveMethod(Nil)

    }
}
Error:(21, 30) could not optimize @tailrec annotated method
someRecursiveMethod: it contains a recursive call not in tail position
someRecursiveMethod(tail)
```

Also, one thing to notice is that we're helping out the Scala compiler by providing the annotation as `tailrec`. When we provide this annotation, the compiler considers your function as a tail recursive function. Evaluation of such a function does not create separate stack frames on each call, but uses the ones already created. This is how we avoid stack overflow and use recursion. What we've tried to do in our example is match to a list of names. Yes, you're already familiar with the notion of pattern matching. If not `Nil`, we check for the name `Raven` in the list, and then we stop further calls. If you're missing `break` or `continue` statements in Scala, this is the way that you can implement them: by using recursion and checking for the condition.

So this was all about tail call optimization. We've also seen that the Scala compiler helps us when we provide the annotation. Well, recursion helps you avoid mutability and at the same time achieve complex logic, adding to the already powerful functional programming. Since we are learning about functional programming constructs, it's really important for us to know that they are rooted in *eternal mathematics*. Mathematics created the notion of functional programming, and almost all functional programming concepts come from some mathematical proof or concept. One of them is a combinator. Learning about combinators or understanding how they are related to mathematics is beyond the scope of this book but we will look at a short introduction and see a simple example. It'll be fun. Let's go through *combinators*.

Combinators

Wikipedia says the following about **combinators**:

> *"A Combinator is a higher-order function that uses only function application and earlier defined Combinators to define a result from its arguments."*

As well as this definition, we could also say that a combinator is a closed *lambda* expression. We have already seen lambda applications in several places and defined them. A lambda is nothing more than an anonymous definition of any function. For example, when you pass an expression to our beloved `foreach` method, you pass it in the form of a lambda expression. Take a look at the following:

```
val brands = List(Brand("Toyota", List(Car("Corolla", "Toyota"))),
                  Brand("Honda", List(Car("Accord", "Honda"))),
                  Brand("Tesla", List(Car("Model S", "Tesla"),
                                      Car("Model 3", "Tesla"),
                                      Car("Model X", "Tesla"),
                                      Car("New Model", "Tesla"))))


brands.foreach((b: Brand) => {
   //Take the brand name, and check the number of Cars and print them.
val brandName = b.name
   println(s"Brand: $brandName || Total Cars:${b.cars.length}")
   (brandName, b.cars)
})
```

Here, the `foreach` method takes a lambda expression and executes it. To be more precise, `(b: Brand)` contained in the brackets is an example of a lambda. Now, let's ask some questions. What do lambdas have to do with combinators? Or let's ask, what's the working (functional) programmer's definition of a combinator? Well, to answer these kinds of questions, we'll use the first Wikipedia definition. If you take a closer look, there are a few things to notice. Firstly, it's a higher-order function and secondly, it's a closed lambda. Closed means it does not contain any *free* variables. For those of you who want to know what a free variable is, take a look at the following lambda:

```
((x) => x * y)
```

Here, y is a free variable. We've seen these kinds of higher-order functions with no free variables before: our `map` and `filter` functions. These are called combinators. In functional programming, we tend to use these a lot. You can also use these as transformations to already available data. If we use these combinators together, they're really helpful for forming data flow logic. This means, if you use `map`, `filter`, and `fold` as combinators together, you can create a domain logic out of your program. This way of writing programs is often used in functional programming. You'll find more of these when you check out the written libraries. Various combinators are used for all sorts of collections and other data structures. The reason for using these combinators is that they provide an abstract or, in other words, a generalized approach to perform some operations. Hence they're used everywhere. It's easy and fun to implement some logic that looks like the following:

```
creditCards.filter(_.limit < 55000)
            .map(cc => cc.accounts(cc.holder))
.filter(_.isLinkedAccount)
  .get
  .info
```

It's really a powerful construct and used a lot in functional programming.

Now that you've learned about combinators, and are also aware of higher-order functions, you're equipped to solve programming problems. So what now? It's time to take the next step. We'll dive into the abstract (sea) levels of Scala programming. If we can make our solutions abstract, it means the solutions we provide should satisfy more than just one problem statement. Let's start with learning about *type parameterization.*

Type parameterization

For an introduction to **type parameterization**, we'll refer to two examples we've already seen to try to make some sense of it. I know you're following the chapter with interest and you've gone through the examples and concepts we've talked about, so let's do an exercise. Think of our savior, `Option[T]` type and try to think why you would want to pass a type (as it requires T to be a type) to `Option`. What purpose can it serve?

I think you've come up with some idea. Maybe you thought that by passing a type of our choice, we can make our code with the `Option` type work in more than one scenario. If you thought so, great! Let's call it generalizing our solution. And moreover, let's call the approach a generic approach to programming. How does it look? Let's take a look at the following code:

```
object TypeParameterization {

  def main(args: Array[String]): Unit = {
      val mayBeAnInteger = Some("101")
      val mayBeADouble = Some("101.0")
      val mayBeTrue = Some("true")

    println(s"Calling mapToInt: ${mapToInt(mayBeAnInteger, (x: String) =>
x.toInt)}")
      println(s"Calling mapToDouble: ${mapToDouble(mayBeADouble, (x: String)
=> x.toDouble)}")
      println(s"Calling mapToBoolean: ${mapToBoolean(mayBeTrue, (x: String)
=> x.toBoolean)}")
    }
    def mapToInt(mayBeInt: Option[String], function: String => Int) =
function(mayBeInt.get)

    def mapToDouble(mayBeDouble: Option[String], function: String => Double)
= function(mayBeDouble.get)

    def mapToBoolean(mayBeBoolean: Option[String], function: String =>
Boolean) = function(mayBeBoolean.get)
  }
```

The result is as follows:

```
Calling mapToInt: 101
Calling mapToDouble: 101.0
Calling mapToBoolean: true
```

So as the code suggests, we have some optional strings, which can be of the `Int`, `String`, or `Boolean` type. Our intention was to convert them to their respective types. So we formed some functions, which take the optional string and then we convert them to their respective types, so we passed a function literal for that. If we can't think of a few counter cases, then it means it's working. However, the solution is bulky; it doesn't feel good. Plus, we can see that there's some repetitiveness in the code. We are doing an almost similar operation to `mapToXXX`, where we think of `XXX` as any type. It seems that we can generalize the solution. Let's think about it, how can we do this?

How can we tell the method about the types we are going to provide? One solution is to pass the types to the method as parameters and then use them in the declaration. Let's try the solution and see what the code looks like:

```
object TypeParameterization {

  def main(args: Array[String]): Unit = {
    val mayBeAnInteger = Some("101")
    val mayBeADouble = Some("101.0")
    val mayBeTrue = Some("true")

    println(s"Calling mapToValue: ${mapToValue(mayBeAnInteger, x =>
x.toInt)}")
    println(s"Calling mapToValue: ${mapToValue(mayBeADouble, x =>
x.toDouble)}")
    println(s"Calling mapToValue: ${mapToValue(mayBeTrue, x =>
x.toBoolean)}")
  }

  def mapToValue[T](mayBeValue: Option[String], function: String => T) =
function(mayBeValue.get)
}
```

The result is as follows:

```
Calling mapToValue: 101
Calling mapToValue: 101.0
Calling mapToValue: true
```

After the generalization, we are able to perform the same logic with just one function. So, let's take a look at the change and the way we gave type parameters:

```
def mapToValue[T](mayBeValue: Option[String], function: String => T) : T =
function(mayBeValue.get)
```

In the preceding `mapToValue` function, after giving the function name, that is, `mapToValue`, we gave `T` in braces as a type parameter. With this, we got the license to use this type parameter in the function declaration and definition. Hence, we used it as a type in a function literal and as return types. We're allowed to give any number of type parameters based on the use. For example, if you want to make it more generalized, the function may look like the following:

```
def mapToValue[A, B](mayBeValue: Option[A], function: A => B) : B =
function(mayBeValue.get)
```

In this definition, we used two type parameters, A and B, and hence made our method more generalized. If you take a look at the map method from Option[T], it looks like the following:

```
def map[B](f: A => B): Option[B] = if (isEmpty)
      None
  else
      Some(f(this.get))
```

Here, we have used type parameters in the function definition of map. So, according to this, for Option[A], we have a map method, which takes a function from A type to B type. So the compiler will infer the A and B type when you give a call to this map method from the context.

This is just an introduction to type parameterization. In the next chapter, we'll get to see more of it along with some advanced concepts. With this, we can end our chapter, let's summarize what we've learned.

Summary

This chapter gave us insights into how we can implement logic with different flavors of implementation. We talked about for expressions and their translation into higher-order functions. We saw how *pattern matching* can make complex logic look very simple. We also talked about constructs such as Option and the lazy keyword. These enable us to write code that is meaningful and optimized. Then we discussed *tail call optimization*. We confronted *combinators*, and then finally we got an introduction to *type parameterization*.

In the next chapter, we'll start from where we ended this chapter. We'll talk more about types, parameterized types, and variance relationships, and let me tell you, that will be fun.

10
Advanced Functional Programming

"Like punning, programming is a play on words."

– Alan Peris

You're a developer, right? Think of a scenario where you're asked to write some software that has certain entities. Take a look at the following:

```
Animal            |        Food
```

We have the `Animal` and `Food` entities. We're working on an automated system that serves food to animals in a zoo. Suppose we're going to write a function which lets two animals share their food. It expects two animal objects, food, and then does the job. The function looks like this:

```
def serveSharedMeal(
    animalOne: Animal,
    animalTwo: Animal,
    meal: Food) = ???
//don't care about the implementation
```

So far, everything's fine, right? Let's introduce two animals now. We have two animal subclasses named `Lion` and `Deer`. Our simple function takes two `animal` instances and shares the `meal` instance among them. Now, you might wonder what happens when we pass instances of `Lion` and `Deer`; what might be the consequences? Hence, we promote strictly typed programs, which can fail at compile time. This means we can write our programs in such a way that the Scala compiler won't allow us to write such programs. You're able to see how types can save lives. Great, so this is the agenda here.

We'll be talking about types and parameterizing our types. We introduced type parameterization in the previous chapter, so we'll take our journey further and learn more about type parameterization, abstract types, and a lot more. Let's take a look at what's coming:

- Genericity/type parameterization
- Parameterized types
- Variance
- Abstract types
- Bounds
- Abstract versus parameterized types
- Type classes

Let me tell you, this chapter's going to be another interesting one. We'll be using constructs that we've already used to make our code more meaningful. But before we dive in to learn about parameterized types in detail, let's talk about why there's so much hype about types.

Why so serious about types?

We've seen that knowing what we're doing can save life. But joking aside, if we really think before writing our applications, it can really help. Our programs consist of two ingredients:

```
Data       |            Operations
```

We can perform operations on the data available. At the same time, not all operations can be performed on all sorts of data. That's what difference types make. You don't want to perform an addition operation between an Integer and a String literal. That's why the compiler does not allow us to do that. Even if it assumes you're trying to concatenate the string with the literal, it's not going to give you a result that's not meaningful. That's why defining types make sense.

Let's discuss a few terms that we just mentioned. It's really good that Scala is a statically typed language because it provides us compile time type safety. The code that we write is less prone to runtime errors, because we were so smart and we wrote it that way (we'll learn about this in this chapter). Our beloved Scala compiler performs a compile time type check on the program we wrote and throws an error at compile time if we try to be too smart. The following diagram may clear your doubts:

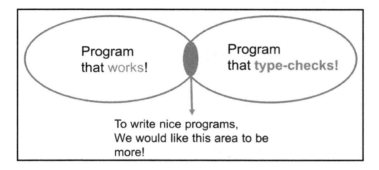

You see? The preceding picture depicts that if your program is working, that's not enough, eventually you may find some corner cases that will cause them to fail. So, we better choose a language that helps you cover that section more, so that your program lives in a happy world:

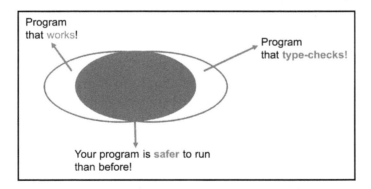

This is essential for us to understand why we're supporting a system where using *types* is encouraged.

We began to understand the importance of types in programming, and as we approached writing optimized and well structured code, we found something called type genericity. We began to write types which can be specified later on. And this gave rise to the notion of type constructors. Now, we can write types that take parameters. For example, think of a type constructor `List[T]`. Here, our known `List[T]` expects you to provide a type. You can also think of it as a function on a type, you provide a parameter while constructing. In our example, if we choose to provide a string, our list will then be called a `List[String]`, that's an applied version of `List[T]` with the `String` type. This concept is called **parametric polymorphism** where we say that our `List[T]` uses a type parameter `T` to abstract over the type of its elements. Let's try out the stuff we talked about in Scala REPL:

```
scala> val xs: List = List("ABC")
<console>:11: error: type List takes type parameters
       val xs: List = List("ABC")
```

In the preceding snippet we got an error. This happened because we tried providing a type constructor `List` instead of a concrete type:

```
scala> val xs: List[T] = List("ABC")
<console>:11: error: not found: type T
       val xs: List[T] = List("ABC")
```

The previous snippet also failed with an error because we knew that we should provide a type parameter but we supplied some element that itself isn't a type. So what should we do now? Let's try the following:

```
scala> val xs: List[String] = List("ABC")
xs: List[String] = List(ABC)
```

This time it worked for us: we provided a type `String` to our type constructor and it worked for us. So I believe we can differentiate between a type constructor and a type. Now that you've insights into why we're doing this, let's dive in and learn about parameterized types.

Here comes type parameterization

Think of the same scenario. You were asked to write a program that contains some different entities, for example, humans and animals. Now, both require food to stay alive. Our colleagues are aware of this and have written code that takes care of the way food is served to humans as well as animals.

They have written the code and provided it as a library (we can access those functions by importing the packages they wrote). Our colleagues were ahead of time and wrote a function that looked like the following:

```
def servseMeal[A, B](serveTo: A, serveThis: Option[B]) = ???
```

We were told the function will work, we just have to provide who to serve the food to as the first parameter and an optional food item as a meal. The rest will be taken care of by the logic they've put. We tried a couple of ways and wrote a few applications of this as follows:

```
serveMeal(Human(Category("MALE")), None)
serveMeal(Human(Category("FEMALE")), Some(Food()))
serveMeal(Animal(), None)
serveMeal(Animal(), Some("NONVEG"))

case class Human(category: Category)
case class Category(name: String)
case class Animal()
case class Food()
```

And somehow, it works as expected. But wait, this is really cool, we were exposed to only one function and everything seemed to work as expected. They didn't want us to specifically call `serveMealToHumans` or `serveNonVegMealToAnimals` functions.

This really helped us write better code at our end. We were both intelligent teams and we separated our concerns. You know, their concern was to take care of the ways of serving food to all, our concern was to ensure each of our entities are getting food they're supposed to get. The job's done. Let's talk about why we chose this example. To understand that, take a look at the function signature they wrote:

```
def serveMeal[A, B](serveTo: A, serveThis: Option[B]) = ???
```

We see the `def` keyword, then the name of the function, but after that they wrote letters A and B, what are these? To learn more, let's go ahead and read out the whole signature. There's a parameter that we were supposed to serve, the type was named *A,* and the food option was given a type named B *(option B)*. Well, these are type parameters. The function itself is an example of *parametric polymorphism.* We know that it means *having multiple forms.* The same goes here. Our function can have multiple parameter types. To better understand, take a look at this:

```
serveMeal(Human(Category("MALE")): Human, None: Option[Food])
serveMeal(Human(Category("FEMALE")): Human, Some(Food()): Option[Food])
serveMeal(Animal() : Animal, None: Option[Food])
serveMeal(Animal(): Animal, Some(Food()): Option[Food])
```

Here in the function calls, we specified the types of our parameters. From the signature of our function it is clear that we can give whichever type we want and the serveMeal function takes care of the rest of the logic. So, the take away is that these A and B parameters are called type parameters. The whole concept can be termed type parameterization. We cannot just write generic methods, but also generic classes and traits. Let's check them out.

Another way around - generic classes and traits

We just saw the effect of *genericity* and it solved more than one problem, we wrote less code and achieved more. The serveMeal function was a generic one because it takes type parameters, in our case A and B. It performs the intended logic, great! Let's talk about *parameterized types*. You know the type List, right? Let's take a look at its declaration in the Scala standard library:

```
sealed abstract class List[+A] extends AbstractSeq[A]
   with LinearSeq[A]
   with Product
   with GenericTraversableTemplate[A, List]
   with LinearSeqOptimized[A, List[A]]
   with Serializable
```

Okay, the declaration seems far too complex, doesn't it? No, wait, we know what sealed means, we know why we used an abstract class, then the name List, and then a few more declarations for showing inheritance relationships. But there's this thing called [+A] in our declaration. Our job is to find out what this is and why we used it.

From the previous few topics, we gained an idea of this notion of *type constructors*. So, let's call this List[+A] a type constructor. We know that if we provide it a concrete type, List will make a meaningful type. We've tried this before so we won't be creating another list of strings. We'll try to learn the significance of this + sign in the next few topics. It shows a *variance* relationship. Let's look at the previous declaration first.

Type parameter names

Here, in the declaration of the List[+T] type constructor (we can use the names parameterized types or type constructors interchangeably), we used the parameter name, T, it's a convention to use such names in generic programming. The names T, A, B, or C have nothing to do with the initializer type you're going to provide when you initiate a list instance. For example, when you give a String type for the previously mentioned type parameter when you instantiate List[String], it really doesn't matter if the declaration has List[T] or List[A]. What we mean is the following two declarations are equivalent:

```
//With type parameter name A

sealed abstract class List[+A] extends AbstractSeq[A]

//With type parameter name T

sealed abstract class List[+T] extends AbstractSeq[T]
```

Container types

We've seen Scala's class hierarchy, hence we are aware of many collection types such as List, Set, and Map. What's different about these types along with types such as Option and Either, is that they all expect you to provide a type and then instantiate. We call List as a container type because it works that way. We use a list to contain elements of a certain data type. Similarly, we can think of an Option as a binary containerized type, as Option can be some value or None. The Either type goes the same way. In Scala, when we create such container types, we tend to use a type parameter to declare and provide a concrete type, such as String, Int, Boolean, and so on when we instantiate. Take a look how Option is declared in Scala (more on Option and Either types in the next chapter):

```
sealed abstract class Option[+A] extends Product
    with Serializable
```

It takes a type parameter A. It's possible to provide more than one type parameter if your type expects more than one type to get instantiated. An example of such a type is Either:

```
sealed abstract class Either[+A, +B] extends Product with Serializable
```

As shown previously, our type `Either` takes two types, A and B. But when I tried the following snippet it didn't work as expected:

```
object TypeErasure extends App {
  val strings: List[String] = List("First", "Second", "Third")
  val noStringsAttached: List[Int] = List(1, 2, 3)

  def listOf[A](value: List[A]) = value match {
    case listOfString: List[String] => println("Strings Attached!")
    case listOfNumbers: List[Int] => println("No Strings Attached!")
  }

  listOf(strings)
  listOf(noStringsAttached)
}
```

The result is as follows:

```
Strings Attached!
Strings Attached!
```

You see? We created two lists, first of strings and the other list of numbers. Then, a function named `listOf` that's a generic function simply to take a list and tell the type of list it is. We performed a pattern match to check the type of list passed to the function and print it. But it didn't work out for us (and might not for anyone). Also, it threw a few warnings telling us there was unreachable code for the second case expression. Let's talk about why!

Type erasure

When the Scala compiler compiles the previous code, it erases the parameterized type information from the previous code and so it doesn't have the necessary knowledge at runtime; the list we passed does not take any further information about itself. In other words, all type information for generic types is discarded by the time the code compiled. This phenomenon is termed **type erasure**. This is the reason our function `listOf` didn't work as we expected or, let's say, assumed. That's the same reason you got a warning of unreachable code, because our statically typed language was able to know that the second case will never be executed, and the first case is a kind of catch all in this pattern match. Let's explain this a bit better. Take a look at a few cases where type erasure will be applicable. Imagine you have a trait named `Tfoo`:

```
trait Tfoo[T]{
  val member: T
}
```

After the process of compilation, the generic type gets converted to object and becomes like the following:

```
trait Tfoo {
  val member: Object    //Cause scala files gets converted to *.class files.
}
```

Similarly, conversion takes place if we use any type parameter in a generic method. It's clear the type information gets erased, no matter if it's at class level or method level. Great! So, now we have some idea about parameterized types. Any code snippet, regardless of it being a method or any class/trait, if it contains a *type parameter*, it's not alien code to us. But, then you ask, what's with the + sign in List [+T]? Yes, this shows variance under an inheritance relationship and this + is called **variance annotation**. Let's go through it.

Variance under inheritance

One of the ways we can learn about a concept is to ask questions that lead you to the concept. So let's ask a question ourselves. Given that a Cat class type extends the Animal class, is it okay to treat a list of *cats* as a list of *animals*? Programmatically, see the following:

```
abstract class Animal()

class Cat(name: String) extends Animal()                // Inheritance
relationship between Cat and Animal

def doSomethingForAnimals(animals: List[Animal]) = ??? //definitely do
something for animals.

Is it possible to pass an argument that's a list of Cats?
val cats = List(new Cat("Mischief"), new Cat("Birdie"))
doSomethingForAnimals(cats)
```

If it's possible, the statement that List [Cat] is a subtype of List [Animal] makes sense. Also, the concept is called **covariance**. Hence, we say List is covariant in its type parameter T:

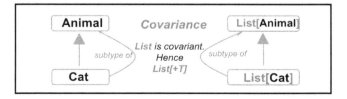

If you take a look at the preceding image, the direction of the inheritance relationship between two concrete classes, namely *Cat* and `Animal`, and their parameterized versions, namely `List[Cat]` and `List[Animal]` types, are the same. But it's not the case every time. There might be cases where you have a container type for which the variance relationship works the opposite way.

Think about it this way: given two types A and B, where A is a super type of B, and some container type `Foo[T]`, so the relationship where `Foo[A]` is a subtype of `Foo[B]` is called contravariance in T, and represented by `Foo[-T]`. Here the – sign represents contravariance.

If you're thinking this is too theoretical, some code examples may make the concept clearer. Let's take a look at a scenario. Nowadays, enterprises like to provide all sorts of arrangements for their employees from food and insurance to their travel needs. It's not a big deal if some corporation decides to work with an airline company to provide corporate bookings for their employees. Airline companies, in order to support such bookings, can support schemes where they book seats for corporate passengers, executive passengers, and regular passengers. So, imagine in our program that books seats in an aircraft, we represent each seat as an aircraft seat. Programmatically, we can represent it as a class:

```
class AircraftSeat[-T]
```

Now, we have a few passengers represented by the `Passenger` class. There are a few subtypes of Passenger such as `CorporatePassenger`, `ExecutivePassenger`, and `RegularPassenger`.

The relationship between them is as follows:

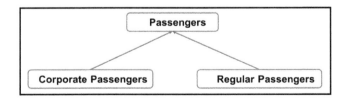

As shown, `CorporatePassengers` and `RegularPassengers` inherit from the `Passengers` class, so there's an inheritance relationship between these types. This can be represented by the following:

```
abstract class Passengers
class CorporatePassengers extends Passengers
class RegularPassengers extends Passengers
```

Now, if you have a function that reserves seats for the corporate employees, its signature may look like the following:

```
def reserveSeatForCorporatePassengers(corporateSeats:
AircraftSeat[CorporatePassengers]) = ??? //Seat booking logic!
```

The previous function expects you to provide an
AircraftSeat[CorporatePassengers], and does its job. If we try writing the whole of
this in a Scala application, it'll look like the following:

```
object ContraVariance extends App {
  class AircraftSeat[-T]

  def reserveSeatForCorporatePassengers(corporateSeats:
AircraftSeat[CorporatePassengers]) = {
    //Performs some logic regarding the seat reservation!
    println(s" Seats Confirmed!")
  }

  abstract class Passengers
  class CorporatePassengers extends Passengers
  class RegularPassengers extends Passengers

  reserveSeatForCorporatePassengers(new AircraftSeat[CorporatePassengers])

  reserveSeatForCorporatePassengers(new AircraftSeat[Passengers])

}
```

The result is as follows:

```
Seats Confirmed!
Seats Confirmed!
```

Now, take a moment, and go through the preceding code. We'll talk about a few points and
try to play with annotations and inheritance:

- AircraftSeat[-T] is a container type in our case that uses contravariance
  annotation, that is, a – sign for its type parameter.
- The reserveSeatForCorporatePassengers(corporateSeats:
  AircraftSeat[CorporatePassengers]) function takes AircraftSeat of
  type CorporatePassengers or its super type such as Passengers, because of
  the contravariance relationship in its type parameters.

- The function call to `reserveSeatForCorporatePassengers(new AircraftSeat[CorporatePassengers])` and `reserveSeatForCorporatePassengers(new AircraftSeat[Passengers])` works because of contravariance in the parameterized type, `AircraftSeat`.
- In the previous code, try changing the type constructor `AircraftSeat[-T]` to `AircraftSeat[+T]`. You'll be greeted with a compilation error saying type mismatch because the parameterized type gets changed to covariant in `T`, and because of that the `Passengers` super type is no longer valid in place of `Aircraft[CorporatePassengers]`.
- Similarly, if we try to make a function call to the `reserveSeatForCorporatePassengers` function with `RegularPassengers`, it won't work and will throw a compilation error about type mismatch. The reason is the same: our parameterized type being contravariant in `T`.

The previous example and experiments clear up what covariance and contravariance are and what the differences are between them. See the following image:

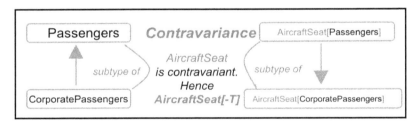

The preceding image explains the inheritance relation between the concrete types `Passengers`, `CorporatePassengers`, and parameterized types `AircraftSeat[Passengers]`, and `AircraftSeat[CorporatePassengers]`. You may have noticed that the inheritance direction for contravariance is in the opposite direction.

With this, we've understood two types of variance relationship within the parameterized types. First is covariance and then contravariance. Now, there's another type of variance relation that's possible and that's called invariant relationship in `T`. We don't use any signs to show that invariance relationship. We simply use the container type along with a type parameter name as in `Foo[T]`, the type is invariant in `T`. Hence, if you want to consume an instance of type `Foo[T]`, you must provide an instance of `Foo[T]`, any super type or sub type of T will not work for that.

Variance is quite an important concept in functional programming. Hence, you may find many examples of it in Scala. We've already seen examples, such as `List[+T]` and `option[+T]`, which are covariant in T.

Another popular example for such variance relationships is the `Function` trait:

```
trait Function1[-T1, +R] extends AnyRef {self =>
  /** Apply the body of this function to the argument.
   *
   * @return the result of function application.
   */
  def apply(v1: T1): R

}
```

Here, we declare something like the following:

```
scala> val func = (i: Int) => i.toString
func: Int => String
```

Here, Scala converts it into an instance of these `Function` traits and this becomes the following:

```
new Function1[Int, String]{
  override def apply(v1: Int): String = v1.toString
}
```

Here, this trait as shown in the signature consumes the type T and produces R. We've put variance annotations in front of T and R, where `Function1` is contravariant in `[-T]`, the consumable type and covariant in `[+R]` the producible type. I hope this clears up the variance relationship. Let's look at when to use covariance and contravariance.

When to use what type of variance relation

It's clear that variance is useful for telling the compiler when it's okay to bind an instance of one parameterized type to a reference of the same parameterized type with a different type parameter. The way we did for `List[Animal]` and `List[Cat]`. But the question arises, whether to use covariance or use contravariance.

In the last example, we saw the `Function1` trait from Scala's standard library. The input/consumable type was contravariant and the output/producible type was covariant. It gives us a sense that when we are about to consume some type, it's okay to use contravariance. (Why? We'll get to that shortly.) When we are about to produce some results we should go for covariance. The idea here is that as a `consumer` you can consume a variety of types or, in other words, you're allowed to consume more general (contravariant) stuff, and at the same time as a `producer`, you are allowed to produce more specific (covariant) stuff. You get the point, right?

So you remember, we talked about our programs made of two entities: *data* and *operations*. We also said not all operations can be performed on all data. Hence, we had the concept of types. Now, our lives are much more exciting because of type parameterization, but we should take care when we declare our parameterized types because there may be some operations that are not defined for all types under T in Foo[T]. For this, we have a thing called *Type Bounds*. Using type bounds we can specify for which types we want to perform the operations. Well, we'll talk about *bounds* too, but before that I want to talk about another way of achieving abstraction in our programs and that's through *abstract types*. Let's go through and try to understand a concept people find difficult when they start using Scala (you won't, we'll make it clear!).

Abstract types

Okay, first things first. We tried to achieve *abstraction* when we introduced *type parameterizing*. We will do the same thing using *abstract type members*. But what's an *abstract type member*? How do we write them, how can we use them, and why do we even need them when we already have *parameterized types*? These are a few questions. We'll try answering them. So let's start with the first question. How do we write an abstract type. This is done as follows:

```
trait ThinkingInTermsOfT {
    type T
}
```

Okay, we just wrote a trait named `ThinkingInTermsOfT` and it has an abstract type member. So, to declare an abstract type member we use the keyword `type` along with the parameter name that in our case is `T`. From our elementary Scala introduction or, let's say, from previous chapters, we know how we can instantiate a trait. So when we instantiate our trait, we'll give a type to our abstract member. That's going to be a concrete type:

```
val instance = new ThinkingInTermsOfT {
  type T = Int
```

```
    def behaviourX(t: T): T = ???
}
```

Here, we instantiated the trait with a `new` keyword and then, while defining the trait implementation, we gave the `Int` type to our abstract type member `T`. This allows us to use `T` type at the declaration side trait without caring about what the type's going to be. And when we instantiate, we assign a concrete type, just like we did here:

```
type T = Int
```

You now have some idea of how to perform these kinds of operations and why we used this *type T* declaration: so that we can write our behavior methods such as `doX` and return `T`, or `doY(t: T)` using type `T` and return something. Abstract members give us the flexibility to write code without worrying about the type at the time of writing. Our functions/methods are fine to work with whatever type we define when we instantiate the trait/class.

Let's take an example to compare how and what we achieved using type members:

```
object AbstractTypes extends App {

    trait ColumnParameterized[T] {
        def column() : T
    }

    trait ColumnAbstract {
      type T

      def column(): T
    }

    val aColumnFromParameterized = new ColumnParameterized[String] {
      override val column = "CITY"
    }

    val aColumnFromAbstract = new ColumnAbstract {
      type T = String

      override val column = "HOUSE_NO"
    }

    println(s"Coloumn from Parameterized: ${aColumnFromParameterized.column}
|   and Column from Abstract: ${aColumnFromAbstract.column} ")
}
```

The result is as follows:

```
Column from Parameterized: CITY    |   and Column from Abstract: HOUSE_NO
```

This example is easy to understand. We have both our parameterized version and the current one, a trait with an abstract type. So take a look at the parameterized version. We have specified that our `traitColumnParameterized[T]` is a parameterized type with parameter `T`. We're comfortable with this kind of syntax, right? We've just gone through it, it's simple and easy to understand. Now, the latter declaration, trait `ColumnAbstract` has a type member, we declared it using the `type` keyword.

Now take a look at the implementation. For parameterized types we knew what we had to do and we instantiated the trait (you know what's happening with these curly braces at the time of instantiation, right?). Similarly, we instantiated the trait with the abstract member and overrode the definition with a `val`, that's possible, you know that already.

And that's why we were able to call both of these and get the values out of them. Now, if you try to assign the following:

```
type T = String
```

Here, we use the following:

```
override val column = 23
```

Here, we get an error, an error saying incompatible types. We know the reason: because an integer cannot satisfy the signature, the signature expects the type to be `T`, and `T` is `String`. So, you're trying to do the wrong thing; the compiler won't let you pass through. I would suggest you try out these two concepts of parameterized types and abstract types. The more you use them and write them, the more comfortable you will get. Remember, these abstract members expect you to provide types and in Scala, a function is also a type. So, you can go deeper by thinking in terms of generating functions dynamically using a trait.

Let's take a moment and think. Suppose you want to form a mechanism for performing an action/operation. The code for such an action generator may look like this:

```
trait ActionGenerator[In] {
  type Out

  def generateAction(): Out
}
```

Now, this looks cool: we've used a parameterized type and also an abstract type member. Also, our type `Out` member can be a function type. Think of it as a rule or pattern. It can be as follows:

```
type Out = Int => String
```

To get more insight, let's think of a scenario where you want to provide a mechanism to generate a rating between 1 to 5 from a list of comments you received on your blog post. Now, different people have different ways of appreciating (or not appreciating) so some people were good enough to give you a rating of 4 or 5. Some people, out of the blue, wrote, Awesome, Nice, or Worst ever. You have to generate a rating for your blog from all these comments.

Now, from the scenario, it might seem cool to write a rule, which, based on the comments, can generate the rating. Look closely: *generate the rating* is an action/operation. We'll abstract this and we'll write the generate the rating generator, we mean ActionGenerator. It could look as follows:

```
object RatingApp extends App {

  type Rating = Int
  type NumericString = String //String that can be converted into Int!
  type AlphaNumeric = String  //Alphanumeric String

  val simpleRatingGenerator = new ActionGenerator[NumericString] {
    type Out = NumericString => Rating

    /* Times when ratings are simple NumericStrings
     * Rating as 1, 2, 3, 4, 5
     * We don't care about numbers more than 5
     */
    override def generateAction(): NumericString => Rating = _.toInt
  }

  val generateNumericRating = simpleRatingGenerator.generateAction()

  println(generateNumericRating("1"))
}
```

The result is as follows:

```
1
```

Here, simpleRatingGenerator is the ActionGenerator. A few takeaway points from the implementation:

- Syntax, like type Rating = Int, is just to make code more readable. It enables the reader to think of Rating as a type that internally accepts *integers*. This is merely type declaration.

- Our `simpleRatingGenerator` specifies from its definition that it can accept a `NumericString` and give a function that is of type `NumericString => Rating`. We can view it as if `simpleRatingGenerator` is an `ActionGenerator` that provides a mechanism to generate a rating from `NumericString`.
- Now, the way we can use such an action generator is to get the mechanism and pass a numeric string value to it to get the rating. That's how we do it:

```
val generateNumericRating = simpleRatingGenerator.genrateAction()
println(generateNumericRating("1"))
```

We can also create another rating generator that takes comments such as `Awesome`, `Good`, `Nice`, and so on. Here is an example of how to create an `AlphanumericRatingGenerator` that can provide a mechanism to generate rating from `AlphanumericString`:

```
val alphanumericRatingGenerator = new ActionGenerator[AlphaNumeric] {
  type Out = AlphaNumeric => Rating

 /* Times when ratings are Awesome, Super, Good, something else like
Neutral
  * Rating as 1, 2, 3, 4, 5
  */
  override def generateAction(): AlphaNumeric => Rating = toRating// Some
other mechanism to generate the rating
}

val toRating: AlphaNumeric => Rating = _ match {
  case "Awesome" => 5
  case "Cool"    => 4
  case "Nice"    => 3
  case "Worst Ever" => 1
  case _ => 3 // No Comments then average rating.
}
```

The way we can use this is the same way we used `simpleRatingGenerator`:

```
val generateAlphanumericRating =
alphanumericRatingGenerator.generateAction()

println(generateAlphanumericRating("Awesome"))
```

The result is as follows:

```
5
```

So these ways can come in handy when we try to provide a simple interface to a consumer of our functionality. For example, if a person wants to see the rating based on the comments, he may not be interested in the complexity and only like to call a particular function.

Why you would want to try out stuff with these concepts such as type parameters and abstract types now makes more sense: to create abstractions such as `ActionGenerator`. Life's easier when you have a set of rules already defined and you only have to code them. So with this, let's go ahead and try to make rules that are more precise. In other words, let's take a look at how we can define limits for using our parameterized type.

Type bounds

We've seen an example where we were allowed to create `AircraftSeat` for passengers. The example looked like the following:

```
class AircraftSeat[-T]
```

From what we know so far, `Aircraft` is contravariant in its type parameter `T`. But the thing is, when it comes to creating instances of `AircraftSeat`, it can be created for any type of `T`. What's expected is that this type parameter can only be of the `Passengers` type or it's subtype. So to achieve that we can introduce a type bound, in our case we'll use an upper-type bound. The reason for this is because we want to specify the type that's on the top of the inheritance hierarchy, in our case it's `Passengers`.

It'll look as follows:

```
class AircraftSeat[-T <: Passengers]
```

Here, the notation *<:* specifies its *upper bound*. What does this do? Let's check out an example to understand it better:

```
object Bounds extends App {

  /*
   * AircraftSeats can be consumed only by Passengers.
   */
  class AircraftSeat[-T <: Passengers]

  def reserveSeatForCorporatePassengers(corporateSeats:
AircraftSeat[CorporatePassengers]) = {
    //Performs some logic regarding the seat reservation!
    println(s"Seats Confirmed!")
```

```
    }

    val corporateSeat = new AircraftSeat[CorporatePassengers]()
    val passengersSeat = new AircraftSeat[Passengers]()


    reserveSeatForCorporatePassengers(new
  AircraftSeat[CorporatePassengers]())

    reserveSeatForCorporatePassengers(new AircraftSeat[Passengers]())

    abstract class Passengers
    class CorporatePassengers extends Passengers
    class RegularPassengers extends Passengers


  }
```

Here, we have the same example we used earlier; the only thing different is that now we can only create `AircraftSeat` for the `Passengers` type. The code will work fine. But we would like to see the behavior for when we try to create an `AircraftSeat` instance with a type that's not a subtype of `Passengers`. For that, let's create another class and try to create an `AircraftSeat` instance out of it:

```
class Person(name: String)

val seat: AircraftSeat[Person] = new AircraftSeat[Person]()
```

If you try to compile code with this instance, the Scala compiler will throw an error at compile time. It says the following:

```
type arguments [chapter10.Bounds.Person] do not conform to class
AircraftSeat's type parameter bounds [-T <: chapter10.Bounds.Passengers]

  val seat: AircraftSeat[Person] = new AircraftSeat[Person]()
```

From the error shown previously, it's clear that the compiler was able to understand what we specified and is not ready to take anything else other than `Passengers`.

Similarly, it's possible to specify a lower bound for our type parameters. We can use the sign `>:` to specify lower bounds. It looks as follows:

```
class ListLikeStructure[T >: AnyRef]
```

Here, we specified a `ListLikeStructure` for any reference types. It's special in the sense that it only takes `Any`, `AnyRef`, or equivalent types in hierarchy. So let's try creating an instance of the same for `Any` and `AnyRef`. The Scala compiler will not complain about the code and will work fine for the following:

```
new ListLikeStructure[Any]()
new ListLikeStructure[AnyRef]()
```

When we try to create the same instance with a different type to `Any` or `AnyRef`, the Scala compiler will give an error as follows:

```
new ListLikeStructure[String]()
Error:(30, 7) type arguments [String] do not conform to class
ListLikeStructure's type parameter bounds [T >: AnyRef]

    new ListLikeStructure[String]()
```

From this error, it's clear that the signature with a lower bound specified will not let you provide a type that comes lower in the type hierarchy. That's why we got an error for the `String` type. These are the ways we can provide lower and upper bounds in Scala. There's another way we can use both the bounds together to specify a specific range of types in the hierarchy.

Think of a class inheritance hierarchy as follows:

```
abstract class Zero
trait One extends Zero
trait Two extends One
trait Three extends Two
trait Four extends Three
```

For such a structure, a `ListLikeStructure` can be declared in the following way:

```
class ListLikeStructure[T >: Four <: Two]
```

It specifies you can only provide a type between `Two` and `Four`, so it's possible to create structures with the following types:

```
new ListLikeStructure[Four]
new ListLikeStructure[Three]
new ListLikeStructure[Two]
```

But once you try passing a type that's not in the bounds, the Scala compiler greets you with a compile time error:

```
new ListLikeStructure[One]
type arguments [chapter10.Bounds.One] do not conform to class
ListLikeStructure's type parameter bounds [T >: chapter10.Bounds.Four <:
chapter10.Bounds.Two]
  new ListLikeStructure[One]
```

As the error indicates, this instantiation does not satisfy the bounds. So now you are aware of the bounds for type parameters. In the same way, we can put bounds to abstract types as well:

```
trait ThinkingInTermsOfT {
    type T <: Two
}
```

Here, as shown in the previous declaration, our type `T` can be instantiated with only types for which `Two` is the upper bound.

With the discussion of bounds and variance, the difference and the use cases of both are clear. It's good to point out again, that variance is merely the rules for inheritance relationships between parameterized/container types. Bounds only write a rule that states a certain range of types can be used to instantiate a type that is parameterized or contains an abstract member.

Now that we have an idea about parameterized types, abstract types, and ways to define them, we should also try and find out why we choose abstract types rather than parameterized types or vice versa.

Abstract versus parameterized types

Both are forms of providing polymorphic abstractions in Scala. Mostly, it's a design choice whether you prefer one over the other. Talking about design choices, let's have a closer look. For that we'll take an example where we have two class hierarchies as follows:

```
abstract class Food
class Grass extends Food
class Meat extends Food

abstract class Animal {
    type SuitableFood <: Food
    def eatMeal(meal: SuitableFood)
}
```

From the knowledge about abstract types and upper bounds we can say `Animal` is an abstract class, which has an abstract type member named `SuitableFood`, which expects only the `Food` type. If we declare two subtypes of `Animal` class namely `Cow` and `Lion` it could look like a cow can eat `Grass` as well as `Meat` because both are subclasses of `Food`. But this isn't the desired behavior. To resolve the issue, we can declare `Cow` like this:

```
class Cow extends Animal {
  type SuitableFood <: Grass

  override def eatMeal(meal: SuitableFood): Unit = println("Cow's eating
grass!")

}
```

We have put a bound on the abstract type member `SuitableFood`. Now, for any cow (instance), the type that we provide has to be of type `Grass` (and yes, we were allowed to put *Grass* only because it's a subtype of `Food`). We can do the same for the `Lion` class:

```
class Lion extends Animal {
  type SuitableFood <: Meat

  override def eatMeal(meal: SuitableFood): Unit = println("Lion's eating
meat!")
}
```

When we try using these classes, we'll have to provide the intended concrete types. Let's take a look at the app:

```
object AbsVsParamTypes extends App {

  abstract class Animal {
    type SuitableFood <: Food

    def eatMeal(meal: SuitableFood)
  }

  class Lion extends Animal {
    type SuitableFood <: Meat

    override def eatMeal(meal: SuitableFood): Unit = println("Lion's eating
meat!")
  }

  class Cow extends Animal {
    type SuitableFood <: Grass
```

```
    override def eatMeal(meal: SuitableFood): Unit = println("Cow's eating
grass!")
  }

  val lion = new Lion(){
    type SuitableFood = Meat
  }

  val cow = new Cow(){
    type SuitableFood = Grass
  }

  cow.eatMeal(new Grass)
  lion.eatMeal(new Meat)


  abstract class Food
  class Grass extends Food
  class Meat extends Food
}
```

The result is as follows:

```
Cow's eating grass!
Lion's eating meat!
```

So, as shown, we can create a cow instance by providing a type that satisfies the bounds specified. These kinds of requirements are best written using abstract types. When you need to provide a type with a parameter, just for instantiation, examples are `List[String]` or similar types. When using the same type to evolve as you write/define members of your class/trait, it's better to consider abstract types.

Now that we've discussed *abstract versus parameterized types*, let's talk about one more concept that you will encounter often when working with Scala. We'll talk a bit about type-classes.

Type-classes

Why would someone need a concept such as a type-class? To answer this, we'll first have to understand what a type-class exactly is. As they say, *"Type-classes allow us to generalize over a set of types in order to define and execute a standard set of features for those types."* Let's try to understand this.

I believe you're aware of the notion of encoding and decoding. Let's think of encoding as applying a certain rule to convert A into a specific pattern. Now, after you encode something, it's in that specific pattern. Decoding is the exact opposite of what we just did: it's changing your type A from the pattern we just created to its original shape. For example, **comma-separated values** (**CSV**) can be considered an encoded pattern. Hence, there's a scheme that converts words from a source to CSV format:

```
trait CSVEncoder[T] {
  def encode(t: T): List[String]
}
```

We've written a *trait* named `CSVEncoder[T]`. It's time to rephrase what we said for type-classes. `CSVEncoder` allows us to generalize over type `T` in order to provide an encoding mechanism for the same type. This means that we can use `CSVEncoder` for all the types we want and use them whenever there's a need. This is the implementation of a type-class. We'll go through the overall type-class implementation in the next chapter after the discussion of implicits. For now, it's good to know what a concept such as type-class does.

With the conception of type-classes, it's time to summarize what we have learned in this chapter.

Summary

From understanding the basic need of types to understanding what a type-class is, we've gone through it all. Along the way, we discussed parametric polymorphism using parametric types and abstract types. With the concept of variance, as well as bounds, we've gone through it all and now it's a bit clearer. For more insights, practice is a must. We can think of scenarios to learn about the concepts. We tried to go through the concepts as they were and look at a few examples, but it'll definitely be fun if you try out some of these on your own. This chapter was the formation or the basis of real Scala programming. Concepts such as type-classes come in very handy when writing effective programs.

In the next chapter, we'll go through concepts such as *implicits* and the ways we can do exception handling in Scala. And of course, we'll play with type-classes.

11
Working with Implicits and Exceptions

"How ironic, when you do business you create exceptions to create new opportunities, when you write code (do a job) you handle exceptions to make it clean."

- Pushkar Saraf

Functional programs are expressions. When we say we want to run a functional program, we mean we want to evaluate the expressions. When we evaluate an expression, we get a value. We also know that functional programming is about composing and evaluating expressions. This means that the function signature you write down holds true for each evaluation. But there are scenarios where it's unlikely to happen. Your code might not work as expected and might result in an exceptional behavior. How do we deal with such scenarios, and how do we handle exceptions in functional programming? These are some fundamental questions, and anyone who's starting with functional programming might ask the same. So, in this chapter, we'll try answering these questions, and then we'll move forward to look at another important and much-talked-about concept in Scala known as **implicits**. We'll take a look at what they are and the instances where we might want to use them. So here's what we'll go through in our chapter:

- Exception handling - the old way
- Using the option way
- Either left or right
- Implicits - what and why
- Implicit class
- Implicit arguments

Let's start by introducing an exceptional behavior to a particular functionality and handling it.

Exception handling – the old way

Let's write some code so that we can talk about exception handling. Take a look at the following:

```
def toInt(str: String): Int = str.toInt
```

In the preceding code, the `toInt` is a function that takes a `String` value, which supposedly can be converted to a corresponding `Int` value. The definition looks okay, but as functional programmers, we are so used to trying out the function to see whether it does what it says (in the definition). Let's try out some calls to this function:

```
println(toInt("121"))
println(toInt("-199"))
```

The preceding code gives the following result:

```
121
-199
```

Things worked fine for us. We passed a number in a string format and got the corresponding integer values. But what if you try something like the following:

```
println(toInt("+ -199"))
```

Say that we get something unexpected, some exception saying this:

```
Exception in thread "main" java.lang.NumberFormatException: For input
string: "+ -199"
    at
java.lang.NumberFormatException.forInputString(NumberFormatException.java:6
5)
```

Instead of responding with an integer result, what we got is an exception—that's bad. But let's be positive; there are a few things that we can learn from this failure:

- The definition of our function was not right. It was telling us, *you give me a string and I'll give you back the corresponding integer.* But it didn't happen.
- We knew that instead of the ideal cases, there might be scenarios where our operation might fail to complete.

So, learning from this experience, we now have an idea that we might want to handle the unwanted scenarios. But how?

In some programming languages, we get a construct that wraps a block of code that might throw an exception and catches exceptions when thrown, and we are allowed to introduce our desired behaviour by putting in catch blocks. These are nothing but `try... catch` blocks. Why don't we try out these blocks?:

```
import java.lang.Exception

object Main extends App {

  def toInt(str: String): Int =
    try{
      str.toInt
    } catch {
      case exp: Exception =>
        println("Something unexpected happened, you may want to check the
string you passed for conversion.")

        println("WARN: Overriding the usual behavior, returning Zero!")
        0
    }

  println(toInt("121"))
  println(toInt("-199"))
  println(toInt("+ -199"))
}
```

The following is the result:

```
121
-199
```

Something unexpected happened; you may want to check the string you passed for conversion:

```
WARN: Overriding the usual behavior, returning Zero!
0
```

Did you try to run the preceding code? If you did, you can see that whatever concerns we had, we are able to overcome them with this code snippet. We wrapped our logic for the conversion of a string to an integer in a `try` block and also prepared what should be the behavior in case something went wrong. That change gave us a synthetic result, along with a pretty warning message.

Does this implementation seem reasonable? To some extent, it's a workaround and it does what it says in the function's signature. But returning zero in exceptional cases is still not a good option.

Using the Option way

Let's try and change the function signature in a way that we can reason about and modify it so that it does what it says:

```
def toInt(str: String): Option[Int] = Try(str.toInt) match {
  case Success(value) => Some(value)
  case Failure(_) => None
}
```

In the preceding definition, we knew that the response was optional. We might or might not get a corresponding integer value for every string we pass to our function. Hence, we made the response type an `Option[Int]`. Also, as you may have noticed, we used another construct available to us from the `scala.util` package, named `Try`. How do we use `Try`? We pass a function for its evaluation to the `Try` block's constructor/apply method. As might be obvious, the `Try` block's `apply` method takes a function as a `by-name` parameter, which tries to evaluate that function. Based on the result or exception, it responds as a `Success(value)` or `Failure(exception)`.

We used the `Try` construct and passed logic as an argument. On success, we responded as `Some(value)`, and in case of failure, we returned `None`. Both worked well, as these are subtypes of the `Option` type. We've already seen `Option[+T]` in Chapter 9, *Using Powerful Functional Constructs*. Let's talk a bit about the `Try[+T]` type. We will start with the signature:

```
sealed abstract class Try[+T] extends Product with Serializable

object Try {
  /** Constructs a 'Try' using the by-name parameter.  This
    * method will ensure any non-fatal exception is caught and a
    * 'Failure' object is returned.
    */
  def apply[T](r: => T): Try[T] =
    try Success(r) catch {
      case NonFatal(e) => Failure(e)
    }
}
```

```
final case class Success[+T](value: T) extends Try[T]

final case class Failure[+T](exception: Throwable) extends Try[T]
```

Now that we are comfortable working with parameterized types, it will be easier for us to understand the signature of `Try`. A couple of things to notice are the `Success` and `Failure` subtypes—no need to explain what they are here for. Let's take a look at the companion object of the type `Try`, which has an `apply` method, as discussed already. It expects a by-name parameter. Our famous `try... catch` block is taking care of the rest of the stuff.

That's one of the ways you may want to change the function signature to handle exceptions and work as it says it's going to work. Let's talk about a scenario where we might want to pipeline a few operations—in other words, we want to perform functional composition. Take a look at the following function definitions:

```
def getAccountInfo(id: String): Option[AccountInfo]

def makeTransaction(amt: Double, accountInfo: AccountInfo): Option[Double]

case class AccountInfo(id: String, balance: Double)
```

Seeing these two functions, it seems they can be pipelined together to perform logic in one go. But how? We can pass an account ID to our `getAccountInfo` function, which in turn returns an optional `AccountInfo`. We can take this account info and the amount and call `makeTransaction` to make a transaction. These two operations look good enough to be composed together, but the only problem we have is that the first one's output is optional, and so the second function might or might not get called. So for this, the `flatMap` operation looks good. So let's try that:

```
import scala.util.Try

object BankApp extends App {

  val accountHolders = Map(
    "1234" -> AccountInfo("Albert", 1000),
    "2345" -> AccountInfo("Bob", 3000),
    "3456" -> AccountInfo("Catherine", 9000),
    "4567" -> AccountInfo("David", 7000)
  )

  def getAccountInfo(id: String): Option[AccountInfo] =
Try(accountHolders(id)).toOption

  def makeTransaction(amt: Double, accountInfo: AccountInfo):
Option[Double] = Try(accountInfo.balance - amt).toOption
```

```
   println(getAccountInfo("1234").flatMap(actInfo => makeTransaction(100,
actInfo)))

   println(getAccountInfo("12345").flatMap(actInfo => makeTransaction(100,
actInfo)))
}

case class AccountInfo(id: String, balance: Double)
```

The following is the result:

```
Some(900.0)
None
```

If we take a look at the preceding code, we can see that our getAccountInfo and makeTransaction functions return optional values and either of these results can be None. It will be hard for us to know which operation went wrong as there's no good error message that tells us what went wrong. So to conclude, Option is a way to handle such scenarios, but it would have been better if we had a way of knowing what went wrong. For that purpose, we can use another construct from Scala, named Either.

Either left or right

Scala has an Either[+A, +B] type for us. But before we talk about Either, let's use it. We'll refactor our code with the Either type:

```
import java.lang.Exception
import scala.util.{Failure, Success, Try}

object Main extends App {

  def toInt(str: String): Either[String, Int] = Try(str.toInt) match {
    case Success(value) => Right(value)
    case Failure(exp) => Left(s"${exp.toString} occurred," +
      s" You may want to check the string you passed.")
  }

  println(toInt("121"))
  println(toInt("-199"))
  println(toInt("+ -199"))
}
```

The following is the result:

```
Right(121)
Right(-199)
Left(java.lang.NumberFormatException: For input string: "+ -199" occurred,
You may want to check the string you passed.)
```

In the preceding code, we knew things might go wrong with the conversion from a `string` to an `int`. So the result can be either an exception or the intended integer. So we tried to do the same: we used the `Either` type with the left value as a `String` message when things go wrong, and an `Int` as the right value. Why so? Let's take a look at the signature of the `Either` type to understand that:

```
sealed abstract class Either[+A, +B] extends Product with Serializable
final case class Right[+A, +B](value: B) extends Either[A, B]
final case class Left[+A, +B](value: A) extends Either[A, B]
```

From the preceding signatures, we can see that the `Either` type takes two type parameters, A and B; by convention, we think of the `Left` value as the exceptional case value and the right value as the intended resulting value. That's the reason we declared the response type as follows:

```
Either[String, Int]
```

This states that we expect either a `String` or an `Int` value. So the use case is clear. We got to know what happened with our operation—that is, the conversion from a string to the corresponding integer value. Now, why don't we go ahead and try to do some function composition using the `Either` type? We can use the same scenario for this:

```
import scala.util.{Failure, Success, Try}

object BankApp extends App {

  val accountHolders = Map(
    "1234" -> AccountInfo("Albert", 1000),
    "2345" -> AccountInfo("Bob", 3000),
    "3456" -> AccountInfo("Catherine", 9000),
    "4567" -> AccountInfo("David", 7000)
  )


  def getAccountInfo(id: String): Either[String, AccountInfo] =
Try(accountHolders(id)) match {
    case Success(value) => Right(value)
    case Failure(excep) => Left("Couldn't fetch the AccountInfo, Please
Check the id passed or try again!")
```

```scala
  }


    def makeTransaction(amount: Double, accountInfo: AccountInfo):
Either[String, Double] = Try {
      if(accountInfo.balance < amount) throw new Exception("Not enough
account balance!") else accountInfo.balance - amount
    } match {

      case Success(value) => Right(value)
      case Failure(excep) => Left(excep.getMessage)
    }

    println(getAccountInfo("1234").flatMap(actInfo => makeTransaction(100,
actInfo)))

    println(getAccountInfo("1234").flatMap(actInfo => makeTransaction(10000,
actInfo)))

    println(getAccountInfo("12345").flatMap(actInfo => makeTransaction(100,
actInfo)))
  }

  case class AccountInfo(id: String, balance: Double)
```

The following is the result:

```
Right(900.0)
Left(Not enough account balance!)
Left(Couldn't fetch the AccountInfo, Please Check the id passed or try
again!)
```

This is interesting. This new construct made our life easier and gave us meaningful messages about the failures. We're also now able to recognize what went wrong, as well as when things went wrong.

We can see that `Either` helps us better in dealing with exceptions. Also, we've seen a couple of ways that we can deal with exceptional cases. What's the take away from the discussion? Let's conclude.

We've seen a few of the constructs available for us to handle exceptional scenarios in Scala programs. You may argue that one of the constructs, `Try[+T]`, does nothing but use a -`try... catch` block to handle exceptions. So the response we have for the argument is in terms of *functional composition*. The reason you may want to go for `scala.util.Try[+T]` instead of a normal `try... catch` block is for reasons of functional composition.

The type provides us some functions, such as `map` for transformation and `flatMap` for composition, so that we can combine two operations together using the `flatMap` operation. If you're wondering what this is, let me tell you that we have already seen examples of this. We wanted to compose two functions together to get the result using the `flatMap` method, which was possible only because our types `Try`, `Option`, and `Either` had this crazy-looking function named `flatMap`. It's worth taking a look at the implementation of the `flatMap` method. This `flatMap` function for `Option` might look as follows:

```
def flatMap[A, B](someValue: Option[A])(functionToPerfom: A => Option[B]):
Option[B] =
    if (someValue.isEmpty) None else functionToPerfom(someValue.get)
```

According to the signature, we're going to pass `Option[A]`. The `A` argument here is nothing but a type parameter and a function of the form `A => Option[B]`, and the definition is going to give us back the type `Option[B]`. That's powerful, and helps us in composing the two functions together. That's one of the reasons you might want to go for `Option`/`Either`/`Try` constructs. Which of the three is going to be used depends upon the use case. The `Either` type gives you the convenience of returning a message when things go wrong.

So that explains how we might want to handle exceptions in our Scala programs. Now let's go ahead and talk about a concept that Scala provides to let you do stuff implicitly. Let's talk about implicits in Scala.

Implicits – what and why

What are *implicits*? When we talk about implicits, we mean implicit parameters or conversions that happen implicitly. Implicit parameters are the ones that come along with a keyword, `implicit`, and we don't have to explicitly pass an argument for these parameters if they were in Scope. Let's see how.

Let's take an example, and create a `Future` value. A `Future` is nothing but a computation (that we provide) that's going to happen at a later point in time. It means a computation that's going to happen in the future. We'll talk about `Future` values in depth when we discuss concurrent programming techniques in `Chapter 13`, *Concurrent Programming in Scala*. Let's write a code snippet for now:

```
import scala.concurrent.Future

object FuturesApp extends App {
```

```
    val futureComp = Future {
        1 + 1
    }

    println(s"futureComp: $futureComp")

    futureComp.map(result => println(s"futureComp: $result"))
}
```

Okay, we are not sure about how this Future thing works, but from the code snippet, it looks like there's a computation, 1 + 1, that is wrapped in a Future block and that we are then printing out this Future instance. After that, we're extracting the computation's result out of the Future value and printing it. Looks like it should work fine. Let's run this. We will get the following result:

```
Error:(7, 27) Cannot find an implicit ExecutionContext. You might pass
an (implicit ec: ExecutionContext) parameter to your method
or import scala.concurrent.ExecutionContext.Implicits.global.
   val futureComp = Future {

Error:(7, 27) not enough arguments for method apply: (implicit executor:
scala.concurrent.ExecutionContext)scala.concurrent.Future[Int] in object
Future.
Unspecified value parameter executor.
   val futureComp = Future {
```

The Scala compiler greets us with two compilation errors. The first one says that it wasn't able to find an implicit value of the ExecutionContext type. Okay, we don't know what this ExecutionContext is, for now. Let's look at the next error. It says not enough arguments for method apply: (implicit executor: ExecutionContext) scala.concurrent.Future[Int].

Now, we've got this idea that there's an argument that is needed that's not available to our code. Let's take a look at the Future block's apply method for that:

```
def apply[T](body: =>T)(implicit executor: ExecutionContext): Future[T]
```

Okay, this seems interesting. We've got this `implicit` keyword for the parameter `ExecutionContext`. It means that it's okay to call the `Future` block's `apply` method; the only thing we need to take care of is the implicit value of the type declared. So things should work fine if somehow we can get the value of type `ExecutionContext` available into our scope. What do we mean by scope? Let's think of the current compilation unit (Scala file) as the scope, for now. So let's do this:

```
import scala.concurrent.Future

object FuturesApp extends App {

  implicit val ctx = scala.concurrent.ExecutionContext.Implicits.global

  val futureComp = Future {
     1 + 1
  }

  println(s"futureComp: $futureComp")

  futureComp.map(result => println(s"futureComp: $result"))
}
```

The following is the result:

```
futureComp: Future(Success(2))
futureComp: 2
```

We've declared an `implicit` value named `ctx` of the type `ExecutionContext`, and then tried to run the application again, and magically things worked fine. We didn't pass any context explicitly or do something extraordinary—we've just brought the value of the desired type into scope and things worked. We've got the results. One thing to note, though, is that we've used this `implicit` keyword; that's the reason `Future.apply` was able to infer the value available in scope. If we tried this without the `implicit` keyword, we'd get similar compilation errors to those that we had previously. So the idea is to get an implicit value in scope, and now we know what's implicit. There's a big question though: why would you want to have this kind of behavior? We're going to have a healthy discussion regarding this idea.

Let's start with the idea that implicits in Scala can be used to automate the process of passing a value to an operation or conversion from one type to another type. Let's talk about the first one: implicit parameters.

Implicit parameters

We use implicit parameters when we want the compiler to help us find a value that's already available for a certain type. We've just seen an example of an implicit parameter when we talked about `Future`. Why don't we define something similar for ourselves?

We can think of a scenario where we need to show the present date in our application and we want to avoid passing a date's instance explicitly again and again. Instead, we can make the `LocalDateTime.now` value implicit to the respective functions and let the current date and time be passed as an implicit parameter to them. Let's write some code for this:

```
import java.time.{LocalDateTime}

object ImplicitParameter extends App {

  implicit val dateNow = LocalDateTime.now()

  def showDateTime(implicit date: LocalDateTime) = println(date)
  //Calling functions!
  showDateTime
}
```

The following is the result:

```
2017-11-17T10:06:12.321
```

Think of the `showDateTime` function as the one that needs the date-time's current value—hence it's possible for us to make it available as an implicit one. That's what we did—in the definition of `showDateTime`, we declared an implicit parameter named `date` of the type `LocalDateTime`. We also have an implicit value named `dateNow` in scope. That's why we didn't have to pass an argument at the call site and things still worked out good for us.

This seems a good use case. You can make your desired values automatically available for yourself using *implicits*.

The implicitly method

Scala's standard library provides a utility method to create concrete instances of types' availability implicitly. The method's name is also `implicitly`. Let's take a look at the function signature:

```
def implicitly[T](implicit e: T) = e
```

This `implicitly` method simply expects a type parameter, finds the implicit value available in scope, and summons and returns it to us. This is a good option available to us to tell whether a particular type's value is available in implicit scope. Let's look at an application of this method:

```
import java.time.{LocalDateTime}

object ImplicitParameter extends App {

  implicit val dateNow = LocalDateTime.now()

  def showDateTime(implicit date: LocalDateTime) = println(date)

  val ldt = implicitly[LocalDateTime]

  println(s"ldt value from implicit scope: $ldt")
}
```

The following is the result:

```
ldt value from implicit scope: 2017-12-17T10:47:13.846
```

In the preceding code snippet, a call to `implicitly`, along with the type, returned us the value available—as we already know, it's the current date-time value.

So this is how we can use the `implicit` parameter in our definitions and make them available to respective scopes.

With some idea about implicits now, let's take a look at *implicit conversions.*

Implicit conversions

The Standard Scala FAQ page describes implicit conversions as: "If one calls a method m on an object o of a class C and that class C does not support method m, then Scala compiler will look for an implicit conversion from C type to something that does support m method".

The idea is clear: it's a synthetic behavior (using a method) that we're forcing on instances of a particular type, and these behaviors (methods) aren't a part of the defined type. It's like we have a library with certain functionalities already available and we want to give some add-on functionality to a certain type from the library. Think about it—this is powerful. Having the ability to add on a functionality for a particular type is itself powerful. And that's what implicits let us do. We'll try our hand at something like the following.

First, think of a scenario where we want to create some syntax methods. We have a few methods available for the date-time library `java.time.LocalDate` that can help us add or subtract days/weeks/months/years, and those methods are:

```scala
scala> import java.time.LocalDate
import java.time.LocalDate

scala> val ld = LocalDate.now
ld: java.time.LocalDate = 2017-12-17

scala> ld.plusDays(1)
res0: java.time.LocalDate = 2017-12-18

scala> ld.plusWeeks(1)
res1: java.time.LocalDate = 2017-12-24

scala> ld.plusMonths(1)
res2: java.time.LocalDate = 2018-01-17

scala> ld.plusYears(1)
res3: java.time.LocalDate = 2018-12-17
```

What we would like to have is a simple + or - for days/weeks/months/years to work as the `plusXXX` or methods. What are all the options we have to achieve such a syntax?

One of the options is to create a `Wrapper` class over `LocalDate`, such as a `CustomDate(date: LocalDate)`, and define these methods for it. In that case, the code might look like this:

```scala
import java.time.LocalDate

case class CustomDate(date: LocalDate) {
```

```
  def +(days: Day): CustomDate = CustomDate(this.date.plusDays(days.num))
  def -(days: Day): CustomDate = CustomDate(this.date.minusDays(days.num))

  def +(weeks: Week): CustomDate =
CustomDate(this.date.plusWeeks(weeks.num))
  def -(weeks: Week): CustomDate =
CustomDate(this.date.minusWeeks(weeks.num))

  def +(months: Month): CustomDate =
CustomDate(this.date.plusMonths(months.num))
  def -(months: Month): CustomDate =
CustomDate(this.date.minusMonths(months.num))

  def +(years: Year): CustomDate =
CustomDate(this.date.plusYears(years.num))
  def -(years: Year): CustomDate =
CustomDate(this.date.minusYears(years.num))

  def till(endDate: CustomDate): CustomDateRange = if(this.date isBefore
endDate.date)
    CustomDateRange(this, endDate)
  else {
    throw new IllegalArgumentException("Can't create a DateRange with given
start and end dates.")
  }

  override def toString: String = s"Date: ${this.date}"
}

case class Day(num: Int)
case class Week(num: Int)
case class Month(num: Int)
case class Year(num: Int)

case class CustomDateRange(sd: CustomDate, ed: CustomDate){
  override def toString: String = s"$sd till $ed "
}
```

As you might have noticed in the preceding code, we have a `CustomDate` class wrapping over the type `LocalDate`, and are using the `LocalDate` type's methods to define our own desired syntax methods. Let's try using it. For this, we can create another object extending `App` trait:

```
import java.time.LocalDate

object BeautifulDateApp extends App {
```

```
val today = CustomDate(LocalDate.now())
val tomorrow = today + Day(1)
val yesterday = today - Day(1)

println(today)
println(tomorrow)
println(today + Year(1))

val dateRange = today till tomorrow + Day(20)
println(dateRange)


}
```

The following is the result:

```
Date: 2017-12-17
Date: 2017-12-18
Date: 2018-12-17
Date: 2017-12-17 till Date: 2018-01-07
```

By taking a look at the preceding code snippet, we can see that things worked fine: we've got the desired syntax for adding extra days to our date. But wrapping LocalDate gives us the feeling that this syntax isn't a part of the standard library we have. So for this, implicits come into the picture. We're going to do a similar syntax hack using the implicit class.

For this, we're going to create an implicit class that takes nothing but a val of the type LocalDate, then similar logic to provide all of our syntax methods. Afterwards, we'll bring that implicit class in scope by importing it. Let's write that:

```
case class Day(num: Int)
case class Week(num: Int)
case class Month(num: Int)
case class Year(num: Int)

case class CustomDateRange(sd: CustomDate, ed:CustomDate){
  override def toString: String = s"$sd till $ed "
}

object LocalDateOps {
  implicit class CustomDate(val date: LocalDate) {

    def +(days: Day): CustomDate = CustomDate(this.date.plusDays(days.num))
    def -(days: Day): CustomDate =
CustomDate(this.date.minusDays(days.num))

    def +(weeks: Week): CustomDate =
CustomDate(this.date.plusWeeks(weeks.num))
```

```
        def -(weeks: Week): CustomDate =
CustomDate(this.date.minusWeeks(weeks.num))

        def +(months: Month): CustomDate =
CustomDate(this.date.plusMonths(months.num))
        def -(months: Month): CustomDate =
CustomDate(this.date.minusMonths(months.num))

        def +(years: Year): CustomDate =
CustomDate(this.date.plusYears(years.num))
        def -(years: Year): CustomDate =
CustomDate(this.date.minusYears(years.num))

        def till(endDate: CustomDate): CustomDateRange = if(this.date isBefore
endDate.date)
        CustomDateRange(this, endDate)
    else {
        throw new IllegalArgumentException("Can't create a DateRange with
given start and end dates.")
    }

        override def toString: String = s"Date: ${this.date}"
    }
}
```

Now, it's time to use the same in our `BeautifulDateApp` class:

```
import java.time.LocalDate
import LocalDateOps._

object BeautifulDateApp extends App {

  val today = LocalDate.now()
  val tomorrow = today + Day(1)
  val yesterday = today - Day(1)

  println(today)
  println(tomorrow)
  println(today + Year(1))

  val dateRange = today till tomorrow + Day(20)
  println(dateRange)
}
```

The following is the result:

```
2017-12-17
Date: 2017-12-18
Date: 2018-12-17
Date: 2017-12-17 till Date: 2018-01-07
```

We can see the difference in the two approaches we took. The second one seems the more native approach. As consumers of these syntax methods, we never tried to call the `CustomDate` class—rather, we created an instance of the `LocalDate` type:

```
val today = LocalDate.now()
```

We used + and – like native methods defined in the `LocalDate` class. That's the power, or let's say magic, of *implicit conversions*. For those who want to know what happened in the background, let's look at the workings of the code in more detail.

The Scala compiler saw this:

```
val tomorrow = today + Day(1)
```

The compiler then tried to look for a method named + that takes a day as a parameter in the `LocalDate` class. It's not surprising that the compiler wasn't able to find such a method there, hence it tried to check whether there was any other class available in the implicit scope that is expecting a `LocalDate` and that was performing operations such as + with a day/week/month/year. Then, the compiler found our `CustomDate` implicit class. Finally, implicit conversion took place and this particular method call worked for us. We were then able to make such method syntax hacks possible.

Now that we've seen such an example, one question that we might want to ask ourselves is what do we mean by *implicit scope?* We also need to see how the Scala compiler searches for implicit values. Let's try to get an answer to this.

Looking for implicits

Your usual application Scala code might contain some constructs that import other classes and objects, or it might also inherit other classes. You write methods that expect types as parameters and also declare parameters. So when the Scala compiler looks for an implicit value, where should it start looking for such a value? The compiler starts to look for an implicit value according to the following criteria:

- Defined in current scope
- Explicitly imported
- Imported using wildcards
- Companion object of a type
- Implicit scope of an argument's type
- Implicit scope of type arguments
- Outer objects for nested types

We know that if we define an implicit value in the current scope (block of code), it gets the highest precedence. Afterwards, you can also import it using an `import` statement, as shown in the following code:

```
import scala.concurrent.Future
import scala.concurrent.ExecutionContext.Implicits.global


object FuturesApp extends App {

  val futureComp = Future {
      1 + 1
  }

  println(s"futureComp: $futureComp")

  futureComp.map(result => println(s"futureComp: $result"))
}
```

The following is the result:

```
futureComp: Future(Success(2))
futureComp: 2
```

A wildcard import can also work for this:

```
import scala.concurrent.ExecutionContext.Implicits._
```

But life's a bit uncomfortable for the compiler, as well as us, when it sees two implicit values eligible for the same type in the same scope. What we then see is a compilation error stating `ambiguous implicits`. Let's try that:

```scala
import scala.concurrent.Future
import scala.concurrent.ExecutionContext.Implicits.global

object FuturesApp extends App {

  implicit val ctx = scala.concurrent.ExecutionContext.Implicits.global

  val futureComp = Future {
    1 + 1
  }

  println(s"futureComp: $futureComp")

  futureComp.map(result => println(s"futureComp: $result"))
}
```

For the preceding code, we'll face this compilation error:

```
Error:(10, 27) ambiguous implicit values:
 both lazy value global in object Implicits of type =>
scala.concurrent.ExecutionContext
 and value ctx in object FuturesApp of type =>
scala.concurrent.ExecutionContext
 match expected type scala.concurrent.ExecutionContext
   val futureComp = Future {
```

So, we need to take care of the implicit value's ambiguity.

If the compiler isn't able to find the implicit value in the current block of code or via imports, it searches for it in companion objects of the type. That's how the compiler searches for implicit values. The standard Scala documentation explains the topic of finding implicits, which you can find at https:`//docs.scala-lang.org/tutorials/FAQ/finding-implicits.html`.

With this discussion of implicits, we've seen few ways in which we can use the concept and let the magic work for us. It's widely used by library designers when they define type-classes and make their instances available via implicit values. We've covered what type classes are, and we can create one on our own. Let's try that.

Type-classes ahead!

When creating type-classes to solve problems, such as providing a mechanism to encode types in a particular format, we have to unleash the power of languages such as Scala. What we desire is a way to encode values of a certain type in **comma-separated value (CSV)** format. For that purpose, we'll create a type-class named CSVEncoder. In Scala, we can do this using a trait of some type by convention:

```
trait CSVEncoder[T]{
  def encode(value: T): List[String]
}
```

What we defined is a functionality provider for our types. The functionality right now is to encode a value of some particular type and give back a list of string values that we can represent in CSV. Now, you might want to use this functionality by calling some functions on it, right? For a simple type such as Person, it can look like this:

```
case class Person(name: String)

CSVEncoder.toCSV(Person("Max"))
```

Some other syntax might look like this:

```
Person("Caroline").toCSV
```

To use something like these, what we need is this:

- A way to encode the type Person in CSV format
- The utility function toCSV

Let's define the ways our type-class-provided functionality can be used:

```
object CSVEncoder {
  def toCSV[T](list: List[T])(implicit encoder: CSVEncoder[T]): String =
    list.map(mem => encoder.encode(mem).mkString(", ")).mkString(", ")

}
```

Here, we have defined a companion object for CSVEncoder and defined our utility function named toCSV, which takes a type parameter and sequence of values of the same type, except that it expects an implicit CSVEncoder instance for the same type. What it returns in turn is a List[String]. We know it's easy to convert a sequence of string values in CSV. The definition is something that we want from this function. Hence, we simply call encoder.encode(value) and convert the values in comma-separated format.

Now, let's define a way to encode the Person type:

```
implicit val personEncoder: CSVEncoder[Person] = new CSVEncoder[Person] {
  def encode(person: Person) = List(person.name)
}
```

In the preceding code, we provided a way to encode our Person type. Now, let's use it:

```
object EncoderApp extends App {
  import CSVEncoder.personEncoder

  println(CSVEncoder.toCSV(List(Person("Max Black"), Person("Caroline Channing"))))

}
```

The following is the result:

```
Max Black, Caroline Channing
```

What we did here in our EncoderApp is import CSVEncoder[Person] implicitly and call a toCSV function with the expected value. Calling this function gives us the desired result. We can now hack the toCSV function syntax using an implicit class and give the consumer of our type-class another way of using our encoder. Let's do that:

```
trait CSVEncoder[T]{
  def encode(value: T): List[String]
}

object CSVEncoder {

  def toCSV[T](list: List[T])(implicit encoder: CSVEncoder[T]): String =
    list.map(mem => encoder.encode(mem).mkString(", ")).mkString(", ")

  implicit val personEncoder: CSVEncoder[Person] = new CSVEncoder[Person] {
    def encode(person: Person) = List(person.name)
  }

}
```

```
case class Person(name: String)

object EncoderApp extends App {
  import CSVEncoder._
  import CSVEncoderOps._

  println(CSVEncoder.toCSV(List(Person("Max Black"), Person("Caroline
Channing"))))

  println(List(Person("Max Black"), Person("Caroline Channing")).toCSV)
}

object CSVEncoderOps {
  implicit class CSVEncoderExt[T](list: List[T]) {
    def toCSV(implicit encoder: CSVEncoder[T]) : String =
      list.map(mem => encoder.encode(mem).mkString(", ")).mkString(", ")
  }
}
```

The following is the result:

```
Max Black, Caroline Channing
Max Black, Caroline Channing
```

In the preceding code snippet, we were able to call the `toCSV` function as a method:

```
List(Person("Max Black"), Person("Caroline Channing")).toCSV
```

We achieved this syntax call using the implicit `CSVEncoderExt` class, which was the approach we took in the case of the syntax methods for `LocalDate`:

```
implicit class CSVEncoderExt[T](list: List[T]) {
    def toCSV(implicit encoder: CSVEncoder[T]) : String =
      list.map(mem => encoder.encode(mem).mkString(", ")).mkString(", ")
  }
```

All we had to do was take care that this particular class was in the scope at the call site, so we imported it. This is how we have created and used our first type-class. It wasn't that hard, was it? Sure, we have covered enough about type-classes in this chapter. Let's go ahead and summarize what we've learned in this chapter.

Summary

First, we discussed exceptional cases that occur when we try programming. We saw how we handle these exceptional cases in functional programming. We even tried exception handling in functional composition. Then, we began to see the magic that implicits bring in Scala. We discussed implicit parameters and then *implicit conversion.* We saw the `implicitly` method, provided by the Scala standard library. Finally, we talked about the already much-talked-about type-classes, and defined/used our first one. Once you practice enough with the concepts that we have discussed, it's worth going through type-classes in detail. Most of the Scala libraries' frameworks heavily use this concept.

In the next chapter, we'll learn about the Akka toolkit. We'll cover *Actor System*, one of Akka's offerings, and much more.

12
Introduction to Akka

"Technology is nothing. What's important is that you have faith in people, that they're good and smart, and if you give them tools, they'll do wonderful things with them."

- Steve Jobs

As developers, we are used to facing programming problems and solving them using abstractions, programming models, or some design patterns. These programming models tend to make ours and consumer's lives easier. This chapter is about learning one such programming model that solves more than one problem. We'll understand and work with Akka, which is based on *Actor models*. We can think of Akka libraries (well mostly) as an open source set of libraries that help you write concurrent, fault tolerant, and distributed applications. We'll talk about what you might expect from this toolkit. As we go through the chapter, we'll try understanding the actor model and how these actors work together, as well as how the actor mechanism is different from any other concurrency mechanism.

Going through all the Akka libraries is outside of the scope of this chapter as well as the book, hence we'll focus on understanding the actor system, which is the basis for any other library available within the Akka toolkit. This will enable us to use them when needed. In this chapter, we'll be going through the following:

- Why do we care about Akka?
- What's up with the Actor model?
- Actors in practice
- Supervising fault in our Actors
- Testing Actors

So why do we care about another programming model? Let's find out.

Why do we care about Akka?

With a large amount of data all around us, our computer/processing systems are striving for performance. With multicore architecture and distributed computing, we are achieving high performance with acceptable availability of services. But this cannot be taken for granted; we have come to a point where we already have mechanisms to deal with problems that arise due to either incapability of systems or the programming models we are using.

Due to the advent of multicore architecture, our systems are capable of processing a large amount of data with high performance. But there is a fault in our programming models, which we use to mutate states, and at the same time use several threads to vary the states present in our programs. This has given us a reason to think.

Two or more threads trying to process a particular shared state might cause a *deadlock* (more on this in `Chapter 13`, *Concurrent Programming in Scala*, where we discuss concurrency and threads in more detail) and your program may not even complete. But still, we are discussing the problem; nowhere do we see the solution. One way in which we can think of dealing with threads and problems is using some sort of locking mechanism so that two separate threads cannot access the same instance/state at the same time.

But think of it this way, by introducing locks, we are making our operating systems interrupt/suspend the thread and restore it later to perform the same task. It's expecting more from your computer's CPU.

It means that without locks we are facing problems with states of our instances, and now with locks in place, the program's performance takes a hit. Now picture a multithreaded distributed environment; life's worse there.

Also, the way we handle failures in multithreaded environments is not pleasing. Hence, what we need for handling these is a different mechanism altogether. In the case of Akka, we let entities interact via messages. We create entities in terms of Actors that communicate by passing messages to each other. You may compare this kind of communication to network communication where we depend on HTTP request-responses to perform the intended operation. Similarly, by encapsulating the state within Actor instances, we tend to pass immutable instances to another actor to perform some logic. That receiving actor, after applying/performing some logic, returns back a response. That's how we can build our systems.

Actor models have proven to be a highly effective solution. Akka provides this actor model and enforces a tree-like structure for actors. Some points to note down about actors:

- By communicating via messages, we omit the possibility of corrupting the state for a particular instance
- Because one actor can process one message at a time, we avoid the deadlock situation
- With a hierarchy in place, it's easier to form a domain logic
- The parent-child relationship between two actors makes it possible for us to handle faulty behavior; in Akka terminology, we call it a *supervision strategy*

We'll go through the way *actors* communicate and how messages are ordered/stored and executed. First, let's try to understand the *Actor Model*.

What's up with the Actor Model?

From our discussion, it's clear that we have some entities that act on receipt of some messages, or let's say requests. We call them Actors. To solve some domain-specific problems, we might want to have more than one Actor. Think of a basic scenario of e-commerce checkout flow. There's more than one area of concern. The following diagram represents the basic intended flow:

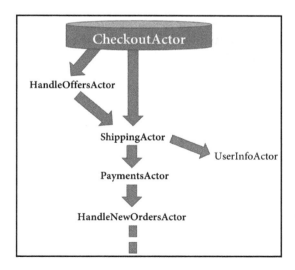

By taking a look at the diagram, it's clear that we have few entities, and these entities are going to take care of specific concerns. We have named these entities based on their area of concern:

- **CheckoutActor** might have the responsibility to fetch details from the cart and show the respective information.
- Additionally, you might want to apply some coupon code or offer. Our system has to validate that coupon or offer code and based on that we might want to modify order details. For this particular process, we have **HandleOffersActor**.
- **ShippingActor** has the responsibility of fetching user-specific information such as address, and based on that we can calculate the estimated time for shipping. It's important to note that **ShippingActor** is not restricted to process the whole logic within, and can call another child actor named **UserInfoActor**, which does nothing but to fetch a user's information. Another point to note is that the operation of fetching user information is so general that this Actor might be useful outside this particular hierarchy.
- After shipping details are in place, we might want to redirect a user to a payment page, where we can perform payment-specific logic. For that, we have **PaymentsActor**.
- Finally, based on the payment's success or failure, we might want to handle orders. For example, upon successful payment, we want to proceed to ordering, and in case of failure we might want to send an email to the user stating that they process payment again! For this purpose, we have **HandleNewOrdersActor**.

In the whole scenario, we can see that the whole flow makes a hierarchy of actors. Let's say **ShippingActor** fails to provide user information from the database, due to network/connection issues. Now it's up to us as to how we want to deal with that. Similarly, upon **PaymentsActor** failure, it's up to the business to make a decision about what to do next. It could be to proceed and take orders with payment status pending and payment method on delivery or to ask the user to retry. So, handling such scenarios is easier when you have your entities in a hierarchical manner, performing logic.

In this simple scenario, we understood that these actors form a hierarchy, or let's call it a group, and live within a system; in Akka terminology, we call it an **ActorSystem**.

Understanding the Actor system

Akka documentation simply explains an **ActorSystem** as a heavyweight structure that will allocate 1 to N threads, and we should create one per *logical* application. Once we create an actor system, we get the license to create actors under that system. We'll take a look at how we can create Actors in the next sections.

When we create actors as part of a system, these actors share the same configuration (such as *dispatchers, paths,* and *addresses)* as the Actor system.

Within an Actor system, there's a **root guardian** Actor; this serves as a parent actor to all actors residing within an actor system, internal actors, as well actors that we create. So, as expected, this is the last actor to be stopped when the system terminates.

The reason why Akka provides these guardian actors is to supervise the first-level actors we create, so for user created actors too, we have a specific **user guardian**. Similarly, for system provided actors, Akka has system guardian.

Take a look at the following diagram to understand the hierarchy of guardian actors in the Akka system:

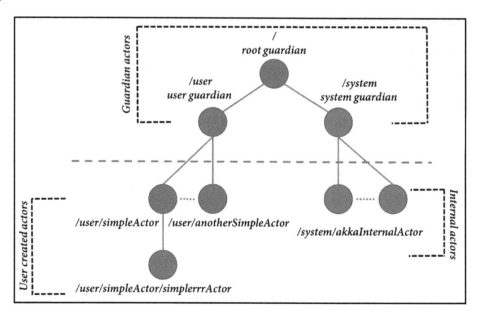

In the previous diagram, we can see there's a path representation of each actor specified:

- **root guardian**: /
- **user guardian**: /user
- **system guardian**: /system

So, whenever we create an actor within an Actor system, we tend to create a first-level. Hence, in the example shown in the diagram, we can see that the actor's path is appended to /user, in our case it is the SimpleActor, hence the path formed is /user/simpleActor. With an Actor system defined as system, for creating these *first-level* (more on this in the next few sections) actors, we use:

```
val system = ActorSystem("SimpleActorSystem")
system.actorOf(Props[SimpleActor], "simple-actor")
```

We'll try out creating an actor ourselves in subsequent sections, but for now it's worth nothing the way we called an actorOf method on system to create a *first-level* Actor. From here, we can create child Actors for our first-level Actor. And for that purpose, we use context instead of a system instance. It'll look as follows:

```
val anotherSimpleActor = context.actorOf(Props[AnotherSimplActor],
"another-simple-actor")
```

Here, by using context instead of system, we are specifying that the actor that we want to create is going to be in the context of the current Actor, making it a child actor. It's important to notice that this call to the following definition can only be made from within an Actor. So, with this method call, we get a child Actor for our simpleActor:

```
context.actorOf(Props[AnotherSimpleActor], "another-simple-actor")
```

Assuming that the call was made from SimpleActor and SimpleActor is the first-level actor, our anotherSimpleActor path may look like this:

```
akka://SimpleActorSystem/user/simple-actor/another-simple-actor
```

Now that we have seen the child actor path, it's obvious that path for our `simple-actor` will be:

```
akka://SimpleActorSystem/user/simple-actor
```

Also, a few points worth noting are the usage of `Props` and the return type of the `actorOf` method.

Props

`Props` can be seen as a configuration object for `ActorRef`. We can create instances of the props configuration with some configuration. The following is an example of that:

```
val props = Props[SimpleActor]()
  .withDispatcher("some-simple-dispatcher")

val simpleActor: ActorRef = system.actorOf(props, "simple-actor")
```

One important thing to know about the `Props` object is that it is immutable and hence thread-safe.

Actor references and paths

When we create an Actor, what we get in response is an `ActorRef`. This is a reference to our created Actor. Why we might need an `ActorRef` is to pass throughout the system to other actors as a reference. These references are used for message passing. Every actor that we create has a reference to itself through self.

From within an actor, it's possible to obtain an *actor reference* of the calling Actor via a method named `sender()`.

We can also give names to actor references. In our case, we named our `SimpleActor` reference `simple-actor`:

```
val simpleActor: ActorRef = system.actorOf(props, "simple-actor")
```

We also know that these Actors are created in a hierarchical fashion and we can give unique names to *actor instances*. Hence, these names together make a path for each Actor. The path is unique for each Actor. Our `SimpleActor` path might look like this:

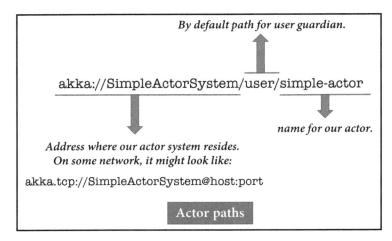

We can see that due to the hierarchy, we have paths for different actors, because actors must have unique names. We can also see that regardless of your actor being created on a remote network, its path is going to have the same structure along with host and port.

Selecting existing actorRefs via actorSelection

Due to every actor having its own unique ID, we can refer to a particular actor via its path using the `actorSelection` method. We can call the `actorSelection` method on `system` or `context` and get the `ActorRef`.

When we call `actorSelection` on `system`, we need to pass the absolute Actor path starting from root, whereas while calling the same on `context`, we can pass the path relative to the current Actor.

Assuming the current Actor (first-level Actor) has a `SiblingActor`, at the same level, we may refer to the sibling Actor's actor reference as:

```
context.actorSelection("../siblingActor")

context.actorSelection("/user/siblingActor")
```

In these two approaches, the first one used to represent the parent Actor. The other approach directly referred to the Actor's path. With this, we were able to get the actor references, but it's discouraged because we might not want to write actor paths explicitly. We can leverage use of `actorSelection`, when suppose we want to make use of a wildcard (*), that is, to send messages to all the actors below a certain (*) level in hierarchy. The following diagram will clear what we mean by that:

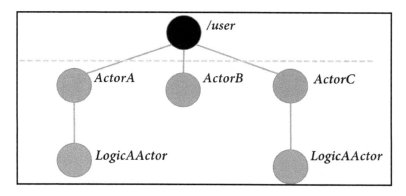

Here, in previous diagram, by providing the following code:

```
context.actorSelection("akka://someActorSystem/user/*/LogicAActor")
```

We can obtain the reference, that point to all the `LogicAActor` parameters in previously mentioned hierarchy. Also it's worth knowing that a call to the `actorOf` method creates an actor on the context or system, depending upon which it's invoked. Whereas a call to `actorSelection` does not create any new actors, it points to `actorpath` which we pass, and doesn't ensure actor's existence there.

Now that we have gone through simple entities in an Actor system, let's try and understand how the Actor life cycle works and what approaches we might want to choose to kill an actor instance.

How the Actor life cycle works

When we make a call to method `actorOf`, what we get in return is an `ActorRef` that in turn also possesses a particular path where we've created the Actor. With this call, we know exactly there's an Actor instance created, been assigned a unique ID, and hook methods are called. There's this method named `preStart()` that gets called as the very first action, after a new Actor is created.

A few points to note when a new Actor is created:

- A new Actor path is reserved for the Actor
- A unique ID is assigned to the Actor
- After the instance is created, the `preStart()` method is called:

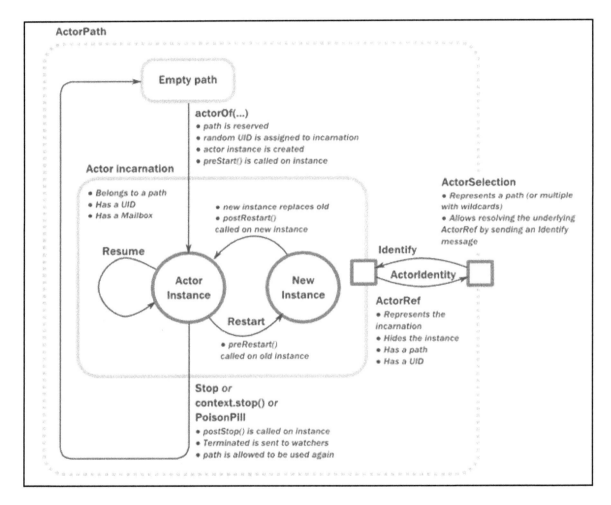

When an Actor is restarted:

1. The `preRestart()` is called on the instance.
2. New instance is created, replaces the old instance.
3. The `postRestart()` method is called.

When an Actor is stopped:

1. The `postStop()` method is called on the instance.
2. Terminated message is sent to watchers.
3. Actor path is allowed to be used again.

The previous diagram illustrates this whole cycle. An important point to note is that we get these hook methods in the form of `preStart`, `preRestart`, `postStop`, and `postRestart`. Using these methods, we can define some logic as required.

So, now that we're aware of the actor model and have also discussed that Actors communicate via messages, let's practice them.

Hello world in Akka

For writing our first Akka actor, we need to add the `akka-actor` library dependency. For dependency management we'll be using SBT and, as we know, we'll be defining these library dependencies in our `build.sbt` file. To do this, we need to have SBT installed on our system.

Setting up the environment

To get started with a simple Akka project, we can simply follow these steps:

1. Go to Lightbend's **TECH HUB** (`https://developer.lightbend.com`) and click on **START A PROJECT**:

2. Search for **Akka Quickstart** Scala under Akka projects:

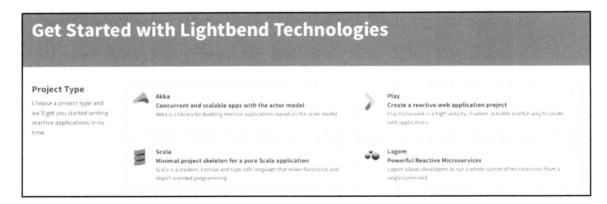

3. Click on **CREATE A PROJECT FOR ME!**:

4. Extract the downloaded ZIP (compressed) file.

We can open the extracted folder in **IntelliJ IDEA** IDE:

1. Open IntelliJ IDE.
2. Click on **File | New | Project from Existing Sources...**:

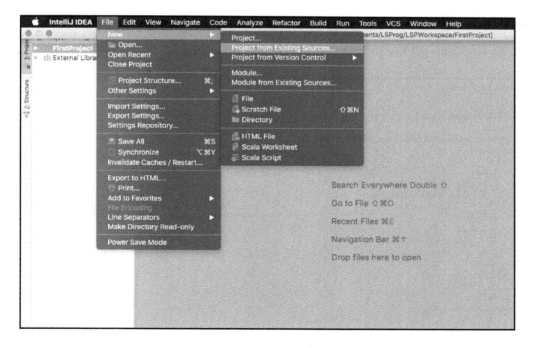

3. Choose the `build.sbt` from the project (`akka-quickstart-scala`) we've just extracted:

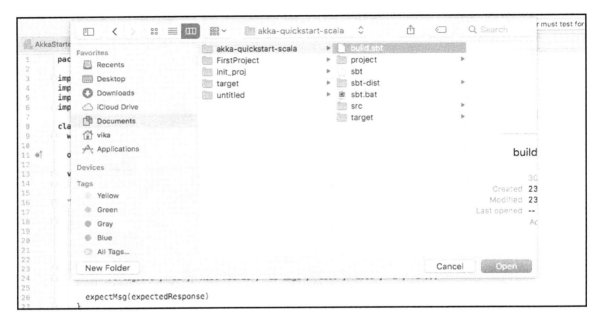

4. And you get the project open in the IntelliJ window:

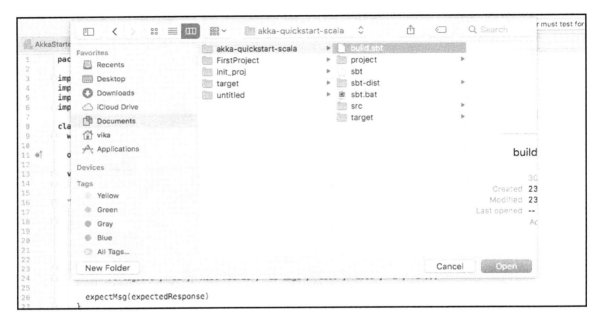

This is one way of starting with an Akka project. This project has already defined all the `akka-actors` specific dependencies. We don't have to define them on their own. But we would like to start by taking the first step ourselves hence let's start with a bootstrapped `sbt-scala` project and define library dependencies.

We can take some steps to do that:

1. Open your favorite command line (Command prompt in Windows/Terminal in Linux and macOS), and go to the desired directory where you want to locate the project.

2. Give the command `sbt new sbt/scala-seed.g8`:

3. Command prompt will ask for the name of the project. Give a name to it:

4. The command will generate the Scala seed project for us. We can follow *Steps 1* to *3* to open the **Acala** seed project in IntelliJ IDE.

5. Open the `build.sbt` file. The file might look like this:

```
import Dependencies._

lazy val root = (project in file(".")).
  settings(
    inThisBuild(List(
      organization := "com.example",
      scalaVersion := "2.12.3",
      version      := "0.1.0-SNAPSHOT"
    )),
    name := "Hello",
    libraryDependencies += scalaTest % Test
  )
```

This file specifies that we have a root project in the current directory named `Hello`. Along with that, we have given some version-specific information, and the final line specifies that we currently have one `libraryDependency`, that is, `scala-test`. This value comes from the `Dependencies.scala` file.

We'll define `akka-actors` specific dependencies in this `build.sbt` file:

```
libraryDependencies ++= Seq(
  "com.typesafe.akka" %% "akka-actor" % "2.5.8",
  "com.typesafe.akka" %% "akka-testkit" % "2.5.8",
  "org.scalatest" %% "scalatest" % "3.0.1" % "test"
  )
```

Here in the preceding code snippet, we've specified three dependencies; the first one is an `akka-actor` specific dependency. The second is for testing Akka Actors. The last one is specific to Scala testing.

With this, we would use the `sbt update` command for updating libraries, and give a command in the current project directory using `cmd/terminal`.

With these steps, we're ready to write our first Akka actor.

Writing our first Actor

Writing an Actor is as simple as writing a class that extends the `akka.actor.Actor` class. And we know that Actors respond to messages, so to identify messages, we have a method named `receive` that we have to define for each Actor we write. Let's write our `SimpleActor`:

```
import akka.actor.Actor

class SimpleActor extends Actor {
  override def receive = Actor.emptyBehavior

}
```

So, we wrote the `SimpleActor` with some empty behavior defined in the `receive` method. But here we've just wrote our Actor; we have to instantiate the Actor as part of an Actor system. After instantiating, we might also want to run our application to see the behavior, hence, let's write the entry point to our application and instantiate an Actor system:

```
import akka.actor.ActorSystem

object AkkaStarter extends App {

  val simpleActorSystem = ActorSystem("SimpleActorSystem")

}
```

This statement gives us an instance for an Actor system with the name `SimpleActorSystem`. Now, we want to create an instance of our `SimpleActor` as a top (first) level actor, hence we'll use the `simpleActorSystem.actorOf` method available:

```
import akka.actor.{Actor, ActorSystem, Props}

class SimpleActor extends Actor {
  override def receive = Actor.emptyBehavior
}

object SimpleActor {
  val props = Props[SimpleActor]
}

object AkkaStarter extends App {
```

```
val simpleActorSystem = ActorSystem("SimpleActorSystem")

val simpleActor = simpleActorSystem.actorOf(SimpleActor.props)
}
```

Right now we have an Actor system available, and we have created an Actor instance. It is to be noted that by convention, we've created a companion object for our Actor class and defined its `props` value in it. We can also name our actor by giving an extra argument as a string:

```
val simpleActor = simpleActorSystem.actorOf(SimpleActor.props, "simple-
actor")
```

This line gives our actor a `namesimple-actor`. For now, the behavior defined for our Actor is empty. We would like to define a `receive` method for our actor. Let's think, what's the simplest thing our actor can do? It may be to call any public finance API to give us stock information or to call any API to perform currency conversion; that's up to us. For this example scenario, we'll call our `football.csv` file to fetch and show information to the user. Lets see how this can work using actors.

First, let's define some utility methods we might need to perform, parsing from string response to `Players` data. We have this case class for `Players`:

```
case class Player(name: String, nationality: String, age:String, club:
String, domesticLeague: String, rawTotal: String, finalScore: String,
ranking2016: String, ranking2015: String)

object Util {

  def bufferedSourceToList(source: BufferedSource): List[String] = {
    val list = source.getLines().toList
    source.close()
    list
  }

  def asPlayers(listOfPlayersString: List[String]) : List[Player] =
listOfPlayersString match {
    case head :: tail => tail map {line =>
    val columns = line.split((",")).map(_.trim)
    Player(columns(5),columns(6),columns(9),columns(7),
      columns(8),columns(10), columns(12), columns(0),columns(2))
    }
    case Nil => List[Player]()
  }

}
```

We defined two utility methods named `bufferedSourceToList` and `asPlayers`; these methods do what they say. So, let's now define our `SimpleActor` receive method:

```scala
class SimpleActor extends Actor {
  import scala.io.Source
  import SimpleActor.ShowFootballPlayersRequest
  import Util._

  override def receive = {
    case ShowFootballPlayersRequest(url) => {
      val playersInfoSource = Source.fromFile(url)

      val players = asPlayers(bufferedSourceToList(playersInfoSource))
      players.foreach(player => println(player + "n"))
    }
  }

}

object SimpleActor {
  val props = Props[SimpleActor]

  final case class ShowFootballPlayersRequest(uri: String)
}
```

We have defined the receive methods, or let's say `SimpleActor` method's behavior, for a particular request such as `ShowFootballPlayersRequest`. The request itself contains the required information to fetch the information from the URI for the file. We defined this request as a final case class in the companion object of `SimpleActor`. This conventional approach specifies the requests our actor supports. On receipt of such a request for players information, our actor fetches information from the file at the location specified, and then it prints the player's information.

Let's use it. We're going to send a request of `ShowFootballPlayersRequest` type using our actor reference:

```scala
val fileSource = "/Users/vika/Workspace/akkaa/akka-
starter/src/main/scala/files/football_stats.csv"

simpleActor ! ShowFootballPlayersRequest(fileSource)
```

In the previous code snippet, we've used a method with this operator-like name, "!", and passed an instance of `ShowFootballPlayersRequest` with the file source URI. This method, let's call it `bang` for now, in an ideal case goes to the actor's mailbox and delivers this message. This happens in a fire-and-forget manner. There's no guarantee of message delivery at the called actor's mailbox. There might be scenarios where you expect a response from called actors; in that case instead of calling `bang`, we make an ask call to our Actors.

We'll consider a request containing a player's name and the source for a list of players. For example, the source can be any public API to get the player's information; in our case, it's a simple `List[Player]` with all the player's data.

The first thing we would like to do is create a simple request and response. For this, we can define these in our `SimpleActor` companion object. First is a simple request with the player's name and a list of players we'll pass along. The second one is a response container which has nothing but an option player:

```
final case class GetPlayerInformationRequest(name: String, source:
List[Player])
final case class PlayerInformationResponse(player: Option[Player])
```

Now, let's define a receive method for such a request, of type `GetPlayerInformationRequest`:

```
import scala.concurrent.Future
import scala.concurrent.ExecutionContext.Implicits.global

case GetPlayerInformationRequest(name, listOfPlayers) => {
  log.info(s"Executing GetPlayerInformationRequest($name, listOfPlayers)")

akka.pattern.pipe(
Future.successful(PlayerInformationResponse(listOfPlayers.find(_.name.conta
ins(name))))
) to sender()

}
```

A few points to note about this behavior:

- We have used a logger implementation to log information specific to this Actor. For this, we have used the `ActorLogging` trait. Simply mix in this trait by using:

```
class SimpleActor extends Actor with ActorLogging
```

- When we receive a message to perform some expensive operation, we perform that operation and wrap that in future, and want to return back future's reference to the calling Actor. For this purpose, we've used a method named `pipe` from the `akka.pattern` package. This method expects an execution context. The way we use pipe or the similar syntax method `pipeTo` is as follows:

```
akka.pattern.pipe(someFuture) to sender()
```

Alternatively we can use:

```
import akka.pattern._
someFuture pipeTo sender()
```

This `pipe` or `pipeTo` method sends back the response to the calling site.

After defining the behavior of our Actor for messages of type `GetPlayerInformationRequest`, let's call the Actor with this message. First, we'll create the source, `List[Player]`:

```
//Storing players in a collection!
val players: List[Player] = Util
  .asPlayers(bufferedSourceToList(
    scala.io.Source.fromFile(fileSource)
  ))
```

Performing an ask call to the simple Actor is as simple as questioning the Actor:

```
simpleActor ? GetPlayerInformationRequest("Cristiano Ronaldo", players)
```

Now this `?` is called *ask method*; we use this method when we expect a response from the called Actor. We need to give an `import` statement to import this method in scope:

```
import akka.pattern.ask
```

Also, we might want to make sure this request gets completed in a given time duration. We'll ensure that particular timeout duration by bringing an implicit timeout value in scope:

```
import akka.util.Timeout
import scala.concurrent.duration._

implicit val timeout = Timeout(5 seconds)
```

Now, on successful completion of our request we can obtain the values from the response. So, let's do that and print the player's information:

```
val playerInformation = (simpleActor ?
GetPlayerInformationRequest("Cristiano Ronaldo", players))

playerInformation
  .mapTo[PlayerInformationResponse]
  .map(futureValue => {
      futureValue.player map println
    })
```

First, we mapped the response to the desired type by providing a `mapTo` method, and then we mapped values from the future and printed. We've used the *fire-and-forget* way of sending a message to one actor and we've waited for some response using the *ask* method. There's another way we can communicate messages and that's using the `forward` method.

The tell versus ask versus forward method

We use one of these three approaches to transmit messages from one actor to another. As we've already established, `tell` transmits messages and does not wait for the response; this way, we ensure *at most once* delivery. We can also use the `ask` method in cases where we expect our called *actors* to respond back with some messages of the response type. There might be scenarios where you want to forward a message of a particular type with the same actor reference (`ActorRef`) to another Actor. For this purpose, we can use the `forward` method:

```
class AnotherActor extends Actor {
  override def receive = {
    case ShowFootballPlayersRequest(url) => {
      val playersInfoSource = Source.fromFile(url)

      val players = asPlayers(bufferedSourceToList(playersInfoSource))
      players.foreach(player => println(player + "n"))
    }
  }
}

object AnotherActor {
  val props = Props[AnotherActor]
}
```

We have defined `AnotherActor`, and we can make this a child actor of our `SimpleActor`. To do that, let's instantiate this actor by giving a `context.actorOf` call from `SimpleActor`. Then, on receipt of a message of type `ShowFootballPlayersRequest`, we'll forward the message to `anotherActor`, as shown in the following code snippet:

```scala
class SimpleActor extends Actor with ActorLogging {

  implicit val ec = context.dispatcher
  // Works as executionContext for actor calls

  val anotherActor = context.actorOf(AnotherActor.props)

  override def receive = {
    case ShowFootballPlayersRequest(url) => {
      anotherActor forward ShowFootballPlayersRequest(url)
    }

    case GetPlayerInformationRequest(name, listOfPlayers) => {
      log.info(s"Executing GetPlayerInformationRequest($name,
listOfPlayers)")

      akka.pattern.pipe(
Future.successful(PlayerInformationResponse(listOfPlayers.find(_.name.conti
ns(name)) ))
) to sender() } } }
```

The `SimpleActor` class simply forwards the message to another actor; now, we can have a look at the whole code we have written and try to run it:

```scala
package lsp

import lsp.SimpleActor.{GetPlayerInformationRequest,
PlayerInformationResponse, ShowFootballPlayersRequest}
import akka.actor.{Actor, ActorLogging, ActorSystem, PoisonPill, Props}
import akka.pattern.ask
import scala.io.{BufferedSource, Source}
import akka.util.Timeout
import lsp.Util.{asPlayers, bufferedSourceToList}
import scala.concurrent.duration._
import scala.concurrent.Future
import scala.concurrent.ExecutionContext.Implicits.global


class SimpleActor extends Actor with ActorLogging {

  val anotherActor = context.actorOf(AnotherActor.props)
```

```
    override def receive = {
      case ShowFootballPlayersRequest(url) => {
        anotherActor forward ShowFootballPlayersRequest(url)
      }

      case GetPlayerInformationRequest(name, listOfPlayers) => {
        log.info(s"Executing GetPlayerInformationRequest($name,
listOfPlayers)")

        akka.pattern.pipe(
          Future {
PlayerInformationResponse(listOfPlayers.find(_.name.contains(name)))
          }
        ) to sender()

      }

    }

}
object SimpleActor {
  val props = Props[SimpleActor]

  final case class ShowFootballPlayersRequest(uri: String)

  final case class GetPlayerInformationRequest(name: String, source:
List[Player])
  final case class PlayerInformationResponse(player: Option[Player])
}
```

The previous code is our main *SimpleActor* and its companion object. Let's take a look at
AnotherActor:

```
class AnotherActor extends Actor {
  override def receive = {
    case ShowFootballPlayersRequest(url) => {
      val playersInfoSource = Source.fromFile(url)

      val players = asPlayers(bufferedSourceToList(playersInfoSource))

      players.foreach(player => println(player))
    }
  }

}
object AnotherActor {
  val props = Props[AnotherActor]
}
```

Finally, the entry point to our application where we boot the Actor system:

```scala
object AkkaStarter extends App {
  import Util._

  implicit val timeout = Timeout(5 seconds)

  val simpleActorSystem = ActorSystem("SimpleActorSystem")
  val simpleActor = simpleActorSystem.actorOf(SimpleActor.props, "simple-
actor")

  val fileSource =
    "/Users/vika/Workspace/akkaa/akka-
starter/src/main/scala/files/football_stats.csv"

  //simpleActor ! ShowFootballPlayersRequest(fileSource)

  //Storing players in a collection!
  val players: List[Player] = Util
    .asPlayers(bufferedSourceToList(
      scala.io.Source.fromFile(fileSource)
    ))

  val playerInformation = (simpleActor ?
GetPlayerInformationRequest("Cristiano Ronaldo", players))

  playerInformation
    .mapTo[PlayerInformationResponse]
    .map(futureValue => {
      futureValue.player map println
    })

  simpleActor ! PoisonPill
}
```

We also have this `Util` object which consists of utility methods. With this, we have defined the `Player` case class:

```scala
object Util {

  def bufferedSourceToList(source: BufferedSource): List[String] = {
    val list = source.getLines().toList

    source.close()
    list
  }
}
```

```
    def asPlayers(listOfPlayersString: List[String]) : List[Player] =
listOfPlayersString match {
    case head :: tail => tail map {line =>
      val columns = line.split((",")).map(_.trim)
      Player(columns(5),columns(6),columns(9),columns(7),
        columns(8),columns(10), columns(12), columns(0),columns(2))
    }
    case Nil => List[Player]()
  }

}

case class Player(name: String, nationality: String, age:String, club:
String,
                domesticLeague: String, rawTotal: String, finalScore:
String,
                ranking2016: String, ranking2015: String)
```

Run:

```
[INFO] [12/27/2017 14:40:48.150] [SimpleActorSystem-akka.actor.default-
dispatcher-2] [akka://SimpleActorSystem/user/simple-actor] Executing
GetPlayerInformationRequest(Cristiano Ronaldo, listOfPlayers)
Player(Cristiano Ronaldo,Portugal,32,Real Madrid,Spain,4829,4789,1,2)
```

After using our Actor, we should terminate its instance.

Stopping Actors

One way of stopping actors is by calling the `stop` method from the `system` or `context` for a particular actor. To do this, we can define a particular message that can be passed to the actor, telling it to stop. For example:

```
case "terminate" => context stop self
```

Most of the times the preferred way of terminating an actor is by sending a `PoisonPill` message to it:

```
simpleActor ! PoisonPill
```

This simple message passing can terminate the actor gracefully. The termination takes place after all the messages in the Actor's queue are processed before the poison pill is processed. Stopping an *actor* stops all of its child actors. Remember, we talked about those hook methods that can be called if we want to perform some logic when the actor is starting up or at termination. Let's take a look at those.

The preStart and postStop hooks

Let's define these methods in the `SimpleActor` class to log the starting and stopping of our `SimpleActor`:

```
override def preStart(): Unit = log.info("SimpleActor starting!")

override def postStop(): Unit = log.info("SimpleActor stopping!")
```

Run:

```
[INFO] [12/27/2017 14:56:54.887] [SimpleActorSystem-akka.actor.default-
dispatcher-3] [akka://SimpleActorSystem/user/simple-actor] SimpleActor
starting!
[INFO] [12/27/2017 14:56:54.915] [SimpleActorSystem-akka.actor.default-
dispatcher-2] [akka://SimpleActorSystem/user/simple-actor] Executing
GetPlayerInformationRequest(Cristiano Ronaldo, listOfPlayers)
Player(Cristiano Ronaldo,Portugal,32,Real Madrid,Spain,4829,4789,1,2)
[INFO] [12/27/2017 14:56:54.938] [SimpleActorSystem-akka.actor.default-
dispatcher-2] [akka://SimpleActorSystem/user/simple-actor] SimpleActor
stopping!
```

Similar methods are also available for restart operations in the form of `preRestart` and `postRestart`.

When we discuss communicating via messages, the question of in which order the messages get delivered to other actors arises, and also at what guarantee of message delivery.

Actor communication via messages and its semantics

We talked about the fashion of *fire-and-forget* regarding message passing; to understand this a bit more, let's take a look at a diagram explaining message delivery semantics.

The following diagram explains the semantics of message delivery; when we send messages over a network, there are chances of it getting delivered and also chances of it being lost. Also, in the case of an unsuccessful or successful attempt to deliver a message, we might try to send a message or we might not. It depends on us if want to try sending a message exactly once and then not the second time or so on.

Based on these assumptions, we can make some formal terminologies specifying what we discussed, and we call them:

- At most once
- At least once
- Exactly once

At most once	*At least once*	*Exactly once*
• *Message may be lost.* • *Message may be delivered zero or once.*	• *Message may be duplicated but not lost.* • *Message will be delivered at least once or more.*	• *Message may not be duplicated or lost.* • *Message will be delivered exactly once.*

Delivery Semantics

The diagram explains each of the three approaches in simple terms. It's important to know that in case of the Actor's communication, we have at most once delivery; in other terms, it means no guaranteed delivery. When actors communicate, a message might or might not be delivered to the called Actor.

Actors are pretty lightweight and can accommodate a large number of messages fired to them; when we send a message to an actor, the messages get delivered to the actor's mailbox. An actor's mailbox is a queue that gets instantiated when we create an actor's instance. We know the way queue works is FIFO, *first in first out*. The ordering of the execution of the messages depends on the order in which they arrive to the mailbox.

Until now, our discussions were based on the possibilities of successful execution of the logic implemented via Actors. But we know that Akka provides a very nice fault handling mechanism in the *form* of a *supervision strategy*. Let's discuss it.

Supervising fault in our actors

There is a possibility that our logic ends up in a network error or some unexpected exception. Imagine a scenario where our service needs to call a particular database instance to fetch some data. We might face *connection timed out* or some other similar errors. In that case, what should be our behavior? Maybe trying to establish the connection a couple of times will help, this can be achieved if our tasks are performed in such a hierarchical manner. We can achieve this task by performing hierarchy via the *actors* in place. And if some actor from down in the hierarchy fails and can communicate the failure to parent actor, the parent actor, based on the type of failure, can restart/kill the actor or perform some other operation as required. This is in a sense supervising the actors below in the hierarchy; let's say parent actors can supervise child actors. The way we define this strategy comes under the Akka defined supervision strategy.

Supervision in a sense is about reacting to *failures* within an actor's hierarchy. Apart from the *root guardian*, every *actor* has a parent/supervisor to supervise. Every actor when instantiated becomes a part of a *default supervision strategy*. It's also important to observe that *failures* need a separate channel to be communicated to supervisors. So, Akka has a separate group of *system level actors,* which deal with the communication of such messages.

Since we deal with actors in case of failures also, our reactions should be in terms of actor-specific actions.

Hence, think about the actions a supervisor can perform:

- Resume child actors
- Restart child actors
- Stop child actors
- Escalate the failure

When a supervisor actor encounters a *failed child actor,* it can perform one of the actions described above. Depending on our preference, we might want to apply the strategy to all the children actors, regardless of if all of them failed or not. It's also possible to only *resume/restart/stop* the failing child actor.

Based on the children on which the *supervision strategy* should be applied, we have two strategies, namely *OneForOneStrategy* and *AllForOneStrategy*. Let's take a look at them.

OneForOne versus AllForOne strategy

Take the scenario where we have `SimpleActor` and `AnotherSimpleActor` actors. There's one child actor for `SimpleActor` named `SimplerrActor`:

- **SimpleActor**: `/user/topLevelActor/simpleActor`
- **AnotherSimpleActor**: `/user/topLevelActor/anotherSimpleActor`
- **SimplerrActor**: `/user/topLevelActor/simpleActor/simplerrActor`

In such cases, the user guardian is going to take care of `topLevelActor` and `topLevelActor` is going to supervise `SimpleActor` and `AnotherSimpleActor`. If something goes wrong in `SimpleActor` and we want all the actors to resume/restart/stop, we can define an `AllForOneStrategy`. If we want to perform such actions only on the failed `SimpleActor` and its subsequent children, we can opt for `OneForOneStrategy`.

These two are defined as case classes in Scala, which takes a few parameters in the form of `maxNrOfRetries`, `withinTimeRange`, and `loggingEnabled`:

```
case class OneForOneStrategy(
  maxNrOfRetries:             Int      = -1,
  withinTimeRange:            Duration = Duration.Inf,
  override val loggingEnabled: Boolean  = true)

case class AllForOneStrategy(
  maxNrOfRetries:             Int      = -1,
  withinTimeRange:            Duration = Duration.Inf,
  override val loggingEnabled: Boolean  = true)
```

The first parameter is to specify the number of times we might want to retry the strategy on the child actor; we can make it an infinite number of times by specifying -1 as the number. After the specified number of times, the child actor will stop. A second parameter specifies the duration after which the next retry should happen. As shown, the value `Duration.Inf` specifies no time window at all. Finally, we have to specify the logging behavior; it expects a Boolean value, and by default, it's true and means enabled.

These two strategy classes extend the parent abstract class `SupervisorStrategy`. The way these two strategies work can be understood via the diagram here:

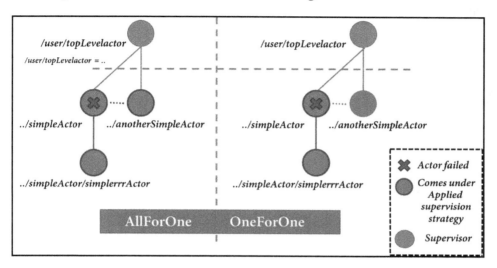

Now, the choice is ours to apply whichever strategy that suits our needs/situation. We define these strategies based on the type of failures; in the case that we've not covered a particular failure occurs, the failure gets escalated to the parent supervisor Actor. There's a defined set of actions performed by supervisors.

Default supervision strategy

By default, the Akka system looks for a few exception types from failure messages received from child Actors. Let's take a look at those scenarios.

The default supervision strategy will stop the failing child Actor in case of:

- `ActorInitializationException`
- `ActorKilledException`
- `DeathPactException`

Note that in case of exception, it'll restart the failing Actor.

With this information, let's try implementing one strategy on our own.

Applying the supervision strategy

While overriding the default `supervisorStrategy`, all we do is define the value with arguments and provide a `Decider`; this decider contains the logic to be implemented in case of exceptions. It looks like this:

```
import akka.actor.SupervisorStrategy.{Resume, Restart}

override val supervisorStrategy =
  OneForOneStrategy(
    maxNrOfRetries = 3,
    withinTimeRange = 1 minute
  ){
    case _: ArithmeticException => {
      log.info("Supervisor handling ArithmeticException! n Resuming!")
      Resume
    }
    case _: Exception => {
      log.info("Supervisor handling Exception! n Restarting!")
      Restart
    }
  }
```

Here, we have defined a `OneForOneStrategy`, and on a case by case basis, the action to be performed in regards to the failing actor. A full example with this strategy in place can look like the following:

```
package example

import akka.actor.{Actor, ActorSystem, OneForOneStrategy, Props,
ActorLogging}
import scala.concurrent.duration._

object SupervisionStrategyInPractice extends App {
  val system = ActorSystem("anActorSystem")

  val topLevelActor = system.actorOf(TopLevelActor.props)

  //Sending StopIt
  topLevelActor ! TopLevelActor.StopIt
  //Sending RestartIt
  topLevelActor ! TopLevelActor.RestartIt
}

class TopLevelActor extends Actor with ActorLogging {
  import akka.actor.SupervisorStrategy.{Resume, Restart
```

```scala
import TopLevelActor._

override val preStart = log.info(s"TopLevelActor started!")
override val postStop = log.info(s"TopLevelActor stopping!")

val superSimpleActor = context.actorOf(SuperSimpleActor.props)

override def receive = {
  case StopIt => superSimpleActor ! SuperSimpleActor.ArithmeticOpRequest
  case RestartIt => superSimpleActor ! SuperSimpleActor.OtherMessage
}

override val supervisorStrategy =
  OneForOneStrategy(
    maxNrOfRetries = 3,

    withinTimeRange = 1 minute
  ){
    case _: ArithmeticException => {
      log.info("Supervisor handling ArithmeticException! n Resuming!")
      Resume
    }
    case _: Exception => {
      log.info("Supervisor handling Exception! n Restarting!")
      Restart
    }
  }
}


object TopLevelActor {
 val props = Props[TopLevelActor]
 case object StopIt
 case object RestartIt
}

class SuperSimpleActor extends Actor with ActorLogging {
  import SuperSimpleActor._

  override val preStart = log.info(s"SuperSimpleActor started!")
  override val postStop = log.info(s"SuperSimpleActor stopping!")

  override def preRestart(reason: Throwable, message: Option[Any]): Unit =
    log.info(s"SuperSimpleActor restarting!")

  override def receive = {
    case ArithmeticOpRequest => 1 / 0
    case OtherMessage => throw new Exception("Some Exception Occurred!")
```

```
    }

  }

  object SuperSimpleActor {
    val props = Props[SuperSimpleActor]

    case object ArithmeticOpRequest
    case object OtherMessage

  }
```

As shown in the code, we have a `TopLevelActor`, which sends messages to its child Actor `SuperSimpleActor`, hence, `TopLevelActor` becomes a supervisor for its child actor. We have overridden the `supervisorStrategy`. According to the new Strategy, we can resume/restart based on the types of exceptions. The rest of the example is self-explanatory. We've logged the start and restart steps of our actors by overriding `preStart` *and* `preRestart` methods. Upon running the example, we'll get the logged output.

Run:

```
[INFO] [12/28/2017 13:35:39.856] [anActorSystem-akka.actor.default-
dispatcher-2] [akka://anActorSystem/user/$a] TopLevelActor started!
[INFO] [12/28/2017 13:35:39.856] [anActorSystem-akka.actor.default-
dispatcher-2] [akka://anActorSystem/user/$a] TopLevelActor stopping!
[INFO] [12/28/2017 13:35:39.857] [anActorSystem-akka.actor.default-
dispatcher-3] [akka://anActorSystem/user/$a/$a] SuperSimpleActor started!
[INFO] [12/28/2017 13:35:39.857] [anActorSystem-akka.actor.default-
dispatcher-3] [akka://anActorSystem/user/$a/$a] SuperSimpleActor stopping!
[INFO] [12/28/2017 13:35:39.864] [anActorSystem-akka.actor.default-
dispatcher-2] [akka://anActorSystem/user/$a] Supervisor handling
ArithmeticException!
 Resuming!
[WARN] [12/28/2017 13:35:39.865] [anActorSystem-akka.actor.default-
dispatcher-2] [akka://anActorSystem/user/$a/$a] / by zero
[INFO] [12/28/2017 13:35:39.867] [anActorSystem-akka.actor.default-
dispatcher-2] [akka://anActorSystem/user/$a] Supervisor handling Exception!
 Restarting!
[ERROR] [12/28/2017 13:35:39.868] [anActorSystem-akka.actor.default-
dispatcher-2] [akka://anActorSystem/user/$a/$a] Some Exception Occurred!
java.lang.Exception: Some Exception Occurred! at
example.SuperSimpleActor$$anonfun$receive$2.applyOrElse(SupervisionStrategy
InPractice.scala:66)
    at akka.actor.Actor.aroundReceive(Actor.scala:517)
    at akka.actor.Actor.aroundReceive$(Actor.scala:515)
    at
example.SuperSimpleActor.aroundReceive(SupervisionStrategyInPractice.scala:
```

```
55) ...
[INFO] [12/28/2017 13:35:39.868] [anActorSystem-akka.actor.default-
dispatcher-3] [akka://anActorSystem/user/$a/$a] SuperSimpleActor
restarting!
[INFO] [12/28/2017 13:35:39.871] [anActorSystem-akka.actor.default-
dispatcher-3] [akka://anActorSystem/user/$a/$a] SuperSimpleActor started!
[INFO] [12/28/2017 13:35:39.871] [anActorSystem-akka.actor.default-
dispatcher-3] [akka://anActorSystem/user/$a/$a] SuperSimpleActor stopping!
```

Since these failures are communicated via system level actors, the order of messages logged does not matter.

With this example, we've pretty much covered how we can implement a supervisor strategy for our Actor.

Akka library also provides `akka-testkit` for the testing of actors. It comes with a construct which make it easier to test actors. Let's go through the library and write unit test cases for our actor implementation.

Testing actors

For the testing of Actors that we create, we might consider few entities that are needed to be present. These entities might be:

- A test actor-system
- A `testActor` (the message sender)
- The actor under testing (whose behavior we want to test)
- Assertions to be made in case of an actors expected message

Akka's `test-kit` library provides us with all of these needed entities ready-made. We can use these to test our actors. Let's write a simple actor test case.

The expect case is to check if our `GetPlayerInformationRequest` works fine:

```scala
package lsp

import akka.actor.ActorSystem
import akka.testkit.{ImplicitSender, TestKit}
import lsp.SimpleActor.{GetPlayerInformationRequest,
PlayerInformationResponse}
import org.scalatest.{BeforeAndAfterAll, WordSpecLike}

class SimpleActorSpec extends TestKit(ActorSystem("testActorSystem"))
  with ImplicitSender with WordSpecLike with BeforeAndAfterAll {

  override def afterAll(): Unit = super.afterAll()

  val players = List(Player("Cristiano Ronaldo", "Portuguese", "32", "Real
Madrid", "La Liga", "1999", "1999", "1", "1"))

  "SimpleActor" must {

    "test for PlayerInformationRequest" in {

      val simpleActor = system.actorOf(SimpleActor.props)

      simpleActor ! GetPlayerInformationRequest("Cristiano Ronaldo",
players)

      val expectedResponse =
        PlayerInformationResponse(Some(Player("Cristiano Ronaldo",
"Portuguese", "32", "Real Madrid", "La Liga", "1999", "1999", "1", "1")))

      expectMsg(expectedResponse)
    }
  }
}
```

The previous code is a very simple example of how we can write an Actor test case. We should make sure that the test case we write is in the test directory:

Before we discuss our *test case,* let's run it. To run it, we can simply right-click using mouse and choose the **Run** option. In our case, the test case should pass. Now, let's take a look at the case we wrote.

The first thing to observe is the declaration we wrote:

```
class SimpleActorSpec extends TestKit(ActorSystem("testActorSystem"))
    with ImplicitSender with WordSpecLike with BeforeAndAfterAll
```

We named our actor test case `SimpleActorSpec`, and extended `Testkit` by passing an `ActorSystem` for testing purposes. We've also mixed in `ImplicitSender`, which in turn returns the response from our actor under test, `SimpleActor`. Finally, `WordSpecLike` and the other `BeforeAndAfterAll` are just to provide DSL-like syntax methods for writing test cases. We can see these syntax methods in the form of must and in.

In the implementation, we've done what's expected, created the actor under the test's reference, and provided dummy data as in the players list. We also created a dummy response that's expected from our `SimpleActor`. The following line sends the message to `SimpleActor`, which in turn responds back:

```
simpleActor ! GetPlayerInformationRequest("Cristiano Ronaldo",
players)
```

The assertion part is handled using the `expectMsg` method. Here, we compared the dummy response to the expected response. For assertion purposes, `scala-test` library provides many alternatives.

With this, we wrote a simple test case for our `SimpleActor`. We've covered all the basics we need to understand and write actors in Akka. There are a few advanced configuration-related topics such as *dispatchers, mailbox implementations*, and *routing* you might want to have a look at. For those, we can first thank the beautifully covered standard *documentation* of Akka available at: `https://doc.akka.io/docs/akka/2.5.8/index-actors.html`.

And if you still have a question in mind about what's next or where to go from here, let me tell you there's way more that Akka provides. We've already talked about Akka as a set of open source libraries. These libraries are available for different problems. Libraries such as `akka-http`, streams, and clustering provide you with respective solutions. The good part is all these libraries are based on the abstraction of actor-model. And we have covered that in our chapter, so let's summarize what we've learnt in this chapter.

Summary

This chapter was an introduction to Akka for us. We tried to understand the basic underlying principle of actors. We've covered one of the most important libraries Akka provides, `akka-actors`. Starting from why we need a library of this sort, to understanding the way we implement Actors in Akka, we covered it all. Then from there, we covered the important supervision strategy in Akka. We talked about and practiced our own custom supervisor strategy. Finally, we had a look at `akka-testkit`, a testkit provided by Akka. With this, we covered what was needed to understand Akka actors and the basics of it. In the next chapter, we'll focus on how we can handle concurrency in Scala. We know it's importance in modern architecture, so the next chapter will be an exciting one.

13
Concurrent Programming in Scala

"Yesterday is not ours to recover, but today is to try and tomorrow is to win or lose."

- Anonymous

The idea that modern computers with multicore architectures give better performance is based on the fact that multiple processors can run separate processes simultaneously. Each process can run more than one thread to complete specific tasks. Picturing this, we can write programs with multiple threads working simultaneously to ensure better performance and responsiveness. We call this concurrent programming. In this chapter, our goal is to understand Scala's offerings in concurrent programming. There are multiple ways we can use constructs to write concurrent programs. We'll learn about them in this chapter. Let's check out what will be here for us:

- Concurrent programming
- Building blocks of concurrency:
    - Process and threads
    - Synchronization and locks
    - Executor and ExecutionContext
    - Lock free programming
- Asynchronous programming using Futures and Promises
- Parallel Collections

Before we start learning about the ways we can write concurrent programs, it's important to understand the underlying picture. Let's start understanding concurrent programming and then we'll go through the basic building blocks of concurrency.

Concurrent programming

It's a programming approach where a set of computations can be performed simultaneously. These set of computations might share the same resources such as memory. How's it different from sequential programming? In sequential programming, every computation can be performed one after another. In the case of concurrent programs, more than one computation can be performed in the same time period.

By executing multiple computations, we can perform multiple logical operations in the program at the same time, resulting in better performance. Programs can run faster than before. This may sound cool; concurrency actually makes implementing real scenarios easier. Think about an internet browser; we can stream our favorite videos and download some content at the same time. The download thread does not affect the streaming of the video in any way. This is possible because content download and video streams on a browser tab are separate logical program parts, and hence can run simultaneously.

Similarly, in programs where we might have the user to perform some I/O operations for input, at the same time we want to run the program. We need these two parts to run simultaneously. Running these parts together makes it responsive to user interactions. Writing a concurrent program comes in handy in such cases. From a very cool web application running on an internet browser to games running on your mobile device, responsiveness and good user experience is possible because of concurrent programs.

This is why learning about concurrency abstractions is important, and what's more important is to keep them simple in our program implementations. So, let's go through the basic building blocks of concurrency.

Building blocks of concurrency

Scala is a JVM-based language, so programs written in Scala run in JVM. **JVM**, as we already know, is **Java Virtual Machine**, and runs as a single process in our operating system. In JVM, one of the basic concurrency constructs is a *thread*; we can create/use multiple threads as part of our Scala program. So, for a basic understanding of processes and threads, let's go through them.

Understanding processes and threads

Think of a process as a program or application that our computer might have to run. This process is going to have some code that's executable, a **process identifier** (pid), and at least one thread of execution. The process might consume some computer resources as well, such as memory. Every process isolates itself from other processes when it comes to consume memory; this means two processes cannot use the same memory block.

Modern computers come with multiple processor cores. These cores are assigned tasks as executable program parts for execution in certain time slices. The task of assigning these executable parts is done by the operating system. Most of the operating systems nowadays use a mechanism called **pre-emptive multitasking**, which is the simultaneous execution of multiple executable parts from all running processes. These executable parts are nothing but threads. It means that each process needs to have at least one thread, we can call it the main thread, in order to run properly.

It's clear that the process within an operating system uses some memory resources, and it can contain multiple threads. Now, these threads from a particular process are free to share the memory block assigned, but two processes cannot do the same. It'll be easier to understand this with the help of the following figure:

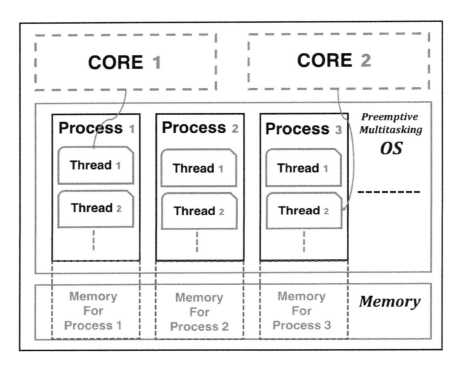

The previous diagram is a simplified version for a system with two processor cores, a *preemptive multitasking operating system* and *memory*. We have a separate memory resource allocated for different processes running, in our case, **Process 1**, **Process 2**, and **Process 3**. The memory block for **Process 1** has no access to the memory block for **Process 2** or **Process 3**. Each process contains more than one thread. Each thread can access the memory allocated from the parent process. These threads can share the memory allocated. Now, what happens is the operating system assigns these executable blocks, in other words *threads*, to process cores for execution, as shown in our preceding diagram.

In a particular time slice:

- **Core 1** is executing **Thread 1** from **Process 1**
- **Core 2** is executing **Thread 2** from **Process 3**

These two executions are happening simultaneously. We already know that JVM runs as a process; the programs we write are going to have threads as entities. For our program to run, we need at least a *main thread* that can be the entry point to our application. We can create more threads as instances of the `java.lang.Thread` class.

Now that we know we can have multiple parts of our application running together, it's important to understand that we need some way to synchronize them. By synchronizing, we can ensure one particular execution is not going to affect any other. Threads within a process have access to the same memory block, hence it might be possible that two threads try to access the memory at the same time—this might cause problems. Threads are low-level concurrency abstractions in Scala, and as the number of concurrent parts or threads increases, complexity also increases with them. To understand how do we restrict other threads to access some block of code simultaneously, first we need to understand how synchronization works.

Locks and synchronization

We talked about threads in previous sections—we'll first try to create a few ourselves before discussing them further. Let's write some code for that:

```scala
object ThreadFirstEncounter extends App {

  class FirstThread extends Thread {
    override def run(): Unit = println(s"FirstThread's run!")
  }

  val firstThread = new FirstThread()
  firstThread.start()

  println(s"CurrentThread: ${Thread.currentThread().getName}")
  println(s"firstThread: ${firstThread.getName}")

}
```

A few pointers for the preceding code:

1. We simply created an object extending `App` to create the application entry point.
2. We created a class named `FirstThread` that extends `Thread`, which is nothing but the same `java.lang.Thread` we talked about in the previous section.
3. When we create a thread, we might want to specify what it needs to run. That can be defined via overriding the `run` method.

4. Until *point 3*, we have defined our thread class; now, to run the thread, we'll create its instance, and then call the `start` method.

5. The `start` method triggers the execution of the thread.

6. Finally, we printed the thread's name. First, the `main` current thread, and then the `firstThread` class name.

Running the application will give us the following output:

```
FirstThread's run!
CurrentThread: main
firstThread: Thread-0
```

So from the first run, it's clear that a thread called `main` runs the application, and as we create more and more threads, these threads also come into the picture. It's great to have multiple threads working together for us to perform some computation. We know from our previous discussions that an OS performs the scheduling of task execution, so it's out of our control which thread will get executed in which order. Now, think of a scenario where you might want to perform a read and write operation to a variable in your program. With multiple threads performing such a task, it might be possible to see inconsistencies in the result. It means that this execution is exposed to *race conditions*; in other words, it depends on the execution schedule of statements by the OS. To better understand this, let's try out the scenario we discussed:

```scala
object TowardsLocking extends App {
  var counter = 0 // counter variable

  def readWriteCounter(): Int = {
    val incrementedCounter = counter + 1  //Reading counter
    counter = incrementedCounter // Writing to counter
    incrementedCounter
  }

  def printCounter(nTimes: Int): Unit = {
    val readWriteCounterNTimes = for(i <- 1 to nTimes) yield
readWriteCounter()
    println(s"${Thread.currentThread.getName} executing :: counter $nTimes
times:  $readWriteCounterNTimes")
  }

  class First extends Thread {
    override def run(): Unit = {
      printCounter(10)
    }
  }
}
```

```
val first = new First
first.start() // thread-0
printCounter(10)    // main thread

}
```

In this small application, we first create a variable `counter`; we are going to read and write to this variable using two threads. Next, we have two methods, first `readWriteCounter` and `printCounter`. The `readWriteCounter` method is doing as the name says. This method increments the counter (reading operation) and assigns the `incrementedCounter` to the `counter` variable. The second method, `printCounter`, takes an integer parameter to increment counter the number of times specified and prints that.

After defining all these, we created a thread with the name `First` and called our `printCounter` method, overriding the `run` method. To observe the behavior, we're supposed to call the `printCounter` from this `First` thread and the main application thread. Since two threads are working simultaneously, it's expected that output of these two shouldn't contain the same number. We also called `printCounter` from the application as the final statement of the program.

Running the program couple of times (if you're lucky, for the first time), you might be able to see some inconsistent behavior.

Run:

```
main executing :: counter 10 times:  Vector(1, 3, 5, 7, 9, 11, 13, 15, 17,
18)
Thread-0 executing :: counter 10 times:  Vector(1, 2, 4, 6, 8, 10, 11, 12,
14, 16)
```

In the output from both the threads, we can see the number 1 appeared twice, while we know it shouldn't have happened. We see that behaviour due to read and write operations happening to our `counter` variable via multiple threads in the following snippet:

```
def readWriteCounter(): Int = {
    val incrementedCounter = counter + 1  //Reading counter
    counter = incrementedCounter // Writing to counter
    incrementedCounter
}
```

By the time the `counter = incrementCounter` statement gets a chance to execute, the `counter` variable gets incremented twice (by multiple threads). This is causing inconsistency. The problem lies in the execution of these two statements; these have to be atomic in nature to give a consistent output where the same number cannot appear for different threads. By *atomic*, we mean these two statements have to be executed together by the same thread.

If we somehow achieve that atomicity for this block of code, it'll provide some satisfactory output to us. It feels like we need some synchronization mechanism which protects the block of code exposed. Using a synchronization mechanism, while the block is being executed by a single thread, no other thread should be able to execute that at the same time. This can be achieved using an *intrinsic locking* mechanism that puts a lock on the block and prevents other threads from executing that snippet of code. There's a *synchronized* statement in Scala, using which we can implement a locking mechanism. Let's try that and see how it looks:

```scala
object TowardsLockingOne extends App {
  var counter = 0 // counter variable

  def readWriteCounter(): Int = this.synchronized {
    val incrementedCounter = counter + 1  //Reading counter
    counter = incrementedCounter // Writing to counter
    incrementedCounter
  }

  def printCounter(nTimes: Int): Unit = {
    val readWriteCounterNTimes = for(i <- 1 to nTimes) yield
readWriteCounter()
    println(s"${Thread.currentThread.getName} executing :: counter $nTimes
times:  $readWriteCounterNTimes")
  }

  class First extends Thread {
    override def run(): Unit = {
      printCounter(10)
    }
  }

  val first = new First
  first.start() // thread-0

  printCounter(10)    // main thread
}
```

In the application, it can be seen that our concerned method block is not guarded by this *synchronized* statement:

```
def readWriteCounter(): Int = this.synchronized {
    val incrementedCounter = counter + 1   //Reading counter
    counter = incrementedCounter // Writing to counter
    incrementedCounter
}
```

By using this, we make the synchronized statement refer to the current object to guard the block. We could also make a particular instance of some type, let's say *Any* and that instance can work as a guard to our synchronised clock. It's shown as following:

```
val any = new Any()

def readWriteCounter(): Int = any.synchronized {
    val incrementedCounter = counter + 1   //Reading counter
    counter = incrementedCounter // Writing to counter
    incrementedCounter
}
```

By using a synchronized statement, we are able to put a lock on this snippet of code and only one thread can execute the code enclosed. Apart from synchronized statements, there are other synchronization mechanisms in Scala, in the forms of *volatile* and *atomic variables*. These are lightweight and less expensive than synchronized statements, and better in performance. They need additional mechanisms to ensure correct synchronization when you only use volatile variables large in numbers. We should be aware that OS scheduler can also freeze any thread for any reason, which might also cause a thread carrying locks to freeze. In this case, if a thread holding a lock gets frozen, it'll block execution of other threads as well; that's not something we want for sure.

Creating a thread is an expensive operation—if you have more computations, you want to perform concurrently and you create several threads to compute those. It'll be less performant and with some shared data access, your life will be worse. So, to prevent this costly operation from happening, JDK has come up with the concept of *thread-pools*. In *thread-pools*, there are multiple thread instances provided. These threads within a pool remain in *waiting* state; when you want to perform some computation, we can run these. The job of running these is done by the `executor`. Let's try to understand it.

Executor and ExecutionContext

Executor is an interface that encapsulates the *thread-pool* and deals with executing computations via one of the threads or the caller thread itself. One example of an executor is `java.util.concurrent.ForkJoinPool`. Scala's implementation of such an executor is `ExecutionContext` which internally uses the same `ForkJoinPool`. Before going further to see an example, why not think of the need for this `Executor` mechanism?

As programmers, while writing performance-efficient concurrent applications, we might have to deal with two major tasks, the first being defining instances of concurrency abstraction, let's say *threads*, and making sure they handle our data/state in the right manner. Second, to use these *threads* in our program. Now, the creation of all these threads, if created by us, are:

- Costly operations
- Complex to manage

Hence, mechanisms like `Executor` take away the work of creating these threads. We don't explicitly decide which thread will execute the logic we provide; we also don't need to manage those. Executor implementations, when used, create daemon and worker threads. When we assign computation via the `execute` method, a particular worker thread is assigned the task. Shutting down a daemon thread shuts down all the worker threads. This'll be easier to understand with the help of the following code snippet:

```scala
import java.util.concurrent.ForkJoinPool
import scala.concurrent.{ExecutionContext, ExecutionContextExecutor}

object TowardsExecutor extends App {

  val executor: ForkJoinPool = new java.util.concurrent.ForkJoinPool()
  executor.execute(new Runnable {
    override def run(): Unit =
      println(s"${Thread.currentThread().getName()} printing this in
execution of juc.ForkJoinPool!")
  })

  val ec: ExecutionContextExecutor = ExecutionContext.global
  ec.execute(new Runnable {
    override def run(): Unit =
      println(s"${Thread.currentThread().getName()} printing this in
execution of sc.ExecutionContext!")
  })
}
```

In the application, we used two `Executor` implementations; the first is from `java.util.concurrent.ForkJoinPool` and the second is similar to Scala-specific `ExecutionContext`:

```
val executor: ForkJoinPool = new java.util.concurrent.ForkJoinPool()
val ec: ExecutionContextExecutor = ExecutionContext.global
```

For both implementations, we have an execute method, which expects a `Runnable` instance. To create `Runnable` instances, we have to define a run method. It's another way to create a thread instance. In the definition of the run method, we just printed the executor thread's name.

But running the above program gives you no output. The reason for such behavior is that both the implementations create a *daemon thread,* which shuts down after the first run. Shutdown of a daemon thread kills all worker threads. Calling the `execute` method wakes up `workerthreads`. These `workerthreads` execute the run method asynchronously. Hence, we'll try to include some timeout to wait for a small duration as the last statement by calling the `Thread.sleep` method:

```
import java.util.concurrent.ForkJoinPool
import scala.concurrent.{ExecutionContext, ExecutionContextExecutor}

object TowardsExecutor extends App {

  val executor: ForkJoinPool = new java.util.concurrent.ForkJoinPool()
  executor.execute(new Runnable {
    override def run(): Unit =
      println(s"${Thread.currentThread().getName()} printing this in
execution of juc.ForkJoinPool!")
  })

  val ec: ExecutionContextExecutor = ExecutionContext.global
  ec.execute(new Runnable {
    override def run(): Unit =
      println(s"${Thread.currentThread().getName()} printing this in
execution of sc.ExecutionContext!")
  })
  Thread.sleep(500)

}
```

Run:

```
scala-execution-context-global-11 printing this in execution of
sc.ExecutionContext!
ForkJoinPool-1-worker-1 printing this in execution of juc.ForkJoinPool!
```

After including some waiting time for the execution by the worker threads, we get the output. As shown, the output tells us the *thread* names: both are *worker threads*. The first one, named `scala-execution-context-global-11`, is from Scala's `ExecutionContext` and the second, named `ForkJoinPool-1-worker-1`, is from Java's `ForkJoinPool`.

These *thread-pools* and their implementations become the basis for higher-level concurrency abstractions. We also encountered a bit of asynchrony in the example when we waited for the result of the execution. It's not wrong to say asynchrony is subsumed in *concurrency*, as asynchronous programs tend to execute outside of the main flow of the program. Hence, multiple async computations can be performed at the same time; once we get back the results for these computations, we can perform the desired operation then.

Scala provides constructs from the standard library for asynchronous programming, as well as multiple libraries that provide async constructs to make it easier to develop programs for us, the developers. Let's go through those constructs.

Asynchronous programming

If we try to define *asynchronous programming,* we come up with something that states that it's a programming approach in which computations, which can be *tasks or threads,* execute outside of the basic program flow. In programming terminologies, these computations execute on different call stacks, not the current one. Because of this, it's possible for us to think of more than one async computation happening at the same time; we can wait for each to happen so that aggregation of a result or some other result manipulation is possible.

Up until now, we've looked at three of these terminologies such as *concurrency, multithreading,* and *asynchronous.* We tend to confuse these but given our discussions, it's clear that *asynchronous* subsumes *concurrency* and not *multithreading.* We know that asynchrony can be achieved using scheduling:

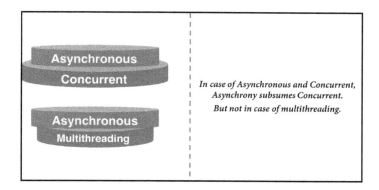

In case of Asynchronous and Concurrent,
Asynchrony subsumes Concurrent.
But not in case of multithreading.

Well, the fact that we have to compose the results of multiple async problems running at the same time means we might end up needing some sort of synchronization. Fortunately, we don't have to deal with managing these cumbersome tasks, as Scala's offerings manage those using the `ExecutionContext`. One of those asynchronous offerings is *Futures* in Scala. Let's talk about `Futures` in Scala.

Working with Futures

The idea here is simple; we have our simple program flow. If we make some complex time-consuming computation in the main program flow, it'll be blocking and the experience won't be good. Hence, we want to perform that time-consuming computation outside of the basic program flow, and continue doing other stuff in the main program flow, keeping the value (that will be available at a later point in time) of computation. Once the value is available, we use it via a mechanism. The way we can picture this is as follows:

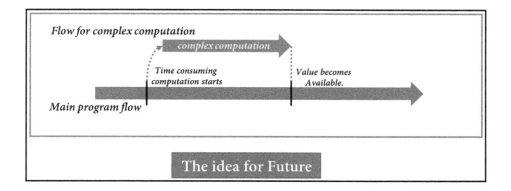

For now, the two entities we can think of are: Futurecomputation and a future value. These two are different; a Future computation is the time-consuming part you want to compute asynchronously and future value is the value reference on which we depend on our program flow. Once the Future computation starts in a separate flow, the program does not stop its execution and when the value becomes available, the part gets executed. The ExecutionContext takes care of the execution of that part, where we may use the value Future.

It's clear that whenever we start some Future computation, we might have to provide an execution context with it. In Scala, the Future type resides in the scala.concurrent package, the same package that has ExecutionContext and its executor ExecutionContextExecutor.

The Future value is represented by Future[T], where T is the type of the value that'll be available at some later point in time. Hence in our programs, whenever we need some value that's a result of some asynchronous computation, we represent that value with this mentioned type. An example will clear this up:

```scala
import scala.concurrent._
import scala.concurrent.ExecutionContext.Implicits.global

object FutureExample extends App {

  val fileSource =
"/Users/vika/Documents/LSProg/LSPWorkspace/FirstProject/src/chapter5/football_stats.csv"

  def listOfPlayers(): Future[List[Player]] = Future {
    val source = io.Source.fromFile(fileSource)
    val list = source.getLines().toList
    source.close()
    giveMePlayers(list)
  }

  println(s"listOfPlayers completed: ${listOfPlayers.isCompleted}")

  Thread.sleep(500)

  println(s"listOfPlayers completed: ${listOfPlayers.isCompleted}")

  def giveMePlayers(list: List[String]): List[Player] = list match {
    case head :: tail => tail map {line =>
      val columns = line.split((",")).map(_.trim)
      Player(columns(5),columns(6),columns(9),columns(7),
        columns(8),columns(10), columns(12), columns(0),columns(2))
```

```
    }
    case Nil => List[Player]()
  }

}

case class Player(name: String, nationality: String, age:String, club:
String, domesticLeague: String, rawTotal: String, finalScore:
String,ranking2016: String, ranking2015: String)
```

Run:

```
listOfPlayers completed: false
listOfPlayers completed: true
```

In this simple application, we specified a file with some content. The file has information about few football players. Now, to read the file contents as well as parsing and encoding them to `Player` instances may take some time, hence we decided to take the `load`, `parse`, and `encode` step as a Future computation, and the resulting value is going to be a Future value of type `Future[List[Player]]`.

Now, after defining such a computation, we checked if computation completed. Then we waited for some time and again tried to check if it completed. Running the application gives us `false` and then `true` respectively. If we think of this example via a diagram the flow might look like this:

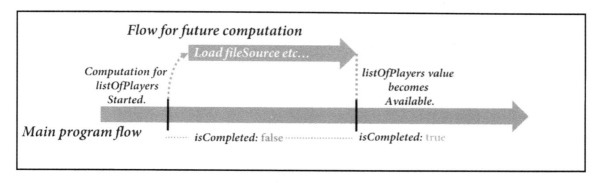

It's easy to understand the execution flow with the help of this diagram; for the duration in which the computation is in progress, the `isCompleted` flag remains false. After completion, it's set to true. After that, we can use the value of future, but in this example, we didn't use the value; also, the question arises of how we can use it. Do we have to check again and again for the value to be available? This sounds bad, so another way is to register a *callback* for this async computation.

Okay, what's a callback? To answer this, let's first extend our program to register one for our Future computation:

```scala
import scala.concurrent._
import scala.concurrent.ExecutionContext.Implicits.global

object FutureExample extends App {

  val fileSource =
"/Users/vika/Documents/LSProg/LSPWorkspace/FirstProject/src/chapter13/footb
all_stats.csv"

  val listOfPlayers: Future[List[Player]] = Future {
    val source = io.Source.fromFile(fileSource)
    val list = source.getLines().toList

    source.close()

    giveMePlayers(list)
  }

  def giveMePlayers(list: List[String]): List[Player] = list match {
    case head :: tail => tail map {line =>
      val columns = line.split((",")).map(_.trim)
      Player(columns(5),columns(6),columns(9),columns(7),
        columns(8),columns(10), columns(12), columns(0),columns(2))
    }
    case Nil => List[Player]()
  }

  // Registering a callback
  listOfPlayers foreach {
    case list => list foreach println
  }

  Thread.sleep(5000)

}

case class Player(name: String, nationality: String, age: String, club:
String, domesticLeague: String, rawTotal: String, finalScore:
String,ranking2016: String, ranking2015: String)
```

So, the previous snippet is the same program; the only difference is that in the few final statements of our program, we've a call to a `foreach` function, on Future value. This is exactly what we mean when we say registering a *callback*. When the value of Future computation becomes available, it gets executed. That's going to work only if we get some value out of our Future computation. But we should be aware of the fact that the computation might fail. In that case, this callback is not going to be executed. The task of callback execution is taken care of by the execution context.

It's worth noting that callbacks are one of the ways we handle the result of an async computation. At the same time, we know that we need to provide some execution context that manages when and where the computation takes place as well as when the *callback* gets executed. This allows us to register more than one callback to a single async computation with a random execution order. The execution of callback in a random manner can be explained by this extended version of the previous diagram; now, we have callback as well in the diagram:

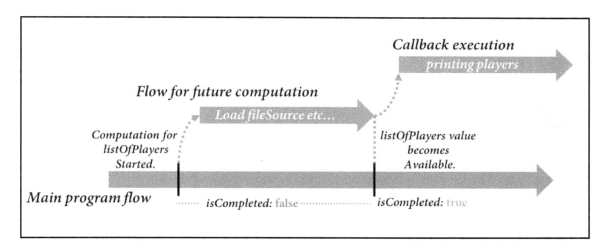

The callback execution only happens after the completion of the Future computation, as depicted in the diagram. The execution of *callbacks* takes place only if the computation gets successfully completed. In other cases, there should be a way to tell the program that things went wrong so that we can do something with it. Let's see what we can do about this big question.

What if Future computations go wrong?

The Future computation might succeed, resulting in a value, or fail, ending up throwing an exception. We need a mechanism to handle both the scenarios. Scala's Future has this mechanism as a method, `onComplete`. First let's see it in practice; to do that, let's comment the callback code snippet we added last time, and add this snippet:

```
listOfPlayers onComplete {
  case Success(list) => list foreach println
  case Failure(_) => println(s"listOfPlayers couldn't be fetched.")
}
```

The previous snippet is also a callback named `onComplete`, which gets called once the Future's value is available; in other words, when Future gets completed. Let's take a look at the `onComplete` method's signature for a `Future[T]`:

```
def onComplete[U](f: Try[T] => U)(implicit executor: ExecutionContext):
Unit
```

The function expects a function to execute; we have to also provide the execution context. The function literal is of type `Try[T] => U`. Fortunately, the execution context is taken from the implicit scope. Hence, we can directly provide the partial function to execute; in our case, we provided the same. Now, there's a possibility that one async call depends on the result of another async call, and in this case we might have to perform nesting of callback functions. This might look something like this:

```
import scala.concurrent.Future
import scala.concurrent.ExecutionContext.Implicits.global
import scala.util.{Failure, Success}

object TowardsFutureComposition extends App {

def firstFuture: Future[String] = Future { "1" }
def secondFuture(str: String): Future[Int] = Future { str.toInt }

  firstFuture onComplete {
    case Success(value1) =>
        secondFuture(value1) onComplete {
      case Success(value2) => println(s"Converted int: $value2")
      case Failure(exception) => println(s"Conversion failed due to
  ${exception.getMessage} ")
    }
    case Failure(excep) => Future.failed(excep)
```

```
    }

    Thread.sleep(5000)
  }
```

In the previous code, we have only two futures nested along with *callbacks,* and this already seems like it should be done in simpler manner. Now think about more of such futures and callbacks together. It'll be a callback hell. Hence, what's needed here is composition. That's one of the powers of Scala Futures; you can compose two futures to perform some complex logic that contains the nesting of callbacks. How can we do that? By using the set of higher order functions given to us in Scala's Future API. Let's check it out.

Why not compose two or more Futures?

Now that we've got the previous toy example where we had two Futures called in sequence, let's compose over those two. What we'll do is first call the `flatMap` function on `firstFuture`, and that'll give us the value. We'll take that value and call `secondFuture`. Finally, we'll call the `map` function to perform the print operation:

```
object FutureComposition extends App {

  def firstFuture: Future[String] = Future { "1" }

  def secondFuture(str: String): Future[Int] = Future { str.toInt }

  firstFuture flatMap ( secondFuture(_) ) map(result => println(s"Converted
int: $result"))

  Thread.sleep(5000)
}
```

Run:

```
Converted int: 1
```

The whole callback logic is magically gone and we have used Future composition to achieve the same. All the magic happens in the line:

```
firstFuture flatMap ( secondFuture(_) ) map(result => println(s"Converted
int: $result"))
```

So, let's try to understand this with the help of a diagram:

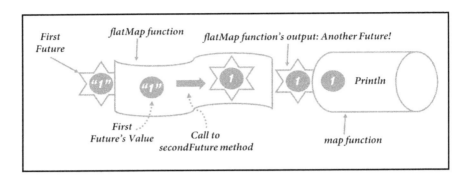

As shown, stars here represent a Future; we take the first future and call the `flatMap` function on it. The `flatMap` function's signature looks like this:

```
def flatMap[S](f: T => Future[S])(implicit executor: ExecutionContext):
Future[S]
```

Comparing the signature to the diagram, we can see that the `flatMap` function takes the future value and calls subsequent calls to get another Future. The output of the `flatMap` function happens to be another Future value, hence we call a `map` function that sucks the value out of future, and then we can perform whatever operation we want to perform; in our case, we just printed the value. And from our previous knowledge, we know, comprehension works as a syntactic hack to our `flatMap` and map call. So, the following code also works well for our future's composition:

```
for {
  value1 <- firstFuture
  value2 <- secondFuture(value1)
} yield println(s"Converted int: $value2")
```

A point to note is that in our `for` comprehension, the second statement only gets executed once the first value, `value1`, is available. That lets us use the first value in the second statement, as shown in the example. So, that's all for future's composition. This mechanism lets us chain several future/async calls together. This composition makes Scala's Future so powerful.

So, we've just discussed the way we create a Future computation by creating a future object; it's worth knowing that Scala also provides a mechanism to assign a particular value to this future object. That mechanism exists in the form of Promises. Let's introduce ourselves to Scala's Promises.

Working with Promises

As we talked about, Promises are used to assign a value to a future object. A Promise itself is an object that corresponds to a particular future object. We can access this `future` object by calling `future` method on the respective Promise. Let's start by creating a Promise object first:

```
import scala.concurrent._
import scala.concurrent.ExecutionContext.Implicits.global

object ItsAPromise extends App {

  val firstPromise = Promise[String]

  for {
    value1 <- firstPromise.future
  } yield println(s"Value1: $value1")

  firstPromise.success("1")

  Thread.sleep(500)
}
```

Run:

```
Value1: 1
```

In the previous code, we created a `Promise` instance by simply calling the `Promise.apply` method:

```
def apply[T](): Promise[T]
```

Here, the `apply` method takes no parameters, hence the `Promise` instance contains no value in itself; the assignment of values to this object can be done using one of the methods available in the Promise API. Methods like `success`, `failure`, and `complete` are used to assign values to a `Promise` instance. Each `Promise` instance's corresponding Future can be obtained by calling the `future` method. In our example, we called the `success` method on the `Promise` object to assign a value to a linked future. We also used this for comprehension to retrieve the future's value and print it. Running this program will yield the result we passed via this call to success:

```
firstPromise.success("1")
```

We can also assign a failure object to linked futures via a call to the `failure` method. There are a few points to note:

- Calling the `Promise.apply` method creates an instance without values, just like we did with Futures
- Promises do not start any asynchronous computations
- Each Promise corresponds to only one `Future` object
- Each Promise object can be assigned a value only once
- Promises provide a way to assign values to `Future` objects

These points clear up the concept of Promises, and also give us a hint about the implementation of the Future API in Scala.

Futures and Promises provide a simple abstraction over low-level constructs to achieve asynchrony in our programs. We've seen the ways we can use and compose these Futures to chain multiple async calls to get things done. There are other async libraries available in Scala to perform asynchronous programming. Some of the examples of these libraries are `scala-async` (`https://github.com/scala/scala-async`) and `monix` (`https://github.com/monix/monix`). You may want to check out these libraries to understand and try out other asynchronous programming constructs.

There might be use cases where a large collection of data needs to be manipulated to perform some logic. Let's take an example of our `football.csv` file. We've read the data and converted the lines from that to `List[String]`, and now every element can be parsed to a `Player` object giving us `List[Player]`. If we think a bit, the step where we need to parse `String` to `Player` does not need to be executed in sequence and can be done in parallel. Now, Scala comes up with the concept of *parallel* collections. Hence, if you need to do some functionality on data in some collections, functionality can be done in parallel. You have an option to convert the collection to its parallel counterpart by calling a simple method `par` on the usual collection. Let's look at parallel collections in Scala and try this out.

Parallel collections

Well, before discussing parallel collections in Scala, it's important to have some insight about what parallel computation is. How's it different from concurrent and asynchronous?

Well, we have spent some time understanding that asynchronous computation is non-blocking, hence we know that async computation happens from outside of the main program flow and gives you the value once the computation gets completed. To understand the difference between *concurrent* and *parallel* computation, let's look at the following example:

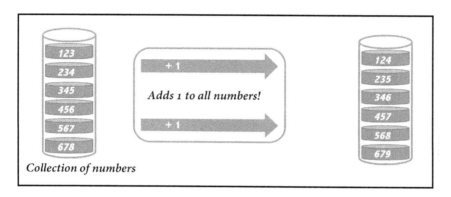

In the example, we are given a collection of numbers where we want to apply a function to each element of the collection to get a new collection. One method is to take a value out from the starting collection, add one to it, and put that value in a new collection, until the first collection is empty. Now, this process can be made faster by introducing *two* threads to perform the task of adding one to an element of the collection; let's put it another way by saying we can create two *threads* to enable *concurrent access* to our collection:

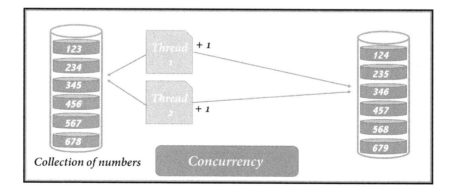

Another way can be to break down the collection into two sub collections and perform the task of adding in parallel. This parallelism is possible because the kind of operation we perform is not related to the sequence of elements in the starting collection, nor does it depend on any other element in the collection. Hence, the operation can be carried out in a separate manner in parallel. That's what the difference between concurrent and parallel computations is. The semantics themselves explain whether parallelism is applicable or not:

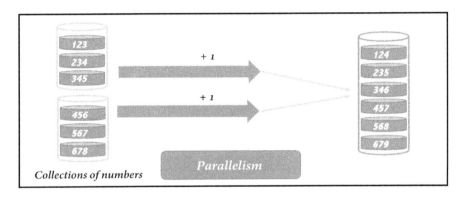

This becomes the basis of *parallel collections* in Scala. Let's try out our well-known example with the `football.csv` file. We'll convert the `List[String]` to its parallel counterpart and then perform the parsing logic in parallel:

```
import scala.collection.parallel.immutable.ParSeq
import scala.concurrent.Future
import scala.util.{Failure, Success}
import scala.concurrent.ExecutionContext.Implicits.global

object TowardsParallelCollections extends App {

  val fileSource =
"/Users/vika/Documents/LSProg/LSPWorkspace/FirstProject/src/chapter13/footb
all_stats.csv"

  val listOfPlayers: Future[List[Player]] = Future {
    val source = io.Source.fromFile(fileSource)
    val list: List[String] = source.getLines().toList

    source.close()

    val parSequence = list.par.tail
    val playerParSequence: ParSeq[Player] = parSequence.map {
      case line => val columns = line.split((",")).map(_.trim)
```

```
        Player(columns(5),columns(6),columns(9),columns(7),
            columns(8),columns(10), columns(12), columns(0),columns(2))
    }


    playerParSequence.toList
}

listOfPlayers foreach {
    case list => list foreach println
}

Thread.sleep(5000)

}
```

In the example, we converted the `List[String]` to a `ParSeq` that is *a parallel* counterpart of our Scala collection `List`. After converting to a parallel collection, we called a `map` method on the parallel collection and performed the parsing operation. The parallel collection API is so consistent that it looks so normal to call the `map` method and perform some operation, but underlying task execution is taken care of by multiple processors at the same time; in other words, computations are happening in parallel. Running the previous code will print out the list of players as expected.

Scala's parallel collections reside in the `scala.collection.parallel` package. To create one parallel collection, we can either use the new keyword along with the collection name or we can convert a sequential collection to its parallel counterpart by calling the `par` function, which we did in our example.

A few of the available parallel collections are:

- `ParArray`
- `ParVector`
- `mutable.ParHashMap`
- `mutable.ParHashSet`
- `immutable.ParHashMap`
- `immutable.ParHashSet`
- `ParRange`
- `ParTrieMap`

We can instantiate these parallel collections the same way we do for sequential collections; that's the power of Scala's parallel collections. This makes a lot of collection-based computations faster to perform. With this, we can go and summarize our chapter.

Summary

In this chapter, we learned about the building blocks of concurrency in Scala. It was fascinating to understand the underlying blocks of concurrency in OS and JVM. We learned the difference between processes and threads. We discussed ExecutionContext and why we need one. Then, we talked about asynchronous programming using Future and Promises. Finally, we discussed parallel collections in Scala.

In our next chapter, we'll be discussing another important and much talked about reactive programming abstraction available in Scala. We'll go through the reactive extensions available in Scala.

14
Programming with Reactive Extensions

"We cannot solve our problems with the same thinking we used when we created them."

- Albert Einstein

It's beautiful when we give a new dimension to thinking while solving a problem. In programming, our approaches to solving problems may differ from each other. Most of the time, there's an interaction between the user and programs. GUI-based and web applications are a few examples of these applications. We can think of ways in which our application gets notified whenever the user tries to interact with it. It may be possible that our program awaits user's interactions or vice versa. In the opposite case, the user's interaction, at times, notifies the application of some kind of event. Let's say we write our programs to react to a user's interactions. This is the essence of being reactive as an application program. We write a program that acts as a system to the surrounding environment, and the environment itself pushes events to our programs. These events drive the whole system, hence they become the core of a reactive programming model. And that's just the beginning of being reactive, there are more concepts that emerge from this kind of model.

From the previous chapter, we have got the essence of asynchronous computations. Async computations include some kind of computation that will be performed in the near future and its callback, which gets executed when the computation gets completed.

Well, in this chapter, we'll continue with our understanding of asynchronous computations to understand reactive extensions, which are nothing but an API created while keeping the reactive programming model in mind. Here's what we'll be discussing:

- Reactive programming
- Reactive extensions
- Reacting to RxScala

Reactive programming, in one line, is the process of programming with asynchronous data streams. If that's not the definition you expect, let's try to get an idea about it. Let's think of it as a journey. We'll start from zero, with no understanding of what being reactive in programming terminologies is. As we proceed, we'll have interactions with a few concepts and mechanisms that form the reactive ecosystem. The final goal is to be able to think in Reactive. So let's start it.

Reactive programming

The best way to understand any new paradigm or concept is to reason about its existence. For this let's think of a very common and simple scenario, as shown here:

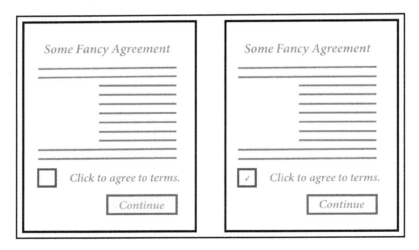

You might have come across the form behavior shown in the preceding figure. There's an agreement to read and then we click on the checkbox to agree to it so that we can proceed further. On the left-hand side, the checkbox is unchecked. Hence, based on its value, we have set the visibility of the **Continue** button (currently for the unchecked box) to false. Once we click and set the checkbox value to true, the visibility of the **Continue** button also becomes true. What is happening is when we click on checkbox, it emits an event with its value, that is, true/false. Now, based on its value, we can set the button's visibility to true/false. This is an example of observing events of a simple checkbox and making use of the event's value. If you picture this, it might look as follows:

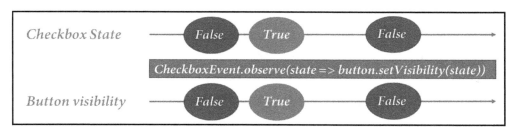

The following diagram shows the **Checkbox** state and button's visibility. We need not care about the code syntax because we're not talking about any language or frameworks for now. In this example, we only cared about a single event getting triggered by the checkbox. It was simple to understand. Now let's think of a computation that's reactive. Think of the following computation:

```
A := 5
B := A
C := A
D := B + C
```

The computation says **A** is going to have a value, **B** and **C** are going to have the same value as A, and, finally, **D** is going to be the result of the addition of **B** and **C**. So in normal programs, once you execute the statement, you get the values for **A**, **B**, **C**, and **D**. Now, let's think what happens when we consider time and also let the value flow in our system. What do we mean by that? Take a look at the following diagram:

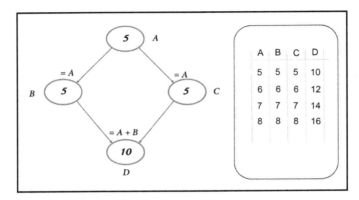

On the left-hand side, we have pictured the scenario which states the same as we mentioned previously. On the right-hand side, we have a table that consists of values of our variables at some instants of time. So let's say we update the value of **A** to 6:

```
A := 6
```

Now, this statement should increment the value of **B** and **C** because it's now in the reactive world. So when data is changes, it flows and changes all the dependent variables. Hence, **B** and **C** get updated to **6**, and finally because of the change in its dependents, the value of D also changes and becomes 12. Taking a look at the table, we can see that the values of B, C, and D get updated each time they observe a change in the value of **A**. Till now, we have not dealt with any particular terminology. But we've seen two examples: the first one gave the essence of *emitting events* and the second one gave the essence of *data flow* in the system containing variables. These are two important concepts of *reactive* programming. But wait, we also mentioned *reactive programming* is programming with asynchronous data streams. To understand this notion, think of the values of the **A** variable as values in a data stream. Now, at a particular instant in time, if we try to access the values of **A**, there are three possibilities:

- You get a value back
- You get an error when you try to fetch a value
- You get a message that the stream is completed and contains no more values

Picturing this, we'll get something similar to the following:

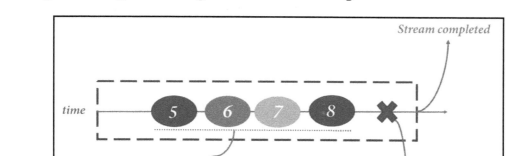

The previous diagram demonstrates the possible outcomes of a data stream. The following are a few important points to take away from the preceding diagram:

- All values are events occurring in time. So the order of these values will be maintained. After the stream completes, there's no possibility of any value getting emitted from the stream.
- Time plays an important role; that's to preserve event order.
- There might be a possibility of an error occurring while accessing the values from the stream.
- Also, as these events are occurring with respect to time, we can make these computations asynchronous in nature and bind a few callbacks to some particular event. We can also filter out a few events based on the values.

These kinds of reactive systems react with respect to time and events. And we can also compare these streams to promises, which we discussed in the previous chapter. Promises are responsible for one value that's going to be available in future. Whereas, streams contain multiple returned values evaluated asynchronously. These are the building blocks of *reactive programming*. The paradigm has its own terminologies for such streams and these are called **Observables**. There are various APIs available that let you create such *observable streams* and allow us to transform, filter, and merge these observable streams to create a reactive system in which data flows.

These APIs are a part of ReactiveX and called reactive extensions. There are asynchronous stream APIs available for a number of languages, some of which are as follows:

- RxJava
- RxJS
- Rx.NET
- RxScala
- RxLua
- RxGo
- RxDart

All these APIs serve the same purpose, that is to provide asynchronous Observable streams in their respective platforms. These APIs revolve around the principle of events and streams. Let's check out what these reactive extensions provide.

Reactive extensions

All these APIs serve the same purpose, that is, to provide asynchronous Observable streams in their respective platforms. These APIs revolve around the principle of events and streams. Let's check out what these reactive extensions provide. It's time to see the term we just introduced ourselves to, that is, Observables.

Observables are the entities that emit a stream of events. Events can be a button click or checking a checkbox, or some other event like providing input to some device via the interface exposed. There has to be an *observer* that reacts to whatever value or sequence of values the Observable is emitting. The way *observers* react to events is by *subscribing* to the Observable. So these *observers* subscribing to Observables to react to events is the main theme of ReactiveX. The process in any of the libraries available for different platforms is somewhat similar to the following:

- We define the Observable, which does the job of emitting events. This will be in an asynchronous fashion, as events can be dependent on some environment/surrounding, for example, user's interaction or some condition being successful.
- We define a method, which does some manipulation with the return value from an asynchronous computation. This method is part of *observers*.
- We attach the *observer* to the *Observable* by *subscribing* to it.

By subscribing the Observer to Observable, we specify that now the mechanism is in place and our observers are ready to react to events. Based on this phenomena, Observables are categorized as hot and cold Observables.

- **Hot Observables**: These start emitting events as soon as they are created, hence if in a later point in time we attach/subscribe an observer to it, the observer continues to react to events from the current point of time.
- **Cold Observables**: These, on the other hand start emitting events when they're subscribed by an observer. In this way, our observers react to events from the beginning.

Also, we have seen while observing events from a stream that there are possibilities of an error or the stream to be completed. So for Observer[T], we provide following methods:

- onNext(T)
- onError(Exception)
- onComplete()

Each call to the observer's onNext method comes with a value from an event. In case you create an observer of the String type, then the onNext method will give you a string value. In a typical reactive programming scenario, a call to the onNext method is made until the event stream gets completed or some error occurs; in these cases, onComplete or onError gets called. After these methods, we don't get any values from that subscription.

If you remember, the iterables we discussed while taking about collections, these iterables work in a somewhat similar fashion, with the only difference being that the Observables are asynchronous in nature. Iterables contain data in sequence, from which we can obtain a value at a time and perform some operation on them. To obtain data from such iterables, we create an iterator. Calling iterator.next() lets us access the value in an iterable. An iterable lets you access a sequence of values in a synchronous fashion:

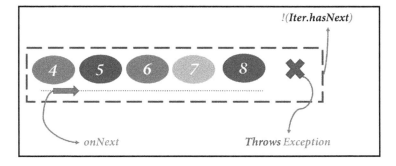

The difference lies in the nature of these two: Observables are asynchronous in nature, while Iterables are not. Taking a look at these two interfaces, we can see the following:

Type of event	Iterator	Observer
Data retrieval	next( ): T	onNext(T)
Error occurrence	throws Exception	onError(Exception)
Completion	!hasNext( )	onCompleted( )

Iterables & Observables

We know about *Observables,* but what makes them powerful is a set of *utility* methods, described as *operators*. These operators allow us to *create, combine, transform, filter,* and *convert* Observables. We can chain these operators to perform these operations in a specific order.

Now that we're sure about the theoretical stuff, it's time to try out what you learned using Scala's offering in the reactive world, that is, *RxScala.* Let's look at the RxScala API to represent the Observables.

React to RxScala

RxScala is a reactive asynchronous streams API provided in Scala. It lets us perform all those concepts we talked about, such as creating *Observables, observers,* and *subscribing* to them. There's a variety of operators available for us to manipulate these *Observables.* Most of the operators return *Observables,* hence chaining of *Observables* is also possible.

To start writing some *Observables,* we'll start by setting up space so that the library becomes available to us. For that, let's follow some steps:

1. On your favorite internet browser, open `https://developer.lightbend.com` and click on the **START A PROJECT** button.
2. You'll get a few options; just choose Scala and click on **CREATE A PROJECT FOR ME!**. It'll download the source in a compressed format:

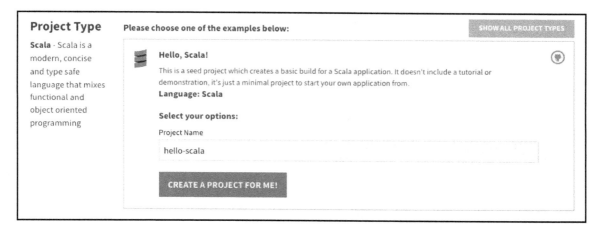

3. We can extract that and open it in IntelliJ IDE.
4. Once it's opened in IntelliJ, we can add the library dependency for RxScala in the build file. This can be done by specifying the following:

```
libraryDependencies += "io.reactivex" %% "rxscala" % "0.26.5"
```

5. After specifying dependency, we can perform the `sbt update` command from the command line, which will download the dependency files. We should do this update from the directory where `build.sbt` is specified.

Now, we are ready to write Observables. So why wait? Let's write some.

Creating Observables

For creating Observables, there are a bunch of operators such as `just`, `empty`, `interval`, `from`, and `defer`. Let's first write some code to create Observables in some of the ways:

```scala
package example

import rx.lang.scala.Observable
import scala.concurrent.Future
import scala.concurrent.ExecutionContext.Implicits.global
import scala.concurrent.duration._


object FirstRxApp extends App {

  //Creates an empty Observable.
  val emptyObservable = Observable.empty

  //Creates an Observable that only emits 1.
  val numObservable = Observable.just(1)

  val sequence = List(1, 3, 5, 7, 9)

  //Creates an Observable, which emits values from the sequence mentioned.
  val sequenceObservable = Observable.from(sequence)

  val someAsyncComputation = Future { 1 }
  //Creates an Observable, from an async computation
  val fromAsyncObservable = Observable.from(someAsyncComputation)

  //Creates an Observable, which emits items at a duration gap specified.
val intervalObservables = Observable.interval(200 millis)


  //Creates an Observable, which starts emitting, once some observer
subscribe to it.
  val deferObservable = Observable.defer(fromAsyncObservable)
  //Creates an Observable, which never emits any value.
  val neverObservable = Observable.never

}
```

In the preceding code snippet, we have only created Observables and there's no subscription to them. Hence, even if they emit some values, we have no mechanism to react to those values. First let's check out the code written:

1. The first statement creates an empty Observable, which means it has no values in it.
2. The second statement calls an operator named `just`, which takes a value and wraps that in the Observable context. Hence, when this observable emits, it'll emit only the value we specified.
3. Next, we provided a sequence of values to our observable with the method named `from`.
4. The `from` method can also take a future value and create an Observable. This Observable emits values that result from async computations specified in Future.

```
def from[T](f: Future[T])(implicit execContext: ExecutionContext):
Observable[T]
```

5. Then there's the `interval` method, which expects us to provide the interval in which we emit values.
6. Finally, there are two more ways we specified. First, we used the operator named `defer`, which takes the `byname` parameter as another Observable and only starts the emission of events once an observer subscribes to it:

```
def defer[T](observable: => Observable[T]): Observable[T]
```

With these operators, we were able to create Observables. Now let's attach subscriptions to these Observables by calling the `subscribe` method. For that, we can add the following snippet to our Scala file. First, let's add some imports:

```
import rx.Subscription
import rx.observers.TestSubscriber
```

Next, we add this snippet following the Observables creation:

```
//Subscribing to Observables
emptyObservable
  .subscribe(value => println(s"From emptyObservable: $value"))

numObservable
  .subscribe(value => println(s"From numObservable: $value"))

sequenceObservable
  .subscribe(value => println(s"From sequenceObservable: $value"))
```

```
fromAsyncObservable
  .subscribe(value => println(s"From fromAsyncObservable: $value"))

intervalObservables
  .subscribe(value => println(value))
Thread.sleep(1000)


new TestSubscriber[Subscription].awaitTerminalEvent(1000, MILLISECONDS)


deferObservable
  .subscribe(value => println(s"From deferObservable: $value"))
```

In the previous snippet, in most cases, we call a `subscribe` method by passing what to do with the value. Take a look at the `subscribe` method's signature:

```
def subscribe(onNext: T => Unit): Subscription
```

The method takes the value and performs, or let's say reacts, to the value. It returns a `Subscription` instance. The advantage of this `Subscription` parameter is that we can cancel the subscription by calling a method named `unsubscribe`.

In the case of `intervalObservables`, we had to provide `Thread.sleep(1000)` too so that our `intervalObservables` type gets some time to emit values. If we don't use some mechanism to wait for these emissions, the thread will be killed and we won't get to see the emitted values.

These are a few ways in which we can create Observables and subscribe to them. But that's more of getting used to APIs. We may want to see some examples which can demonstrate the use of this reactive pattern.

Let's think of a scenario. Suppose a user has to fill a form with information about a football player. He has to provide the player's name, age, nationality, and the league. After filling the information, the user will press **Submit** and that form data comes to us for processing:

Now it's up to us to provide a data flow for the player's information. By this, we mean that with the specific information, we can create a player's instance, validate the information, show the information in some particular format, or any other thing you can come up with. The flow is going to be the same for every form submission. In that case, we can create an Observable to the event, let's call it, the form submit event. Subscribed observer for the same will get data from each form submission. And then we can define onNext to manipulate the form data whichever way we want. Regardless of the user's speed of entering information and pressing the **Submit** button, we have the system in place with the Observable, which gets notified by the event's occurrence. And the process starts.

Now, to see this in practice, let's think that the data source is our favorite CSV file, instead of someone filling out the form for us, and see how the code might look:

```
package example

import rx.lang.scala.Observable

object SmartApp extends App {

  val src =
"/Users/vika/Documents/LSProg/LSPWorkspace/First_Proj_Rx/src/main/scala/exa
mple/football_stats.csv"


  val playerObservable =
```

```
                Observable.from(PlayerService.readPlayerDataFromSource(src))

            playerObservable
              .map(playerString =>
              PlayerService.parseToPlayer(playerString))
              .subscribe(player => PlayerService.showPlayerInformation(player),
              error => println(s"Error Occurred: ${error.getMessage}"))


            Thread.sleep(10000)
        }
```

In the preceding code, think of the `playerObservable` type being created from some event source. It's type is `String`, in our case it's supposed to contain the player information in string format. Now what we are supposed to do with the string is to parse this string information to a Player instance. The methods `readPlayerDateFromSource`, `parseToPlayer`, and `showPlayerInformation` are part of another object named `PlayerService`:

```
package example

import scala.io.BufferedSource
import scala.util.{Failure, Success, Try}

object PlayerService {

  def readPlayerDataFromSource(src: String): List[String] = {
    val source: BufferedSource = io.Source.fromFile(src)
    val list: List[String] = source.getLines().toList

    source.close()
    list
  }

  def parseToPlayer(string: String): Option[Player] = {
    Try {
      val columns = string.split((",")).map(_.trim)
      Player(columns(5), columns(6), columns(9).toInt, columns(7))
    } match {
      case Success(value) => Some(value)
      case Failure(excep) => None
    }
  }

  def showPlayerInformation(playerOp: Option[Player]): Unit = {
    playerOp.map { player =>
      println("----------- Here's our Player Information ----------- ")
```

```
        println(s"Name: ${player.name}")
        println(s"Age: ${player.age} | Nationality: ${player.nationality} |
League: ${player.league}")
        println
    }
  }

  case class Player(name: String, nationality: String, age: Int, league:
String)

}
```

Let's see the magic of operators in our case. The first one is the map itself, which takes a player string as expected and makes a call to parseToPlayer:

```
playerObservable
    .map(playerString =>
       PlayerService.parseToPlayer(playerString))
```

If you try to infer its result type, it's nothing but Observable[Option[Player]], so nothing has changed; it's still an Observable. We've just made a transformation in the Observable world and got a result. After that, we subscribed to the Observables and called our desired showPlayerInformation(player) method:

```
.subscribe(player => PlayerService.showPlayerInformation(player),
      error => println(s"Error Occurred: ${error.getMessage}"))
```

This itself is pretty amazing because the system is set up for a particular event, in our case the *form submit* event that gives us Observable[String]. Thanks to our hypothetical user, who enters the information and submits it so that the system gets a String to operate upon.

Now to clear the picture again, we'll get the help of the following diagram:

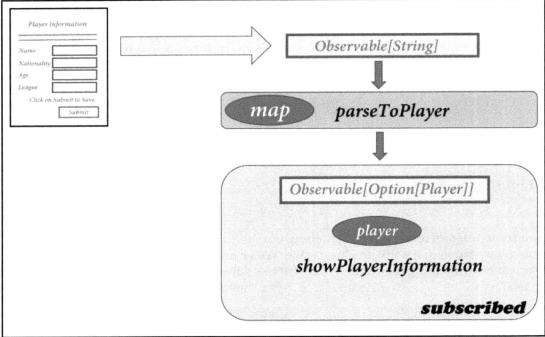

As shown in the preceding diagram, currently, there's only one source of player information attached and the whole pipeline works well. Now think of another scenario where our hypothetical user can also select a player from some suggested input. What will that look like?

In this case, we might get the whole player information as `Option[Player]` instead of string. Hence, the observable working in this case will be of the type `Observable[Option[Player]]`. Now if we want to execute the same logic as we did in the case of form submission, all we have to do is use the merge operator. This will combine the Observables, hence we'll be able to achieve what we desire. The important thing is to merge our new Observable at the right place. From the diagram, we get a hint that it'll be better if we merge Observable when we have `observable[Option[Player]]` as shown in following diagram:

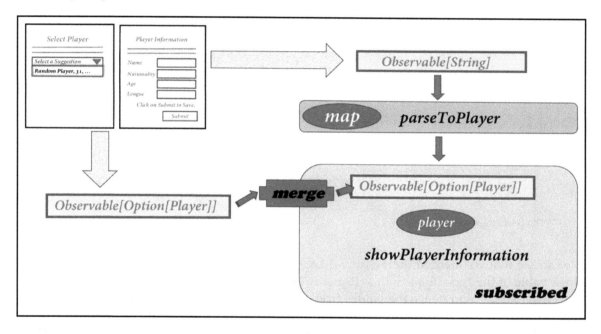

Take a look at the preceding diagram. As you can see on the left-most side, the suggestion input form gives us `Observable[Option[Player]]`, which we merge with our transformed Observable of the same type. We can do the same in our code. Let's create an Observable from a custom optional player and then merge that.

We'll just refactor our code to the following:

```
package example

import rx.lang.scala.Observable

object SmartApp extends App {

  val src =
"/Users/vika/Documents/LSProg/LSPWorkspace/First_Proj_Rx/src/main/scala/exa
mple/football_stats.csv"

  val playerObservable: Observable[String] =
    Observable.from(PlayerService.readPlayerDataFromSource(src))

  val somePlayer = Some(PlayerService.Player("Random Player", "Random
Nation", 31, "Random League"))

  playerObservable
    .map(playerString =>
      PlayerService.parseToPlayer(playerString))
    .merge(Observable.just(somePlayer))
    .subscribe(player => PlayerService.showPlayerInformation(player),
      error => println(s"Error Occurred: ${error.getMessage}"))

  Thread.sleep(10000)
}
```

We can see that we merged the `observable.just(somePlayer)` type with the Observable of the type `Observable[Option[Player]]`. This call to merge combines these two Observables, and hence the values from these combined sources go through the pipeline. We can try this out by running the application. We'll get to see values from our CSV file as well as the `somePlayer` Observable we created if the CSV file is in the correct place. This way, we can use operators to make our system work with several event sources. This is just the tip of the iceberg. There's a lot we can achieve with these operators available. I strongly recommend that you go through the documentation (`http://reactivex.io/documentation/operators.html`) from ReactiveX. Their marble diagrams explain each of these operators, and you can use them according to your needs.

With this recommendation, we would want to summarize what we've covered in this chapter.

Summary

This chapter introduced us to the notion of reactive programming. We understood the concept of Observable events and reacting to them. This gave us an essence of what reactive programming is. After that, we went through reactive extensions and explored the API a bit. We saw how we can create Observables and subscribe to them. Finally, we looked at an example that explained the way we can compose Observables using some operators available to us.

In next chapter, we'll cover one of the most important topics, that is, testing our programs. We'll go through the much talked about nowadays development model, that is, **test-driven development** (**TDD**). We'll start by answering the why and what of TDD and then understand the toolkits available in Scala for testing.

15
Testing in Scala

"Change is the end result of all the true learning."

- Leo Buscaglia

Software development is an ever transforming process. We have seen in recent decades that many patterns have been discovered/rediscovered. These programming techniques/paradigms have become an important part and have changed the way we approach programming. One of them is **Test-Driven Development (TDD)**. In the TDD approach, we first specify the requirement for our application through new tests. Then, one by one, we write concrete code to pass all those tests. In this manner, we complete our requirements by writing new test cases, implementing code to pass them, and end up building an application that runs as expected. Scala provides many frameworks for testing (for example, **ScalaTest**, **Specs2**, and so on) and we have **Mockito** and **ScalaMock** for mocking objects. Testing, in a way, is a small concept with a vast number of explanations possible. In this chapter, we'll focus on understanding the TDD approach and the way we can follow this approach to successfully apply it in Scala. For that, we'll go through:

- The why and what of TDD
    - The process of TDD
    - **Behavior-driven development (BDD)**
- ScalaTest
- ScalaCheck

So, let's start with why this rocket called TDD is flying so high in the software development space nowadays.

The why and what of TDD

To write expected and well-designed software, we tend to clarify the requirements before starting the development process. With agile practices in place, we translate our requirements to what we call user/functional stories. Transforming these stories into a simple specification of what we're going to implement adds an advantage. That's where writing test cases comes in handy. We specify our program's behavior in the form of test cases and then implement those behaviors.

There are some advantages to this approach. Writing test cases first and then providing the implementation drives the design of our program. It means that as we approach toward implementing the behavior, we can think of our design and code for that. If one of your classes, A, is dependent on another class, B, we can make sure that *B* is injected into *A*. In a way, we can make it a practice to follow these ways, for example, inject dependencies from other classes. Apart from driving the design of your application, TDD also helps us think about the use cases and the way in which users of our application might use it. It helps us think clearly about the interface the user is going to get so that we can code accordingly.

In TDD, just because we tend to write test cases first, we cover almost all lines of our software implementation. This provides automatic code coverage to us. Let's take a look at the process of TDD.

The process of TDD

As per the approach, we can break down the process of TDD into the following steps. The process can be included in your development workflow:

1. Write a test that will fail.
2. Write some code to pass the failing test.
3. Refactor your code to improve quality without any changes in the behavior.
4. Repeat *steps 1 to 3*.

We broke down the process into these steps. Let's take a look at each of these steps to better understand the reasoning behind each of these.

Step 1 - write a test that will fail

Writing to fail is not something we feel confident about, but that's how TDD works. After we've determined what's needed from our application and are sure about a certain functionality, we can write a test case for functionality in the way we want it to work. We want to make sure that we run this test case and that it fails. The failure of our test case is expected because we have not implemented any code yet to make it successful. The initial failure we mean is step one of TDD.

Step 2 - write code to pass the failing test

The best thing about this step is to know how we have to pass a failing test case. For that, we'll implement a functionality. In this step, we'll have to write some code. We can try to implement a function, not in the best way possible, but enough to pass the failing test. Passing a test guarantees the particular behavior of a functionality.

Step 3 - refactor the code to improve the quality

Now that we are confident that our functionality is working, we can go ahead and improve the code quality. If the functionality isn't too big, then this step can be a part of the previous one. It's logical to have a review of our code once the functionality is working. This might improve the quality of our code. After the refactor, we should ensure that the feature/functionality is in a working state and is intact.

Step 4 - repeat steps 1 to 3

Now, for this particular functionality, for which we wrote test cases and implemented code, we have ensured that it's working and the code quality is proper. We are done with this particular feature/functionality and now can write another test case and repeat the process steps.

We can visualize the working of TDD as follows:

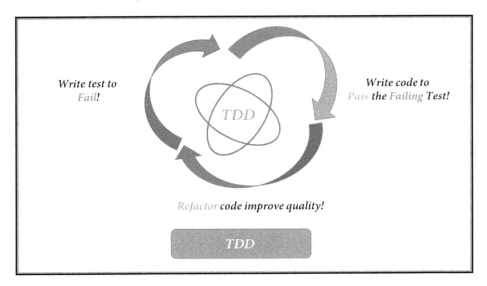

From the previous diagram, it's clear that TDD is a repetitive process, where you specify a use case and write code for it.

One of the benefits of TDD is that our tests serve as a documentation. Library/framework developers tend to write test cases that serve the purpose of documentation too. How? By making use of DSL or, let's say, English-like sentences for designing our test suites. A test suite consists of multiple test cases for our program. Let's take a look at the scenario we have used in a couple of our chapters. The example we will be using is where we will read Football player's data from a CSV file named `football.csv`, convert those to `Player` objects, and further use the data to display the player's information or perform some analytics based on the information. How would we want to proceed with the test cases for such a scenario, or at least, how should it look when we say "English-like sentences" for our specifications?

Scenario

Read the player data and showcase that on the console:

```
"PlayerService" should {
    "return a Player object." in {//some code}
    "return an empty collection if there's no data." in {//some code}
    "return a Nothing on call to getPlayer method with right player
string." in {//some code}
```

```
    "return a Some Player instance on call to getPlayer method with right
player string." in {//some code}
    "print a Player's information on console." in {//some code}
}
```

In the given example scenario, we specified a service and named it `PlayerService`. Now, this service should have the methods that perform the specified cases. These cases are not too complicated, but each case expects our service to provide a simple functionality. This example is for explanation purposes, since we've already seen the code. We'll also try and implement the same using the TDD approach.

The point worth nothing about the preceding test specification is that before even trying to code, we are sure about certain things:

- There should be a `PlayerService` service.
- In `PlayerService`, we should have a `Player` entity.
- In `PlayerService`, we should have a functionality to read the player's data. It has to be a collection; when the source can't be read or the source contains no data, the functionality should return an empty collection.
- In `PlayerService`, there should be a `getPlayer` functionality that expects us to provide some data to it and return a concrete `Player` entity. When we provide wrong data (as in the format), the functionality doesn't throw an exception, but specifies that it couldn't create a concrete `Player` entity.
- In `PlayerService`, there should be a `getPlayer` functionality which expects us to provide some data to it and return a concrete *Player* entity on receiving correct data.
- In `PlayerService`, there should be a `showPlayers` functionality which expects us to provide a collection of `Player` entities and print the player's information on the console.

The fact that the preceding points and specifications we mentioned are similar in semantic meaning and that we can use one of these to write test cases makes TDD fun. These test specifications are too close to real-world test specs that we'll be writing. Take a closer look at the specification we just described; nowhere does it state about the programming language choice we had to make. We didn't get any hint about the language specifications, so these test cases will work in any language if the programming language we use can support such **domain-specific language (DSL)** lookalike mechanisms.

This specification does not limit you to write test cases only in a specified format, but you can choose your own style of writing them. This is one of the conventions that emerged from TDD, and it's called **behavior-driven development** (**BDD**). This term BDD drives itself by specifying behaviors in order to start the development of any functionality. It also serves as documentation to our program. If you see the specification we wrote, in a way, we documented the way we can use functionalities. If these specs were written in Scala, we could have provided the method names according to the functionalities.

Let's discuss a bit about this way of driving development by specifying the behaviors.

Behavior driven development (BDD)

We already saw the *should ... in* way of specifying the behavior of our functionality. There are other ways to specify the behaviors, or let's say, ensure the validity of our functionality. One of the example is *given... when... then....*

Here, we specify the following:

- **Given**: This is what is available at the time of executing some functionality
- **When**: We confront a condition that is based on the data that's given
- **Then**: Execute the part which is expected to happen

In this way, we validate the behavior of our functionality. One of the best practices when we write test cases for one of the functionalities is to specify all the possible scenarios (ideally, that's not possible, but we try our best to include all possibilities we can think of). These scenarios include the *empty case, unit case,* and *failure case.* Finally, we cover all the conditional possibilities. With these, we ensure the specifications are valid and that our implementations are too. These specifications serve as acceptance criteria for our functionality. There are lesser chances of you slipping past some important case. It's important to know that there's no hard and fast rule to describe our test cases.

One of the benefits of behavior-driven development is that instead of talking in terms of tests, we talk in terms of specifications or scenarios. Hence, not just developers, but most of the business stakeholders and domain experts can also specify the requirements for an application.

Now, talking about Scala's offering for frameworks or toolkits provided for testing, there are a bunch of them. **ScalaTest**, **ScalaCheck**, and **Specs2** are a few that developers are using to write tests for their code. We'll go through one of the mostly widely used testing tools, ScalaTest, and try to see the way specs are implemented using examples.

ScalaTest

ScalaTest, as we mentioned, is famous for multiple styles provided to write specifications. Not just multiple styles, this kit also serves as a testing tool for **Scala.js** and even Java classes. ScalaTest covers most of the Scala ecosystem and allows you to choose different ways to write specifications based on the behavior of your functionality.

Setting up for testing

To use ScalaTest, let's go through some of the basic steps. We can create a fresh SBT project and add a dependency for **ScalaTest** via the `build.sbt` file or use Lightbend's tech hub to download a simple Scala project. Let's try out the second approach as it'll give us ScalaTest already added as a dependency in our `build.sbt` file. Let's follow these steps:

1. In your favorite browser, open: `https://developer.lightbend.com`.

2. Click on the **START A PROJECT** button:

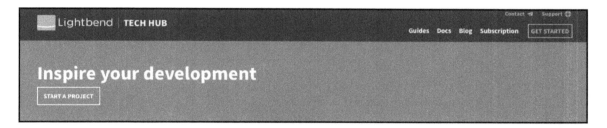

3. Choose **Scala** from project types:

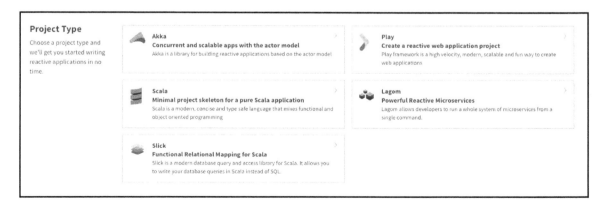

4. You can name the project and click on **CREATE A PROJECT FOR ME!**:

This will download a compressed file for you with the name you specified. Extract the compressed file to a specific location and open it in the IntelliJ IDE.

We can open `build.sbt` to check the dependencies and project settings specified. Our `sbtbuild` file should look like as follows:

```
import Dependencies._

lazy val root = (project in file(".")).
  settings(
    inThisBuild(List(
      organization := "com.example",
      scalaVersion := "2.12.4",
      version      := "0.1.0-SNAPSHOT"
    )),
    name := "Hello",
    libraryDependencies += scalaTest % Test
  )
```

Here, in the `libraryDependencies` settings, `scalaTest` is specified. Hence, we can use that. The sample project comes with some source code and test covering it. So, we'll first try to run the test case. If you can see the `scalatest` library in the external dependencies directory, as shown in the following diagram, then we're ready to execute tests:

test library

If these libraries are not shown in your project structure, we can fire the `sbt update` command so that SBT can download all the dependencies specified. There're a few more SBT commands that we will use to run our test cases. Let's take a look at them:

- `sbt test`: SBT assumes that test sources for Scala are located in the `src/test/scala` directory and resources like the configurations for test sources are located in the `src/test/resources` directory

   Based on previously described assumptions, when we fire a command described in the preceding text, SBT compiles all test files present in the respective locations and tests all of them. What if you're only concerned about specific test cases?

- `sbt testOnly`: Based on similar assumptions that we had for the `sbt test` command, when we fire the `testOnly` command, SBT compiles and tests only test cases that we specified along with the command. Consider the following example:

   ```
   sbt testOnly example.HelloSpec
   ```

- `sbt testQuick`: Based on similar assumptions that we had for the `sbt test` command, when we fire the `testQuick` command, SBT compiles and tests only those test cases that fulfil the following conditions:
   - Failing tests from the previous runs
   - Tests that have not run yet
   - Tests with transitive dependencies

These are a few Scala commands we use to test our cases. Also, while testing our specs, we'll use triggered execution. We initiate triggered execution by putting ~ before our test command. With this, SBT expects a save change, and saving the file again triggers a test execution. So with this, try out this command, assuming that we have the SBT shell opened (open the project directory, where build.sbt is located and the trigger sbt command) in the command prompt of our choice. Let's locate our project in the SBT shell and fire the following command:

```
                                                      opens sbt shell
Vikashs-Air:First_Proj_Testing vika$ sbt
[info] Loading project definition from /Users/vika/Documents/LSProg/LSPWorkspace
/First_Proj_Testing/project
[info] Set current project to Hello (in build file:/Users/vika/Documents/LSProg/
LSPWorkspace/First_Proj_Testing/)
> testOnly example.HelloSpec
[info] Compiling 1 Scala source to /Users/vika/Documents/LSProg/LSPWorkspace/Fir
st_Proj_Testing/target/scala-2.12/classes...
[info] 'compiler-interface' not yet compiled for Scala 2.12.4. Compiling...
[info]   Compilation completed in 19.479 s
[info] Compiling 1 Scala source to /Users/vika/Documents/LSProg/LSPWorkspace/Fir
st_Proj_Testing/target/scala-2.12/test-classes...
[info] HelloSpec:
[info] The Hello object
[info] - should say hello
[info] Run completed in 975 milliseconds.
[info] Total number of tests run: 1
[info] Suites: completed 1, aborted 0
[info] Tests: succeeded 1, failed 0, canceled 0, ignored 0, pending 0
[info] All tests passed.
[success] Total time: 27 s, completed 13 Jan, 2018 6:10:57 PM
>
```

testOnly command

There's this HelloSpec class, located in the test directory of the project we downloaded. If everything works right, as it should, we'll get our tests passed and you'll start loving the *green* color. But if the code is red, this means it has failed. So, we're ready to delve into ScalaTest.

Testing in style using ScalaTest

We've tested the `HelloSpec` class, so we'll take a look at the test, and the way it's written. So, we can open the file `Hello` located in `src/test/scala/example`. The source code looks as follows:

```
package example

import org.scalatest._


class HelloSpec extends FlatSpec with Matchers {
  "The Hello object" should "say hello" in {
    Hello.greeting shouldEqual "hello"
  }
}
```

Taking a look at the code sample, we can observe a few points:

- We've imported `org.scalatest._` to bring all the traits we want to use.
- The class definition named `HelloSpec` extends `FlatSpec` along with the mix-in `Matchers` class. It's a convention to name our test specifications as class name followed by `Spec`.
- The definition consists of only one *specification*. The specification states that "there's an object named Hello that says hello in the specified code snippet". That's how cool it is—the specification is written in a way any English sentence can be written.
- The specification is written in a DSL-like manner. The language looks natural, and further down, the specification states that there's going to be a method call that returns a string equal to `hello`.
- The call to `shouldEqual` is a `Matcher`. The job of a `Matcher` is to match the left operand with the right operand. There are several other ways to write such `Matchers`, but we'll talk about those in subsequent sections.

That's very simple and everything's good till now. Now, let's take a look at the corresponding code file written in the location `src/main/scala/example`. Let's look at the file named `Hello.scala`:

```
package example

object Hello extends Greeting with App {
  println(greeting)
}
```

```
trait Greeting {
  lazy val greeting: String = "hello"
}
```

There's this object named `Hello` according to our specification. We can make a call to `greeting`, which does nothing but print this string, `hello`. Well, this example was already available for us to observe, hence we didn't follow TDD. But we'll try writing something similar to this using the *test first approach* by specifying the behavior.

Before writing the first spec on our own, let's follow some convention or one of the good practices and create an abstract class that extends `FlatSpec` with `Matchers` by default so that we don't have to extend those in every spec we write. We can do this by creating a spec file, and let's name it `SomeSpec` and save it in the `src/test/scala/example/` directory. It should look like this:

```
package example

import org.scalatest._

abstract class SomeSpec(toBeTested: String) extends FlatSpec with Matchers
```

Now that we've created some abstract class that extends the `FlatSpec` and `Matchers` classes, we are ready to follow our first step in TDD to write one failing test spec. Our `SomeSpec` abstract class takes a parameter named `toBeTested`, which is nothing but the name of the functionality.

Let's create another test spec, name it `PlayerSpec`, and save it as `src/test/scala/example`:

```
package example

class PlayerSpec extends SomeSpec("PlayerService") {

  it should "compile" in {
  """PlayerService.Player("Cristiano Ronaldo", "Portuguese", 32, "Real
Madrid")""" should compile
  }


}
```

The preceding test spec is written in DSL. The `it` keyword corresponds to the argument we passed to `SomeSpec`. In our case, it's the functionality under test, that is, `PlayerService`. So the spec states the code snippet compiles, that is, we can create `Player` instances. When we try to run the test case, it's going to fail as expected, because we have not written the `Player` class till now:

```
> testOnly example.PlayerSpec
[info] PlayerSpec:
[info] - should compile *** FAILED ***
[info] Expected no compiler error, but got the following type error: "not
found: value Player", for code: Player("Cristiano Ronaldo", "Portuguese",
32, "Real Madrid") (PlayerSpec.scala:6)
[info] Run completed in 281 milliseconds.
[info] Total number of tests run: 1
[info] Suites: completed 1, aborted 0
[info] Tests: succeeded 0, failed 1, canceled 0, ignored 0, pending 0
[info] *** 1 TEST FAILED ***
[error] Failed tests:
[error]   example.PlayerSpec
[error] (test:testOnly) sbt.TestsFailedException: Tests unsuccessful
```

Let's write the Player case class:

```
// src/main/scala/example/PlayerService.scala

object PlayerService extends App {


  case class Player(name: String, nationality: String, age: Int, league:
String)


}
```

With this code, we can save the file, and as our test is running in the *triggered mode,* we can see that the test case passes:

```
[info] PlayerSpec:
[info] - should compile
[info] Run completed in 199 milliseconds.
[info] Total number of tests run: 1
[info] Suites: completed 1, aborted 0
[info] Tests: succeeded 1, failed 0, canceled 0, ignored 0, pending 0
[info] All tests passed.
[success] Total time: 1 s, completed
```

We'll follow the same steps again. So, let's write a few more test cases:

```scala
package example

class PlayerSpec extends SomeSpec("PlayerService") {

  it should "compile" in {
    """PlayerService.Player("Cristiano Ronaldo", "Portuguese", 32, "Real
Madrid")""" should compile
  }

  it should "throw an exception when source is wrong" in {
    val src = "some source"
assertThrows[java.io.FileNotFoundException](PlayerService.readPlayerDataFro
mSource(src))
  }

  it should "return collection of String when data is read from correct
source" in {
    val src =
"/Users/vika/Documents/LSProg/LSPWorkspace/First_Proj_Testing/src/main/scal
a/example/football_stats.csv"
    PlayerService.readPlayerDataFromSource(src) should not be empty
  }

  it should "return None while parsing wrong player string data into player
instance" in {
    val data = "some wrong player string"
    PlayerService.parseToPlayer(data) shouldBe None
  }

  it should "return Some Player while parsing player string data into
player instance" in {
    val data = """1,1,2,1,2,Cristiano Ronaldo,Portugal,Real
Madrid,Spain,32,4829,40,4789,124,63"""
    val player = PlayerService.Player("Cristiano Ronaldo", "Portugal", 32,
"Real Madrid")
    PlayerService.parseToPlayer(data) shouldBe Some(player)
  }

}
```

As we are clear about the behavior of our functionality, we wrote a few more test cases. Now, our spec includes more test clauses. We have used a few `Matchers` available to us. Let's see how our tests work:

1. After checking for our code, it should compile. In the next clause, we specified that our code should throw `FileNotFoundException` when we try to access the wrong file path. We used an assertion `assertThrows` to specify such behavior. Here, we didn't have to specify any `Matchers` since specifying an *Assertion* was enough.

2. In the next clause, we mentioned that the result of `readPlayerDataFromSource` should not be empty, empty as in a collection.

3. The next spec clause expects to return `None` when we try to call `parseToPlayer` with the wrong formatted data to a `Player` instance.

4. Finally, we expect the `parseToPlayer` method to return a player object when we call it with data in the correct format.

It's clear from our specification and clauses mentioned what we exactly want from our functionality. When we try to run the test case, it doesn't compile because we don't have our methods `readPlayerDataFromSource` and `parseToPlayer`. We can define all these methods and the corresponding code. The code should look like this:

```scala
package example

import scala.util.Try
import scala.util.{Failure, Success}

object PlayerService extends App {

  def readPlayerDataFromSource(src: String): List[String] = {
    val source = io.Source.fromFile(src)

    val list: List[String] = source.getLines().toList

    source.close()
    list
  }

  def parseToPlayer(string: String): Option[Player] = {
    Try {
      val columns = string.split((",")).map(_.trim)
      Player(columns(5), columns(6), columns(9).toInt, columns(7))
    } match {
      case Success(value) => Some(value)
      case Failure(excep) => None
```

```
    }

  case class Player(name: String, nationality: String, age: Int, league:
String)

}
```

After writing the code, we can refactor it if needed. In our case, we've already refactored the code. We may try to run the test cases if you have placed the corresponding file in the right path. All our test cases will pass successfully, meaning that they will all be green:

```
[info] PlayerSpec:
[info] - should compile
[info] - should throw an exception when source is wrong
[info] - should return collection of String when data is read from correct
source
[info] - should return None while parsing wrong player string data into
player instance
[info] - should return Some Player while parsing player string data into
player instance
[info] Run completed in 324 milliseconds.
[info] Total number of tests run: 5
[info] Suites: completed 1, aborted 0
[info] Tests: succeeded 5, failed 0, canceled 0, ignored 0, pending 0
[info] All tests passed.
```

Now, we have a some idea about the toolkit and the way TDD makes it fun to write software. We have used FlatSpec in our example. There are more of these; some of the frequently used Specs are as follows:

- FunSpec
- WordSpec
- FreeSpec
- PropSpec
- FeatureSpec

These styles only differ in the way they look. If we consider our test specs written in an English-like language, we can say these styles consist of different ways in which we can write/speak our sentences. We've already seen `FlatSpec`. The `FunSpec` Spec uses nested clauses with keywords like `describe` and `it`. Let's take a few examples of all of these Spec styles:

- FunSpec

```
describe("In PlayerService object"){
    it("should compile") {
        assertCompiles("""PlayerService.Player (
                        "Cristiano Ronaldo",
                        "Portuguese", 32,
                        "Real Madrid")""")
    }
}
```

- WordSpec

```
"PlayerService.Player.parseToPlayer" when {
    "wrong parsing data passed" should {
        "return None" in {
            PlayerService.parseToPlayer("some wrog data") shouldBe None
        }
    }
}
```

- FreeSpec

```
"PlayerService.Player.parseToPlayer" - {
    "wrong parsing data passed" - {
        "return None" in {
            PlayerService.parseToPlayer("some wrog data") shouldBe None
        }
    }
}
```

These are a few styles that we can use to write our test specs in `ScalaTest`. You should definitely check out `ScalaTest`'s documentation (`http://www.scalatest.org/user_guide`) to learn more about these styles.

We've seen the way we made assertions and used `Matchers` to check for test clause validity. Let's learn more about these. We'll start with the *Assertions* trait.

Assertions

The trait *Assertions* contains assertions that we can make while specifying behaviors for our test cases. There are three default assertions available in all the style specs. These assertions are as follows:

- `assert`
- `assertResult`
- `assertThrows`

We've already used `assertThrows`, and the other two can also be used in a similar fashion. The `assertResult` assertion expects us to provide a value that is going to be the result of some calculation we specify. Similarly, `assert` expects us to provide a Boolean predicate, which has left and right parts. Some equality checks can be performed on some conditions, which result in a Boolean value, based on which the test clause passes.

Apart from these, there are more assertions available. A few of them are `fail`, `cancel`, `succeed`, `intercept`, `assertCompiles`, `assertDoesNotCompile`, and so on. Apart from these assertions, we can also use `Matchers` to check for the validity of our test specifications. We've used `Matchers` along with keywords in a few of our example clauses.

Matchers

We've already seen a few `Matchers` in place when we were going through our example. These `Matchers` are DSL's way of writing assertions. `ScalaTest` provides a rich set of assertions that work with Strings to collections. We can also write `Matchers` for custom classes. With these `Matchers`, we can perform the most basic assertions like equality checks to custom ones, where we have to deal with aggregations and sequencing.

These `Matchers` are cool, because of native language-like methods. Consider the following example:

```
someCollection should have length 7
someString should include ("world")
twenty should be > 10
number shouldBe odd
sequence should contain ("thisvalue")
```

There are so many ways in which you can speak a particular sentence to convey the same information. Similarly, using `ScalaTest`'s `Matchers`, we can specify some clause using different methods. `Matchers` come in handy for this.

We also know that sometimes, while writing software, we get to create mock objects to pass as arguments. For that, we don't have to write mock objects ourselves, but, there're libraries that do this for us. Let's take a look at one of them available in Scala.

ScalaMock – a native library to mock objects

As we discussed, at instances where we need some other services that we are yet to define or it's harder to create their instances since using them is a matter of complexity, we tend to use some Mocking framework.

ScalaMock is a native framework available in Scala. To include ScalaMock in our project, we'll add a dependency for it in our `build.sbt` file. Let's do that. We'll add the following line in the build file:

```
libraryDependencies += "org.scalamock" %% "scalamock" % "4.0.0" % Test
```

We've specified the test scope, because we're sure that `scalamock` is only going to be used in our test cases. After writing this dependency, we'll perform an `sbt update` command by calling the `sbt update` command in the SBT shell. This update is going to add the `scalamock` dependency to our project. We can ensure this by taking a look at the external sources folder. There's going to be a dependency with the `scalamock` name. If that's available there, we are ready to mock some services:

We'll try to mock our `PlayerService` object in our application where we want to show a list of a few players. Let's specify a spec for that:

```scala
import org.scalamock.scalatest.MockFactory

class PlayerAppSpec extends SomeSpec("PlayerAppSpec") with MockFactory {

  it should "give us a collection of 2 players" in {

    val mockPlayer = mock[PlayerService.Player]

    val list = List(mockPlayer, mockPlayer)
    list should have length 2
  }

}
```

The preceding code snippet is a very simple example of a mock object for a class. All we had to do is import the `scalamock` dependency, the `MockFactory` trait in the scope, all by importing the dependencies and calling the `mock` method, specifying which type of object to create as a mock. It's as simple as that. We can also mock functions and set some expectations to that mocked function. Let's see the following example:

```scala
val someStringToIntFunc  = mockFunction[String, Int]
someStringToIntFunc expects ("Some Number") returning 1
```

Now, we can perform some test case execution, which includes a call to this mocked function. Our test case has to somehow call this function at least once in order for it to pass. Mocking of objects is a usual practice we do while writing test cases. It relieves us of the burden of manually writing instances of several classes/functions, letting us concentrate on what matters, that is, validating our program's behavior upfront. And that's why we have such frameworks available, making our lives easier as developers. With this, we've come to the end of the final chapter of this book. Let's summarize whatever you've learned.

Summary

This chapter never seemed like the last one; it was fun. After going through several Scala programming constructs and frameworks, you learned how to ensure the validity of our programs. We knew that testing the code we write is essential, but this new TDD style of programming was a different experience. We understood what TDD actually is—a design scheme driven by specifying the behaviors at the beginning, rather than after we complete our code. We talked about why this approach is good. Then, we started with the testing tools available in Scala, and learned about `ScalaTest`. We wrote the specifications and then coded for the same. Finally, we also took a look at the mocking framework available in Scala named ScalaMock.

Though this is the last chapter, we can think of what more we can do to make our understanding of this language better. One of the best ways is to practice more; this will help us understand the concepts well, and we'll also be well versed with the constructs. But we'll get the real insight when we go about learning functional programming, because that's where all the magic is. Trying to think in a functional way, where we do not mutate stuff it, is one of the most important aspects. Finally, let's thank the wonderful and ever growing Scala community. Join the community, ask questions, and contribute in your own way.

Other Books You May Enjoy

If you enjoyed this book, you may be interested in these other books by Packt:

Learning Concurrent Programming in Scala - Second Edition
Aleksandar Prokopec

ISBN: 978-1-78646-689-1

- Get to grips with the fundamentals of concurrent programming on modern multiprocessor systems
- Build high-performance concurrent systems from simple, low-level concurrency primitives
- Express asynchrony in concurrent computations with futures and promises
- Seamlessly accelerate sequential programs by using data-parallel collections
- Design safe, scalable, and easy-to-comprehend in-memory transactional data models
- Transparently create distributed applications that scale across multiple machines
- Integrate different concurrency frameworks together in large applications
- Develop and implement scalable and easy-to-understand concurrent applications in Scala 2.12

Scala Microservices
Jatin Puri, Selvam Palanimalai

ISBN: 978-1-78646-934-2

- Learn the essentials behind Microservices, the advantages and perils associated with them
- Build low latency, high throughput applications using Play and Lagom
- Dive deeper with being asynchronous and understand the superiority it provides
- Model your complex domain data for scale and simplicity with CQRS and Event Sourcing
- Be resilient to failures by using message passing
- Look at best practices of version control workflow, testing, continuous integration and deployments
- Understand operating system level virtualization using Linux Containers. Docker is used to explain how containers work
- Automate your infrastructure with kubernetes

Leave a review - let other readers know what you think

Please share your thoughts on this book with others by leaving a review on the site that you bought it from. If you purchased the book from Amazon, please leave us an honest review on this book's Amazon page. This is vital so that other potential readers can see and use your unbiased opinion to make purchasing decisions, we can understand what our customers think about our products, and our authors can see your feedback on the title that they have worked with Packt to create. It will only take a few minutes of your time, but is valuable to other potential customers, our authors, and Packt. Thank you!

Index

www.ingramcontent.com/pod-product-compliance
Lightning Source LLC
Chambersburg PA
CBHW060649060326
40690CB00020B/4566